Out of Left Field

SPORT AND SOCIETY

Series Editors
Aram Goudsouzian
Jaime Schultz

Founding Editors
Benjamin G. Rader
Randy Roberts

For a list of books in the series, please see our website at www.press.uillinois.edu.

Out of Left Field

A Sportswriter's Last Word

STAN ISAACS

Edited and with an Introduction by
ARAM GOUDSOUZIAN

Manufactured in the United States of America
1 2 3 4 5 C P 5 4 3 2 1
∞ This book is printed on acid-free paper.

Library of Congress Cataloging-in-Publication Data
Names: Isaacs, Stan, author. | Goudsouzian, Aram, editor.
Title: Out of left field : a sportswriter's last word / Stan Isaacs ; Edited and with an Introduction by Aram Goudsouzian.
Description: Urbana : University of Illinois Press, [2024] | Series: Sport and society | Includes bibliographical references and index.
Identifiers: LCCN 2023035012 (print) | LCCN 2023035013 (ebook) | ISBN 9780252087882 (paperback) | ISBN 9780252056659 (ebook)
Subjects: LCSH: Isaacs, Stan. | Sportswriters—United States—Biography. | Sports—United States—History. | African American athletes—History.
Classification: LCC GV742.42.I83 A3 2024 (print) | LCC GV742.42.I83 (ebook) | DDC 070.4/49796092 [B]—dc23/eng/20230828
LC record available at https://lccn.loc.gov/2023035012
LC ebook record available at https://lccn.loc.gov/2023035013

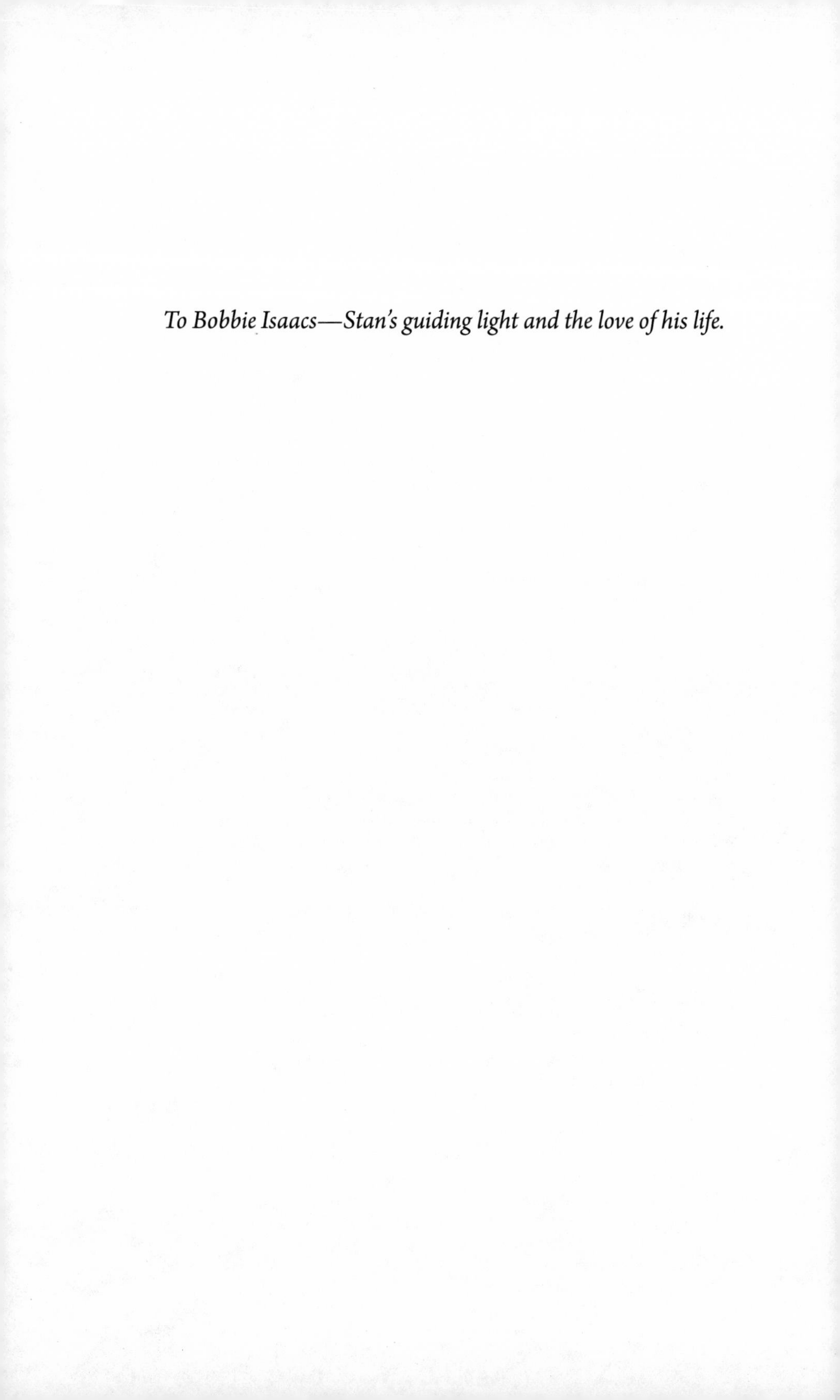

To Bobbie Isaacs—Stan's guiding light and the love of his life.

Contents

Introduction

ARAM GOUDSOUZIAN

Can one moment illustrate the appeal of Stan Isaacs? If so, it might be on October 20, 1969, as confetti twinkled down upon the caravan of convertibles rolling through Manhattan's "Canyon of Heroes." New Yorkers were cramming Lower Broadway to celebrate the Mets, champions of the World Series, just as they had once hailed Charles Lindbergh and Douglas MacArthur and the astronauts on Apollo 11. There was Isaacs, riding in the parade alongside a middle-aged art director named Karl Ehrhardt, who carried signs with proclamations of joy, such as "HOOOORAY" and "WUNNERFUL, WUNNERFUL." The fans recognized him and exclaimed, "Atta way to go, sign man!"

In his next column for *Newsday,* Isaacs described Ehrhardt's climb to celebrity. Since the Mets' futile beginnings at the old Polo Grounds and new Shea Stadium, Ehrhardt had brandished clever signs that tweaked management and players. Isaacs admired the crafty wordplay and jovial disregard for authority. Along with his fellow mischief-makers in the press corps, he urged Ehrhradt to keep it up. As the Mets crawled from chumps to champions, the funny signs won more attention. Ehrhardt, in the words of Isaacs, was "the people's representative."[1]

That tag could also be applied to Isaacs. His column, "Out of Left Field," was irreverent, mischievous, and skeptical of the straitlaced sports establishment. In both sports and life, Isaacs was a champion of the underdog, a seeker of details, a herald for oddballs.

In his memoir, Isaacs preserves the title and spirit of his column. He wrote *Out of Left Field* with a wink and a grin. The book is stuffed with the lore of sportswriters, describing the joys and burdens of the job. It expresses disillusion with self-involved athletes and self-righteous sports barons, but it delights in the dynamic personalities that breathed life into his columns. While paying homage to titans of journalism and literature, it exposes the author's pride in his own contributions, including a long history of fighting for sport's liberal crusades. Finally, it reveals a lifetime of quirky pursuits. It is safe to call Stan Isaacs the only sportswriter in American history who penned multiple columns over many decades about the name of Paul Revere's horse.

Isaacs has an enduring legacy as a cofounder of a group of writers known as the "Chipmunks," along with Larry Merchant of the *Philadelphia Daily News* and Leonard Shecter of the *New York Post*. In the early chapters of this book, Isaacs recounts the rise of his generation of sportswriters. Abandoning the lofty perch of the press box, they sought to humanize athletes. They asked probing questions and scorned hypocrites. They gravitated to big personalities. They looked at sports from fresh angles, including those of fans. As the civil rights movement, Vietnam War, and women's movement opened cracks in America's political culture, they pricked the hypocrisies of conservative sports authorities. But they also reminded readers to keep sports in their place. "It's not the end of the world," said Merchant. "It's just the end of the season."[2]

In a 1966 profile in *The Sporting News,* Leonard Koppett identified some of the Chipmunks' main attributes: a search for offbeat perspectives, a penchant for persistent questions, an ethos of cheeky fun, a mutual admiration for the literary talents of their fellow Chipmunks, and "Beatnik tendencies in dress and manner." They annoyed the older writers with their indifference toward traditional stories, but "they represent the hustle, energy and lively talents absolutely essential to journalistic health." The next year, Frederick C. Klein of the *Wall Street Journal* portrayed the Chipmunks as the vanguard of the new sportswriting: "Quick-witted men themselves, they are prone to write mainly about quick-witted, off-beat athletes—good or bad—who can see the light side of sports." He described Isaacs as a columnist in constant search of the "zany and lovable," and he recounted a landmark moment in Isaacs's career: the "breast or bottle?" story from the 1962 World Series. Isaacs begins his first chapter with the same tale.[3]

In the last chapter, Isaacs speculates that he was the first baseball reporter to decline to serve as an official scorer, despite the extra pay. His cohort resisted the paternalism of big-league franchises, which plied them with food, drink, travel, and tickets in return for soft coverage. By the 1960s, the gulf between athletes and writers was widening. Fueled by television, the sports stars won bigger incomes and adopted the trappings of celebrity, and they resented any criticism, mockery, or prodding into their personal peccadilloes. The Chipmunks considered themselves a breed apart. They were literary men. Instead of drinking at sports joints like Toots Shor's, they hobnobbed with novelists at the Lion's Head. "Not only were they younger than their predecessors," wrote David Halberstam, "they were generally better educated, definitely more iconoclastic, certainly more egocentric, and probably less grateful to be covering the great New York Yankees."[4]

The Chipmunks were not a formal organization, even if by 1965 they had printed up sweatshirts featuring a chipmunk icon, which some donned for touch football games at the *Newsday* offices. They were more a loose fraternity, mostly based in New York and Philadelphia, with some confederates in other cities. Koppett wrote that "Chipmunkery" was "a state of mind, a philosophical question too deep to probe here." More than anything else, the distinction was generational. The lively styles, social attitudes, and literary affections of these young men shaped the future of American sportswriting.[5]

As Isaacs relates, the Chipmunks got their name by appropriating a snarky comment from Jimmy Cannon, the legendary old-school columnist at the *New York Journal American*. The younger writers admired Cannon's literary grace, as well as his style, humor, connections, and charisma. But the Chipmunks also resisted Cannon's sentimental veneration of icons such as Joe Louis or Joe DiMaggio. They sought to write with the depth and detail of the best city-side columnists, while also exploiting the looser standards of the sports page. Their heroes included A. J. Liebling of the *New Yorker,* whose prodigious output included magnificent essays on boxing, and Dick Young of the *New York Daily News,* who asked tough questions in the locker room and then crafted illuminating, well-written articles. Many also drew inspiration from the fine-grained, cinematic "New Journalism" of magazine writers such as Gay Talese and Norman Mailer, who sometimes took sports as their subject.[6]

The Chipmunks capitalized on the larger forces transforming sports journalism. In his first book, published in 1964, a handbook called *Careers and Opportunities in Sports,* Isaacs described how the number of newspaper jobs was declining, but the big papers still had enormous cultural currency. Television not only magnified sports' visibility and profits, but also compelled newspapers to raise their standards. Sports reporters now needed college degrees. They had to be "word conscious" and aware of political debates, business practices, and the diversity of the American people. The Chipmunks, moreover, wrote for afternoon newspapers, which meant that their readers already knew the events from the previous night. They had to present fresh stories or funny takes. In reward, Isaacs wrote, "they are part of a society of some of the most interesting people collected together in any one landscape in America."[7]

• • •

Isaacs loved sports his entire life. Born April 22, 1929, he grew up in Williamsburg, Brooklyn, during the Great Depression, neither poor nor prosperous. He played stoopball and skelly and marbles. His first memory of the World Series was in 1936, when he joined the crowd in a city square, staring at a big board that looked like a baseball diamond—as the Western Union ticker updated the happenings, a man moved the pieces on the board. The New York Giants won that opening game but lost the Series to the Yankees. Isaacs grew to love Giants' outfielder Mel Ott almost as much as he hated Adolf Hitler.[8]

In this memoir, Isaacs recounts lively childhood tales and renders portraits of colorful characters from his family and neighborhood. Though not religious, he expressed pride in his Jewish identity. That background helped shape his life. As his professional career flourished, Isaacs exemplified many trends associated with Jews in the post–World War II United States. Anti-Semitism was on the decline, and professional opportunities were opening. Second- and third-generation Jewish Americans were moving from cities to suburbs, from the working class to the middle class. They possessed high levels of education and upward mobility. They were more secular than their forebears. They advocated liberal politics. They shaped the nation's intellectual life, including literature, and probed what it meant to be an American. They also embraced sports, a clear path toward cultural assimilation. By writing about sports, Isaacs joined this vibrant conversation.[9]

Isaacs first considered becoming a sportswriter during his sophomore year at Eastern District High School, and by 1946, he was already a stringer for the *New York Times*. By 1948 he was writing "The Sports Scene" for his college newspaper, the *Brooklyn Vanguard,* and earned his first byline in the *New York Star*. When the *Star* folded in 1949, Isaacs joined its leftist successor, *The Daily Compass*. He soon had his own column, first called "Big Town Campus" and then just "Stan Isaacs," reporting most notably on the 1951 point-shaving scandals in college basketball.[10]

In 1954 Isaacs came to *Newsday*. At first, he wrote about high school sports, but by 1956 he was covering the World Series, including the perfect game by Yankees pitcher Don Larsen. In 1957 he briefly reported on politics for the Sunday edition, covering stories such as the decline of the American Communist Party, the mysterious disappearance of a Columbia

University professor in the Dominican Republic, and a territorial dispute between Indonesia and the Netherlands. By this time, however, *Newsday* was shifting to more intensive reporting of big-league sports. Isaacs's career was about to launch.[11]

Industrial magnate Harry Guggenheim owned the controlling stake in *Newsday,* but it was his wife, Alicia Patterson, who transformed the newspaper. As editor-in-chief, she had terrific instincts, and she possessed a warm touch with her employees. *Newsday* adopted a tabloid style, with large type and wide columns, almost like a magazine. Mixing light human-interest stories with anti-corruption crusades, it appealed to the masses flocking to Long Island during the postwar boom, as the region transformed from a sleepy expanse of villages and potato farms into a dense suburban network of new homes, new highways, new businesses, new schools, and new residents. Patterson fashioned *Newsday* to serve as its journalistic voice before the New York City papers caught up. The national and international news coverage grew more substantial, and the advertising section got fatter. In 1963 Patterson died, and Guggenheim took over as editor, but *Newsday* kept booming, with a circulation of 415,000 by 1966.[12]

Sports helped forge the paper's reputation. The sports editor was a gregarious, salty ex-Marine named Jack Mann. He was a stylistic opposite to the teetotaling homebody Isaacs, but they shared views on sportswriting, and they worked well together. Their section waged a crusade against clichés and myths, while encouraging creativity and experimentation. "Mixing irony, satire, and solid reporting with liberal grains of salt, the sports section seeks to skip past the publicity handout and the pat phrase and concentrate instead on the heroic villain, the villainous hero, the dramatic incident," stated an admiring profile in *Newsweek.* "If it goes overboard at times and completely misses its mark, at least it aims in the right direction." While the department maintained its vigorous coverage of high school athletics, Isaacs, Mann, and veteran reporter Ed Comerford took turns on a general column. They also nurtured talented young writers such as George Vecsey, Bob Sales, and Steve Jacobson.[13]

In August 1959, Isaacs's column first bore the title "Out of Left Field." In early 1962, he won the National Headliners Club Award for the best overall sports column. In 1963 he began writing "Out of Left Field" five days a week, growing so popular that readers complained when he went on vacation. His columns consistently appeared in *Best Sports Stories,* a book series that compiled the year's finest sportswriting. Isaacs recounts some of those stories here, including the tale of Shail Kumar, the Nepalese student who entered the U.S. Open and lost in straight sets; the joys of the

Mets, a wretched yet endearing expansion team; and the saga of Anthony Lieberman, the star-crossed tennis player who prematurely leaped the net in celebration and then lost his match.[14]

"There isn't another paper that would let him write the way-out stuff he does for us," proclaimed Mann. That was a hard point to argue. Isaacs wrote recurring columns such as "Lieberman's Leap," about athletes who mentally goofed; "Muted Cries from the Bullpen," featuring his silly poetry; and the "Menck Award," in honor of H. L. Mencken, which snarked at the "boobs, quacks, frauds and peacocks who strut across the sports landscape." Over the years, his columns discussed his manifold idiosyncratic passions: the Calaveras County Fair Jumping Frog Jubilee, marching bands, the National Anthem, small-college football, the Boston Marathon, and, of course, the name of Paul Revere's horse.[15]

His signature column was the "Isaacs Ratings of Esoteric Distinction," which debuted in 1960 and appeared in *Newsday* until 2004, usually arriving near April Fool's Day. There were always some sports categories ("Overrated Underrated Athletes," "Reserve Giant Quarterbacks," "Hockey Meanies I Wouldn't Want My Sister to Be Married To"). But he also ranked the Four Horsemen and the Seven Santini Brothers. He graded Pool Balls, Orators, Appendages, People from Montana, and Public Statues of Lions. He rated Bridges Across the Seine and U.S. Cities in Which It Is Inadvisable to Look for a Chinese Restaurant. The categories changed every year, except for the lead item: Chocolate Ice Cream.[16]

The readers connected with Isaacs, often literally. One regular feature was the "Left Field Grab Bag," where he created surveys that readers cut out, filled in, and mailed to *Newsday* headquarters. Isaacs then replied with some promotional swag from the sports beat, stuffed into envelopes by his conscripted children. He also printed letters from readers, including one from 1968, when a bitter teenage intellectual railed against the nationwide sports obsession. As one sample of its tone, it stated, "Sport is fine if you are culturally and intellectually retarded." From the subsequent flood of angry correspondence, Isaacs fished out a measured counterpoint about sport's positive benefits.[17]

Isaacs revealed how sports shaped our everyday existence—he once wrote a column about the different ways to toss a coin at a toll booth. But he also reveled in sports' connections to literary life. In 1959 he talked sports with Jack Kerouac in Northport, Long Island, where the Beat Generation icon lived with his mother. Two years later, Isaacs visited again to play Kerouac's version of fantasy baseball with homemade cards. He wrote about Norman Mailer making a spectacle of himself at heavyweight title fights, Ernest Hemingway alluding to baseball in his writing, and Erich Segal running the Boston Marathon. Isaacs loved both sports books and "high" literature. That appreciation of writers and writing filtered into his column.[18]

Isaacs loved baseball: the subtle adjustments and moments of frenzy, the community of fans gathered on a summer day, the nostalgia connected to childhood and American identity. But he hated any haughtiness about the sport. He often summoned the perspective of the "anti-Yankee fan," resentful of the squad that won ten World Series titles between 1947 and 1962. "Yankee Stadium has always been a gloomy catacomb where the emphasis is not on the fun of being outdoors watching men at play, but on the worship of the pinstriped demi-gods," he wrote. Isaacs begrudged how the press painted Mickey Mantle as an aw-shucks hero. In his own experience, Mantle acted like an arrogant jerk, burdened by celebrity. Isaacs preferred baseball men who were authentic, smart, and lent him column fodder, from the rambunctious owner Bill Veeck to the pitchers-turned-authors Jim Brosnan and Jim Bouton. He was fascinated by Roger Maris, the grumpy, candid anti-hero who broke Babe Ruth's single-season home run record in 1961.[19]

When the Mets arrived in 1962, veteran sportswriters questioned why anyone would rather cover a historically hapless squad than the World Series champions. But the upstarts gravitated to the Mets. Isaacs was among the ringleaders. "Of all the sportswriters, he was the most open and welcoming and generous and helpful to younger writers," recalled Robert Lipsyte of the *New York Times,* who first met Isaacs at the Mets' initial spring training. Lipsyte did not identify as a Chipmunk, but he also resisted casting athletic contests as larger than life. He admired Isaacs for his intelligence, compassion, and sense of fun. "He was doing it the right way," said Lipsyte. "I think he gave courage to a lot of people to be smarter, to be funnier. To not see this as either sacred or profane."[20]

The Mets stunk, but they had characters. Manager Casey Stengel was a bottomless well of rollicking, long-winded stories full of hilarious phrases. Team owner Joan Whitney Payson was an aristocratic grande dame with a common touch. Players like "Marvelous" Marv Throneberry were so bad they made people feel good. The fans were more working-class, more sardonic, and more raucous than the Yankee Stadium crowd. "The Met fans have to be among the most daffy and delightful collection of people ever collected," marveled Isaacs in 1963. "They are dreamers, bon vivants and professional losers. They are rebels with a comic cause." One of his favorite subjects was John Pappas, a young man from Queens who flew to Florida to try out for the Mets, even though he once got cut from his high school team. For a month, he had practiced by throwing a ball at a square on a wall under the Triboro Bridge. In his determined-if-ridiculous failure, Pappas embodied the spirit of the fledgling Mets, and Isaacs loved him for it.[21]

This history of buffoonery lent a special context for the 1969 World Series. "What makes the Mets the joy of baseball and New York is not only Tom Seaver and Ron Swoboda and Gil Hodges and the rest," wrote Isaacs. "No, a bow and a nod must go to Richie Ashburn and Marv Throneberry and all those redoubtable losers." That improbable autumn, the Mets were touched by magic, igniting a remarkable civic enthusiasm. Sportswriters live by the credo of "no cheering in the press box," but Isaacs admitted to some satisfied chuckling alongside his fellow writers. Almost four decades later, Isaacs devoted a chapter to "The Amazins" in his book, *Ten Moments That Shook the Sports World*.[22]

In another chapter, Isaacs recalled another earthquake from 1969: the New York Jets' upset victory in Super Bowl III, which not only established the legitimacy of the American Football League, but also catapulted the hard-living, lady-killing quarterback Joe Namath to new heights of celebrity. When the New York Knicks won the NBA championship the next year, it reinforced that Isaacs was chronicling the glory years of Gotham sports. He was the right man at the right time, with the right lens and the right voice for interpreting the excesses, contradictions, follies, and sheer joys of American sports.[23]

During this same era, Black athletes were challenging the status quo in sports and society. Isaacs backed their cause. Early in his career, he criticized reporters who quoted Black and Latin players in dialect, defended athletes who boycotted Jim Crow facilities, and championed the tumbling of racial barriers. Yet Isaacs analyzed Black athletes from across a racial gulf, and their perspectives did not necessarily align.[24]

In his famous column from July 23, 1964, Isaacs quoted Alvin Dark, the Louisiana-raised manager of the San Francisco Giants, who stated, "We have trouble because we have so many Negro and Spanish-speaking players on this team." Isaacs reported their conversation in a matter-of-fact way. He offered counterpoints but refrained from open criticism. He omitted that Dark had ratcheted up tensions by banning the speaking of Spanish in the locker room. When the column sparked a media firestorm, Isaacs stood by his reporting, but he called Dark a "well-meaning man." In this sense, Isaacs reflected the type of white liberalism that often rankled racial minorities. Although he shone a spotlight on Dark's racism, he did not call the manager a racist. Isaacs viewed their conversation as an intellectual exercise, rather than an attack rooted in prejudice. In the aftermath, he focused on the harm it caused the manager, rather than his Black and Latin players.[25]

Yet more than most writers, Isaacs lent Black athletes a platform, and he took them on their own terms. He sought to paint fully fleshed portraits of socially conscious athletes such as Arthur Ashe, Kareem Abdul-Jabbar, and Frank Robinson. In a young-adult book and in many columns about Jim Brown, the spectacular running back for the Cleveland Browns, Isaacs depicted a fiercely proud man who blasted racism—even if his brusque style muddled his message. Amid the calls for a boycott of the 1968 Olympics in Mexico City, Isaacs questioned the militant theatrics of activist Harry Edwards and sprinter John Carlos, yet also sought the perspectives of Bill Russell and Jackie Robinson, who championed the protests as part of the Black freedom movement.[26]

Isaacs typed more words about Muhammad Ali than any other subject. Old-school writers hated the gloriously loudmouthed boxer, but Isaacs appreciated that Ali was fun. "Happiness is Cassius Clay talking . . . talking . . . talking," began one column in 1964, even before Clay shocked Sonny Liston for the heavyweight title, converted to the Nation of Islam, and adopted his new name. Isaacs was there when Ali met the Beatles, and he saw them all as witty youngsters who entertained the masses from brightly lit stages. Yet he also considered the Nation of Islam a poisonously racist sect, and he made no apologies for Ali's limited intellect, instead analyzing his complicated persona of "clown, host, mystic." As Ali sparked debates over race, religion, war, and citizenship, Isaacs adopted a liberal position, defending his right to self-expression. When Ali refused induction into the Vietnam War, Isaacs explained the situation with balance, annoying many conservatives. One reader complained, "I'd like to know how *Newsday* allows Stan Isaacs to pursue—almost weekly—his reportorial love affair with that big mouth, Cassius Clay."[27]

The title *Out of Left Field* captures not only a writing approach but also a political perspective. "Stan was further to the left and more of a character than anyone writing sports in New York," said George Vecsey, who moved from *Newsday* to the *New York Times* in the late 1960s. By that era, the Vietnam War, Black Power, the women's movement, and a declining economy were polarizing the American people. Isaacs charted the intersections of sports and politics. At the tumultuous Democratic National Convention in 1968, he described the disaffection of progressive athletes such as boxer José Torres and football player Rosey Grier; he also wrote about the notorious Birmingham city commissioner Eugene "Bull" Connor voting to nominate University of Alabama football coach Bear Bryant. In 1970, during a road trip with the Knicks, he stopped in Berkeley to interview Jack Scott, the activist at the heart of the "Athletic Revolution," a movement that questioned sport's hypermasculinity, exploitation of athletes, and obsession with winning. He then went to Stanford, where an appearance by President Richard Nixon triggered protests against the Vietnam War. Isaacs often mocked Nixon for trying to boost his standing by posing as America's No. 1 sports fan. On this day, he admired the passionate idealism of the students who were tilting the political conversation.[28]

• • •

By the dawn of the 1970s, *Newsday* was in transition, and so was Isaacs. Guggenheim sold out to Otis Chandler, publisher of the *Los Angeles Times,* and editor Bill Moyers left the paper. Isaacs, one of the main assets at *Newsday,* took on a new role. In a general column called "Stan Isaacs' Long Island," he wrote about whatever captured his fancy: local politics, labor strikes, phone books, street names, street signs, streets with the most gas stations, restaurants, buttons. He portrayed all types of Long Islanders, from teachers to actors to potato merchants to Vietnam veterans. He still wrote the occasional "Out of Left Field," and in January 1972, he was named sports editor. Though administration was not his forte, Isaacs assumed responsibility for assigning reporters and editing stories. "There are more problems as an editor than as a writer," he said. "But it's harder to be a good writer." He still wrote sporadic columns, including humorous chronicles of stints doing jury duty, taking a lie detector test, pumping gas, and participating in a pickle tasting.[29]

Upon return from a fellowship at Stanford University, Isaacs again reinvented himself. In the 1960s, sportswriters had grumbled about the incursion of television, but by the 1970s, ABC, NBC, and CBS reigned without question. Television producers and announcers dictated how Americans consumed sports, casting it in terms of entertainment. In February 1978, Isaacs debuted his "TV Sports" column. He critiqued broadcasts of major events such as the Super Bowl and Belmont Stakes, took readers into TV production booths, chronicled the rise of all-sports cable network ESPN, and praised and pilloried broadcasters. His favorite television personalities included Bob Costas, Tim McCarver, and especially John Madden. He was more ambivalent about Howard Cosell, whose ego and bombast overshadowed his talents. Although Jack Craig of the *Boston Globe* was the first TV sports columnist, Isaacs operated near the nation's media capital, and he won attention for his engaging work, including some freelance assignments from *Sports Illustrated*. He kept the "TV Sports" column until retiring from *Newsday* in 1992.[30]

Isaacs never stopped writing. After his retirement, *Newsday* kept publishing his travel pieces, sports-related op-eds, and Isaacs Ratings of Esoteric Distinction. The *New York Times* ran some freelance sports articles and funny anecdotes for "Metropolitan Diary." In his local paper, the *Roslyn News,* he celebrated friends who had passed away. He pitched a "Talk of the Town" piece on horse trainer Howie Tesher, but the *New Yorker* declined. Isaacs collaborated with Marty Glickman on the broadcaster's memoir, *Fastest Kid on the Block,* and wrote the book *Ten Moments That Shook the Sports World.*[31]

In the primordial days of the Internet, Isaacs wrote a sports media column for ESPN, when the site was called "ESPNET Sports Zone." (In his files, he called his initial article "Computer Piece No. 1"). In 2000 he started writing for TheColumnists.com, a site that indulged any whimsical swing that he cared to take, including many remembrances of his career and colleagues. His last original column, published in November 2012, relived his favorite caper: the tale of the "purloined pennant," when his gang stole a Brooklyn Dodgers championship flag after the franchise moved to Los Angeles. It is the classic Stan Isaacs story, lush with mischief and righteousness.[32]

Naturally, he included the story of the stolen banner in *Out of Left Field.* Isaacs started writing his memoir around 2004, as he and his wife Bobbie moved from Long Island to a retirement community outside Philadelphia. The book pulls together material from many of his columns, but it fashions them into an engaging narrative about the changing worlds of sports and newspapers, lightened by the outlook of a man Merchant once called "an impish intellectual."[33]

Isaacs died on April 3, 2013. "Tonight the world is a little more safe for mediocrity," mourned Keith Olbermann. In 1981, when Olbermann was a young radio broadcaster, Isaacs recognized a fellow clever, offbeat sensibility. Isaacs wrote a column about him, which led to a television job at CNN. Olbermann forever appreciated Isaacs for catapulting his career. He was not the only one who recognized the impact of Isaacs. Old friends such as Larry Merchant and George Vecsey considered him a mentor. Tony Kornheiser had grown up on Long Island reading "Out of Left Field," and when he joined the sports staff at *Newsday,* Isaacs was his editor. Kornheiser took his typewriter. Along with Henry Hecht of the *Post* and David Hirshey of the *Daily News,* he later formed "The Munchkins," a sportswriting society modeled on the Chipmunks. "My idol growing up, all I wanted to be, was Stan Isaacs," said Kornheiser.[34]

Back in February 1970, Isaacs had reflected on his job. In a typically creative column, he answered questions from himself. He believed that sportswriting served journalism's imperatives to "enlighten, inform and entertain." He admired great personalities like Ali, Veeck, and Stengel, while disparaging churlish heroes such as Mantle. He tried to avoid thinking like the millionaire celebrities he wrote about. Instead, he considered the perspective of his readers. Most important, he had fun. How, Isaacs asked himself, did he get ideas for columns? "By witnessing events; through interviews in person or on the phone; by working myself up into a high dudgeon about injustices real or imagined; and by taking off with a gallop from left field and dishing up some tomfoolery."

Which did he prefer? "The tomfoolery."[35]

Notes

1. *Newsday*, 21 October 1969. After the World Series triumph, Isaacs's column on Opening Day at Shea Stadium often focused on Ehrhradt. See *Newsday*, 15 April 1970, 2 April 1971, 9 April 1975. For other Ehrhradt columns by Isaacs, see *Newsday*, 9 December 1979, 8 January 1984.

2. Larry Merchant, interview with the author, 16 November 2022.

3. Leonard Koppett, "Eager Beavers + Rat Pack = Chipmunks," *The Sporting News*, 16 April 1966, 9–10; *The Wall Street Journal*, 6 October 1967. Koppett further reflects on the Chipmunks in Leonard Koppett, *The Rise and Fall of the Press Box* (Toronto, Canada: Sport Classic Books, 2003), 114–16. See also Isaacs's oral history in Dennis D'Agostino, *Keepers of the Game: When the Baseball Beat was the Best Job on the Paper* (Washington, D.C.: Potomac Books, 2013), 1–10.

4. David Halberstam, *October 1964* (New York: Villard Books, 1994), 172–81. Isaacs wrote about the problems of official scorekeepers from an early stage of his career; see *Daily Compass*, 11 June 1952. See also *Newsday*, 25 January 1964, for a critique by Isaacs of sports celebrity: "The star personality emerges from the corruption at work on the star's good sense."

5. Koppett, "Eager Beavers + Rat Pack," 9; Bryan Curtis, "No Chattering in the Press Box," *Grantland*, 2 May 2012; George Vecsey, interview with the author, 6 January 2023.

6. Bryan Curtis, "In Memoriam: Sportswriting Iconoclast Stan Isaacs," *Grantland*, 4 April 2013; Robert Lipsyte, interview with the author, 10 January 2023; Larry Merchant, interview with the author. For Isaacs's appreciation of Liebling, see *Newsday*, 6 January 1964, 9 September 1975.

7. Stan Isaacs, *Careers and Opportunities in Sports* (New York: E.P. Dutton, 1964), 140–48.

8. *Newsday*, 1 June 1960, 14 November 1963, 7 October 1964, 2 October 1965, 1 November 1967.

9. Edward S. Shapiro, *A Time for Healing: American Jewry since World War II* (Baltimore: Johns Hopkins University Press, 1992); Gerald Sorin, *Tradition Transformed:*

The Jewish Experience in America (Baltimore: Johns Hopkins University Pres, 1997), 194–233; Peter Levine, *Ellis Island to Ebbets Field: Sport and the American Jewish Experience* (New York: Oxford University Press, 1993), 235–69; Allen Guttmann, "Becoming American: Jewish Writers on the Sporting Life," in Steven A. Riess, ed., *Sports and the American Jew* (Syracuse, NY: Syracuse University Press, 1998), 241–55.

10. The Stan Isaacs Collection at Special Collections at Hofstra University contains a vast archive of his published writings dating from 1945 to 2013.

11. For his first byline at *Newsday*, see *Newsday*, 25 October 1954. On Larsen's perfect game, see *Newsday*, 9 October 1956. On Sunday politics pieces, see *Newsday*, 16 February 1957, 1 August 1957, 6 December 1957.

12. Robert F. Keeler, *Newsday: A Candid History of the Respectable Tabloid* (New York: William Morrow, 1990), 126–46, 309–20; "Alicia in Wonderland," *Time*, 13 September 1954, 52; "Dynasty's End," *Time*, 12 July 1963, 69–70; "Captain Takes Command," *Time*, 4 November 1966, 80–81.

13. George Vecsey, interview with the author; "Mann in Charge," *Newsweek*, 27 March 1961, 88–89; Keeler, *Newsday*, 226–28.

14. *Newsday*, 1 August 1959, 6 April 1962, 23 August 1963; Stan Isaacs, "There Once Was a Tennis Player," in Irving T. Marsh and Edward Ehre, eds., *Best Sports Stories 1961* (New York: E.P. Dutton, 1961), 232–34; Stan Isaacs, "Marvelous Marv," in Irving T. Marsh and Edward Ehre, eds., *Best Sports Stories 1963* (New York: E.P. Dutton, 1963), 83–85; Stan Isaacs, "In One Jump, He Joined the Immortals," in Irving T. Marsh and Edward Ehre, eds., *Best Sports Stories 1964* (New York: E.P. Dutton, 1964), 248–49; Stan Isaacs, "He Made the Mets Fun," in Irving T. Marsh and Edward Ehre, eds., *Best Sports Stories 1966* (New York: E.P. Dutton, 1966), 57–59.

15. "Mann in Charge," 89; *Newsday*, 22 April 1959, 21 October 1959, 2 May 1961, 19 May 1961, 24 May 1961, 23 April 1963, 20 November 1963, 21 April 1964, 8 June 1966, 27 June 1969, 7 November 1969, 8 November 1971, 12 November 1971, 21 April 1974, 6 May 1983, 20 May 1984. Isaacs wrote fewer freelance articles for magazines that many of his contemporaries, but one concerned small college football: Stan Isaacs, "Green and Leafy Football," *Look*, 20 October 1970, 70–77.

16. *Newsday*, 20 January 1960, 22 February 1961, 28 April 1961, 4 January 1963, 18 February 1964, 4 April 1966, 31 March 1967, 1 April 1968, 21 April 1969, 31 March 2004. See also Stan Isaacs, "Confessions of a Chocolate Ice Cream Authority," *LI Magazine*, 7 October 1973, 11, 37.

17. *Newsday*, 31 March 1960, 8 March 1961, 11 December 1963, 6 January 1965, 23 January 1965, 6 April 1965, 17 December 1968, 24 December 1968.

18. *Newsday*, 5 January 1959, 17 February 1961, 5 October 1966, 18 May 1966, 2 May 1967, 3 May 1967, 27 February 1969, 13 March 1970, 7 October 1970, 24 November 1970, 1 October 1975; Stan Isaacs, "Norman Mailer: 'I'm Like a Minor Champ,'" *LI Magazine*, 21 September 1975, 10–25. Upon publication of Robert Coover's *The Universal Baseball Association, Inc., J. Henry Waugh, Prop.*, Isaacs drew parallels between the imaginary baseball worlds created by Kerouac and the protagonist of Coover's novel. See *Newsday*, 30 July 1968.

19. *Newsday,* 12 January 1962, 28 March 1962, 18 May 1965, 16 September 1965, 10 May 1966, 14 October 1966; Isaacs, *Careers and Opportunities in Sports,* 164–69.

20. Robert Lipsyte, interview with the author.

21. *Newsday,* 6 June 1962, 29 March 1963, 31 January 1963, 21 June 1963, 5 November 1963, 23 March 1964, 1 March 1965, 2 March 1965. For a similar take on the early Mets, see Jimmy Breslin, *Can't Anybody Here Play This Game? The Improbable Saga of the New York Mets' First Year* (Chicago: Ivan R. Dee, 2003; original 1963).

22. *Newsday,* 17 October 1969; Stan Isaacs, *Ten Moments That Shook the Sports World: One Sportswriter's Eyewitness Accounts of the Most Incredible Sporting Events of the Past Fifty Years* (New York: Skyhorse Publishing, 2008), 75–103. For more on Isaacs and the meaning of the Mets title, see *Newsday,* 26 September 1969, 7 October 1969, 14 October 1969.

23. Isaacs, *Ten Moments That Shook the Sports World,* 187–207. Isaacs had an inkling of the Jets' Super Bowl chances: "If Joe Namath, with all his flaming-youth and outrageous lack of humility, can find it in that powerful arm to strike for those long touchdowns, it will make for one of the stunning upsets of all time." See *Newsday,* 11 January 1969.

24. *Daily Compass,* 14 February 1952; *Newsday,* 26 January 1959, 24 March 1960.

25. *Newsday,* 23 July 1964, 24 July 1964, 5 August 1964; "Faith or Works," *Sports Illustrated,* 27 August 1964, p. 7; "Giant Sized Trouble," *Time,* 14 August 1964. For an earlier Isaacs column on Dark, see *Newsday*, 14 July 1961. See also Adrian Burgos, *Playing America's Game: Baseball, Latinos, and the Color Line* (Berkeley: University of California Press, 2007), 210–12; Samuel Regalado, *Viva Baseball!: Latin Major Leaguers and Their Special Hunger,* 3rd ed. (Urbana: University of Illinois Press, 2008; orig. 1998), 84–87.

26. On Black athletes, see *Newsday,* 12 October 1966, 2 January 1969, 11 September 1970. Isaacs wrote about Jim Brown from his high school years through the publication of his second memoir; see *Newsday,* 27 December 1955, 2 December 1959, 24 September 1964, 28 December 1964, 2 January 1965, 20 September 1989; Stan Isaacs, *Jim Brown: The Golden Year 1964* (Englewood Cliffs, N.J.: Prentice-Hall, 1970). On the 1968 Olympics, see *Newsday,* 28 November 1967, 29 November 1967, 26 June 1968, 27 June 1968, 9 August 1968, 18 October 1968, 24 October 1968, 28 October 1968.

27. *Newsday*, 25 March 1963, 14 March 1964–25 March 1964, 31 March 1967, 22 June 1967, 13 January 1968, 28 March 1968, 5 March 1970. See also Bryan Curtis, "How Muhammad Ali Woke Up Sportswriting," *The Ringer,* 4 June 2016.

28. *Newsday,* 19 April 1967, 27 August 1968, 28 August 1969, 20 August 1968, 23 July 1969, 11 December 1969, 8 May 1970; 13 May 1970, 14 May 1970, 23 November 1970, 8 January 1972, 11 May 1973, 25 March 1975.

29. Keeler, *Newsday,* 394–403, 467–524; *Newsday,* 12 March 1971, 22 March 1971, 22 April 1971, 25 May 1971, 9 June 1971, 19 July 1971, 22 September 1971, 23 September 1971, 13 October 1971, 14 October 1971, 25 October 1971, 18 January 1972, 13 July 1972; 4 November 1973; 23 December 1973; 24 March 1974.

30. Benjamin G. Rader, *In Its Own Image: How Television Has Transformed Sports*

(New York: The Free Press, 1984), 100–155; *Newsday,* 12 February 1978; 5 May 1987, 12 February 2008. On Costas, see *Newsday,* 5 January 1985, 13 August 1985, 11 October 1985, 18 May 1986, 4 June 1987, 7 August 1988. On McCarver, see *Newsday,* 5 April 1987, 7 August 1987, 11 October 1987, 23 April 1989. On Madden, see *Newsday,* 24 January 1982, 4 February 1983, 11 November 1984, 12 January 1986. On Cosell, see *Newsday,* 16 April 1978, 14 August 1984, 19 April 1985, 27 June 1986, 27 September 1986. On *Sports Illustrated,* see Stan Isaacs, "No Armageddon Bowls For Him," *Sports Illustrated,* 1 October 1979; Stan Isaacs, "The Orioles Play Stop the Music," *Sports Illustrated,* 8 October 1979; Stan Isaacs, "A Local Game for the Locals Only," *Sports Illustrated,* 19 November 1979; Kelso F. Sutton, "Letter from the Publisher," *Sports Illustrated,* 21 January 1980; Stan Isaacs, "The Shot Heard 'Round the Links," *Sports Illustrated,* 21 January 1980.

31. *Newsday,* 15 May 1994, 25 June 1995, 13 June 1995, 30 July 1996, 18 October 1996, 13 April 1997, 20 July 1997, 14 December 2003, 22 January 2004, 4 February 2004; *New York Times,* 5 September 1993, 9 January 1994, 26 March 1994, 3 June 1994, 27 July 1994, 7 May 1995; *Roslyn News,* 4 August 1994, 17 April 1997; Marty Glickman with Stan Isaacs, *The Fastest Kid on the Block* (Syracuse, N.Y.: Syracuse University Press, 1996); Isaacs, *Ten Moments That Shook the Sports World.*

32. Isaacs wrote for the ESPNET Sports Zone from 1996 to 1997 and for TheColumnists.com from 2004 to 2012. These articles are no longer on the Internet, but print versions can be found in the Stan Isaacs Papers at Hofstra University.

33. Larry Merchant, interview with the author.

34. Keith Olbermann, "Stan Isaacs: 1929–2013," http://keitholbermann.mlblogs.com/2013/04/04/2115315/; George Vecsey, interview with the author; Larry Merchant, interview with the author; Curtis, "No Chattering in the Press Box"; *Newsday,* 10 February 2006.

35. *Newsday,* 24 February 1970.

A Note on Terminology

In the 1950s and 1960s, Isaacs used the term "Negro," an ordinary and respectful way to refer to Black people in that period. In this memoir, he uses "Negro" only when quoting from columns of that era.

When Isaacs wrote *Out of Left Field* in the first decade of the twentieth century, he adhered to the then-standard identifier of "black," uncapitalized.

PROLOGUE

The Shots Heard 'Round the World

I have stories. Family stories, baseball stories, horse-racing stories, tennis stories, Olympic and celebrity stories. During a fifty-year career of cheering, exhorting, damning, beefing, bitching, kibitzing, glorifying, critiquing, preaching, grieving, ranking, and laughing, I wrote "Out of Left Field," the *Newsday* column from which I threw bouquets and darts at figures from the sports world and beyond. These days, the past bleeds into the present.

September 11, 2001 was to be another day in the continuing progress of a statue of Pee Wee Reese and Jackie Robinson. The project was precious to me. The plan to erect a statue honoring the great Brooklyn Dodgers stemmed from my speech at a memorial to Reese shortly after he died, on August 14, 1999. I suggested commemorating the significant moment during fielding practice before a 1947 game when Robinson, in his first season as the first black man in major league baseball, was being vilified by Cincinnati players and fans. Reese—a southerner from Louisville—responded by walking over to Robinson and putting his arm around him. This quelled the vitriol. Reese is remembered for this act now as much as for his career as an outstanding shortstop and Dodger captain.

The statue idea took hold with the help of columnist Jack Newfield and became part of Mayor Rudy Giuliani's project to renovate the Coney Island section of Brooklyn. Money was raised and sculptors were selected to compete for the assignment of creating the statue that would stand outside the new minor league stadium in Brooklyn, home of the Mets' farm team, the Cyclones.

At the meeting at City Hall early in the morning on September 11, judges got their first look at the five maquettes (small versions of statues) submitted by the sculptors. Among the committee members were Reese's wife, Dotty, and son, Mark; Jackie's wife, Rachel, and daughter Sharon; and former Brooklyn Dodger Ralph Branca.

City Hall was six blocks from the World Trade Center. Tamra Lhota, the woman who was spearheading the selection process, suddenly stopped the proceedings and began to speak haltingly. She relayed a report that something terrible had happened, something about a plane hitting the World Trade Center. She seemed so stunned that we didn't quite understand what she was saying. We asked her to repeat herself. At just about that point, we heard a loud boom. The building shook. That, we found out soon enough, was the sound of the second plane smashing into the other World Trade Center tower.

Rachel Robinson, who had just arrived at the meeting, said, "I heard an earlier boom when the car bringing me here was going under the trestle at the World Trade Center." Stunned and not quite sure what had happened, we moved into an adjoining office and watched the re-runs of the second plane crash on a small television set.

The reality of a terrorist attack began to dawn upon us. We were told to remain at City Hall because it is one of the most secure buildings in the city; arrivals there are screened at security entrances. After a while, my wife and I went out to the front steps of City Hall and saw the smoke gushing from the towers six blocks away. We watched people, some looking panic-stricken, rushing north past City Hall, away from the World Trade Center.

We waited in the building for almost an hour, then made our way over to a subway station two blocks west on Chambers Street. We walked among crowds at corners looking up at the Twin Towers. On the north tower we saw a ribbon of fire some twenty yards across and a huge hole high up in the building. We never dreamed those towers would collapse.

We rode one of the last subway trains uptown, and when Penn Station at 34th Street was shut down, we spent the next hour in the Garment Center offices of a friend. We were stunned to hear on the radio about the collapse of the buildings. On that subway ride uptown, strangers talked to each other, relating where they had been, what they had seen. On the street, people listened to radios from newsstands and parked trucks. There was a oneness among people, not unlike what we heard about Londoners during the World War II Blitz bombing campaign.

• • •

At the end of that awful Tuesday, I was struck by a weird thought. When we heard the huge boom of the second plane crashing into the tower, I was talking to Ralph Branca. Fifty years earlier, he had thrown the pitch that Bobby Thomson hit for a home run that has since become known as "The Shot Heard 'Round the World."

That brings us back to October 3, 1951. I am in the Polo Grounds. Beloved by many, maligned by others, the Polo Grounds is in the upper reaches of Manhattan. It is an overcast day for the celebrated third game of the National League playoffs between the New York Giants and the Brooklyn Dodgers.

I am a Giants fan and my assignment for the *New York Daily Compass* is to cover the Giants' clubhouse at the end of the game. Usually in such a situation, a reporter will make his or her way out of the press box in the top of the ninth inning and inch toward the clubhouse area to be ready to enter the complex when it is opened to the press at the end of the game.

It had been fourteen years since the Giants had won a pennant. Those fourteen years seem like an eternity to me—an eternity of suffering Giants' defeats, ineptness, failures, frustrations, humiliations. I am still as much a fan as a reporter. I want to see the game to its bitter end. I decide to linger as much as I can before leaving for the clubhouse.

I leave the press box with the Dodgers ahead, 4–1, as the Giants are about to come to bat in the bottom of the ninth inning. I walk from the press box in the upper stands behind home plate toward the right field section that leads to the clubhouses in center field. By the time the Giants' leadoff hitter in the ninth inning, Alvin Dark, moves into the batter's box for the Giants' last at-bat, I am on the long runway in right field. This is the path that fans walk up upon entering the Polo Grounds, moving out of the shadows into the light. At this point the huge greensward of the old, oval-shaped ballpark comes into view in the gap between the upper and lower right field stands. Now I am crouching down and looking between those stands to see the unfolding action.

I hope against hope. Dark sends a ground ball single past the lunge of Dodgers' first baseman Gil Hodges. Don Mueller swats another ground ball to Hodges's right and into right field just below me. Monte Irvin fouls out and the old demons of close-but-not-close-enough agitate me. What a pessimist I am. Whitey Lockman then slices a ball on a low line to the opposite field, down the left field foul line. It is a two-base hit. Dark scores. Mueller slides into third base.

There is a delay. Mueller hurt his ankle sliding into the base. Clint Hartung lumbers out to replace him. Now, Dodger manager Charlie Dressen comes out to talk to starting pitcher Don Newcombe. He calls for Ralph Branca. During the delay I talk to a black man wearing cream-colored slacks and a porkpie hat, both of us kneeling to peer through the stands. He is also a Giants fan. We are instant soulmates.

The broad-shouldered Branca, number 13 on his back, trudges in from the Dodgers bullpen. The walk from the bullpen in left-center field to the mound at the Polo Grounds is the longest walk in baseball for a relief pitcher. There is a hush over the ballpark, an occasional shout of encouragement by Giants fans.

Branca pitches to Bobby Thomson with Willie Mays in the on-deck circle. Thomson lets the first pitch go by. It is called a ball. He swings on Branca's next pitch. He hits a low line drive toward left field. I have to bend down as much as I can to follow its flight. I am hoping the ball will hit the upper stands for a home run or miss the upper stands overhang and bounce off the left field wall. I dread—and this would be the final crusher—that the ball will not carry far enough and drop into the hands of Dodgers left fielder Andy Pafko. The ball misses the upper stands, but in its downward flight it falls just over the top of the wall into the front seats of the left field stands. Home run. Giants win, 5–4. Giants win the pennant.

It will be called "The Shot Heard 'Round the World." My first thought is, "I've got the winning dressing room." I am assigned to cover the Giants' clubhouse and now, suddenly, the Giants are the winning team. I shout unintelligibly, part of the noise engulfing the ballpark, and sprint down the ramp, down a flight of stairs to the Giants' clubhouse to join the other reporters. After five minutes or so, we enter into the midst of merriment and delight.

I revel in a scene that is as much a joy for me as a time to interview the celebrating Giants players in the raucous clubhouse. After interviewing Giants manager Leo Durocher, sitting in his sweaty undershirt in a chair in his office, I go over to the funereal Dodgers clubhouse across the way. The never-to-be-forgotten scene is of a distraught Branca lying across a few steps while his teammates tiptoe around him.

I will write sports for more than fifty years and never cover any event as joyous, historic, or meaningful to me as that game on that day in the old Polo Grounds. I will cover four Olympics, including the tragedy of the killing of the Israeli Olympians at Munich in 1972; many World Series; and a half-dozen early Super Bowls, including the New York Jets' historic upset of the Baltimore Colts in 1969. I will cover outstanding horse races, track meets, Islanders' Stanley Cup victories. I will be exposed to some of the most colorful figures in sports. And I will cover tumultuous heavyweight boxing championships, serving as a witness to the early madcap, explosive career of Muhammad Ali.

Bobby Thomson's "Shot Heard 'Round the World" on that gray day in the Polo Grounds stands as my most memorable moment in a long career writing about sports, politics, human interest, entertainment, and whatever stimulated an urge in my noggin to reach out to a populace that I trusted was out there. After newspapers, I followed the crowd to the Internet and had an ego-gratifying run as a blogosphere columnist. As I write this, I am eighty-two years old. So far, so good.

1

The Chipmunks

At the end of the 1962 World Series, reporters surrounded Ralph Terry of the New York Yankees. The pitcher had just beat the San Francisco Giants in the deciding seventh game. Terry had also won an earlier game and was voted the Most Valuable Player of the Series, so the press crowded around his locker. Those of us who covered the Yankees knew the shy, amiable Terry quite well, and there was good-natured banter in the questioning. In the middle of it, Terry excused himself to answer a phone call in another room.

When he got back, he said the call was from his wife.

"What was she doing?" somebody asked.

"She was feeding the baby," he said.

Whereupon I lightheartedly asked, "Breast or bottle?"

Some were floored by my question. Others laughed. Terry gave a shy grin. There was so much laughter I don't think the world ever got to know which method of baby feeding Mrs. Terry was using.

I regarded my question as a joke, but it has come to be a part of baseball lore. I have seen the incident quoted again and again through the years. The descriptions of what was a light-hearted scene have most often been inaccurate. One documentary on baseball writers had the question being asked not in 1962 when Terry was the hero but in 1960, after he gave up the Series-ending home run by Pittsburgh's Bill Mazeroski.

Some have used the question as an example of the arrogance of the press in prying into athletes' lives. Others have regarded it as merely outlandish. I laugh. My wife and I have had three girls. She breast-fed the youngest of them. I have never thought it was strange to talk about breast-feeding. But if I am around, and the name Ralph Terry comes up, I am sure to hear a chuckle about "breast or bottle."

• • •

The "breast or bottle" story is part of the history of the chipmunks. I could capitalize the C to make it seem as if we were a heralded team or something, but I desist. Instead, let me describe the chipmunks—who we were, how we came to be.

It all started with the waggish trio of Leonard Shecter of the *New York Post,* Larry Merchant of the *Philadelphia News,* and me. Shecter and I were kindred spirits on the Yankee beat. We were drawn together because we had an irreverent attitude about the team. We didn't think it was a rare privilege to be allowed to associate with the ballplayers, however talented and lordly they were. We treated the Yankees and baseball for what it was—grown men playing a little boy's game. We asked questions that weren't always appreciated.

Shecter was a heavy-set guy with a thick black mustache and an infectious chuckle. More acerbic than I, he was a thorn in the Yankees' side. Because he worked for a New York City paper, the players and management could read him immediately.

I didn't have that problem. To the people of the sports establishment in the late 1950s and early 1960s, *Newsday* was some half-baked paper out in the Long Island suburbs. If I wrote something pungent, it was overlooked or passed on to one of the players by word of mouth sometime later. Once, when Bill Skowron of the Yankees told me, "Don't interview me, I'm stupid," I quoted him in the paper. Whitey Ford, a *Newsday* subscriber who lived in Lake Success on Long Island, laughed at this, and passed it on to Skowron a few days later. He confronted me. I was secretly pleased that I had at least drawn notice.

Shecter and I migrated to Yankee players who didn't fit the mold. Often, they were marginal players who had the wit and will to convey what life as major leaguers was like. One of them was Mark Freeman, a pitcher of no great physical prowess but an engaging, intriguing young man with a soft Bayou accent. He was a graduate of Louisiana State University who struggled in the Yankee system. Freeman battled for a job on the Yankee staff for several spring training seasons. He finally made the team in 1959, played part of a season with the Yankees, and then was shipped to Kansas City. He pitched with the Chicago Cubs the next season and then faded to the minors and out of baseball. The last I heard, he became an executive in Denver.

Unlike most ballplayers, Freeman was an introspective man. He once said he probably failed as a pitcher because his father had pushed him too hard to be a ballplayer; by failing, he was getting back at his father. With a keen analytical mind, he studied his fellow players. Throwing around psychoanalytic theories, he was a terrific anonymous source for Shecter's three-part series on Mickey Mantle. Shecter ate it up—as did *Post* readers. Mantle, the least introspective of men at the time, paid hardly any attention to it.

Phil Linz and Jim Bouton were other Yankee nonconformists. Bouton was extremely intelligent, articulate, and funny. He lusted for the limelight, and he was too outspoken and rakish for his teammates. Bouton quickly became a favorite of the reporters, because he liked attention and enjoyed our company. He was one of the few athletes who ever inquired about how I went about my work. He asked how I thought of ideas for pieces, dealt with deadlines, and the like.

Shecter grew close to Bouton, who said that before he first met Shecter he thought Len's first name was "Fucking" because Yankee players would tell him, "Watch out for that Fucking Shecter," or "That Fucking Shecter can't be trusted."

Shecter prevailed upon Bouton to take notes and keep a diary of a season. That led to the writing and publication of the acclaimed 1970 book *Ball Four*. An earlier book by Cincinnati Reds pitcher Jim Brosnan, called *The Long Season,* had first provided an accurate inside view of baseball that differed from the gee-whiz approach of baseball literature up to that time. Bouton was funnier than Brosnan, and Shecter was a skilled collaborator. *Ball Four* was a more pointed and critical look at the baseball environment. It made Bouton a pariah in baseball, but it delighted readers.

Merchant was sports editor and columnist for the *Philadelphia News*. He was cheerful, bright and quick to laugh. He looked so much like me—both shorter and stockier than we preferred to be—that we frequently were mistaken for each other. Merchant was an avid reader of out-of-town papers, and he picked up on my work fairly early. He seemed to be more familiar with my writing than the insular guys in New York.

Merchant and his people at the *News* were treating sports with the same kind of irreverence we exhibited in the pages of *Newsday*. When we met at national events, we became friends. Merchant would go on to the *New York Post* before starting a television career. As the highly respected boxing analyst for Home Box Office (HBO), he is as astute and witty on the tube as he had been as a newspaper stalwart.

After a while, because of the similarity of our approach, Shecter, Merchant, and I began referring to ourselves as the Rat Pack. We were taking off on the name associated with Frank Sinatra and his Hollywood pals, in recognition of the view of people who didn't particularly appreciate our work.

The Rat Pack became the chipmunks, a name that traced to a postgame session with Bouton. As usual, when Bouton pitched, he got a good deal of attention from reporters and, as usual, there was a good deal of revelry in the dialogue with him at his locker. The laughter was picked up by columnist Jimmy Cannon on the other side of the clubhouse. He didn't particularly appreciate the irreverence of the younger reporters. He spotted Phil Pepe of the *World Telegram,* one of the younger guys. Pepe's front teeth protruded somewhat, and Cannon, always a quick man with a put-down, said, "Look at them, look at them—a bunch of chipmunks!" He meant it as an insult. I heard Cannon say it and passed it on to Merchant. We adopted it as a badge of honor.

Over the years the term "chipmunk" took on different connotations. Some approved of our attempts to go beyond the details of the game, to show the athletes for better or worse. They saw the chipmunks as a new breed. The establishment used the term derisively.

The chipmunks were about writing well, free of clichés. We cared about our stories more than whether a team won or lost. We saw ourselves as not very different from good city-side reporters, but with the good luck of having the freedom of the sports pages. The group rejected the approach of the cliché-ridden sports reporters of old. We didn't see the sports world as Life and Death. Some of the old-timers were good writers but were more like cheerleaders than reporters. In the main, we felt we were bringing an adult perspective to sports, enlightening the outside world with some of our stories. We were not Olympian observers from on high, but down-on-the-field scramblers looking for the offbeat and the funny.

We gravitated to unconventional characters, such as Cincinnati Reds utility infielder Giraldo Ruiz y Sablon, who was known as Chico Ruiz. For one of my columns, he once rated the National League dugouts for qualities such as ambience and view. Once, his wife was puzzled when she didn't see him in the dugout. She couldn't find him because he was, of all places, in the starting lineup.

Sometimes we may have gone overboard. During one spring training, Shecter wrote a feature about Rich Barry, a Yankee rookie catcher with a huge appetite who set some kind of record for eating chicken wings. On this same day, Mickey Mantle came down with a sore knee. Joe Trimble, the longtime beat man for the *Daily News,* couldn't understand why Shecter would write about an inconsequential rookie's eccentricity on a day when the Yankee star may have suffered an injury that could have huge implications for the team. Shecter responded that Mantle's injuries were a constant thing, and this one was not particularly worthy of breast-beating.

In retrospect, one could argue that the rookie's chicken-wing-eating record could have been held for another day.

• • •

Periodically, in all aspects of journalism, comfort and lethargy set in among those who have been on a beat too long. Inevitably, younger reporters come along to do things with more energy, more fervor. It happens more rapidly these days. The chipmunks of old do not necessarily approve of some of the newer breed's scabrous work.

Along with Shecter, Merchant, and me, the ranks of the chipmunks included, among others, Jack McKinney and Stan Hochman of the *Philadelphia Daily News,* Bud Collins of the *Boston Globe,* John Crittenden of the *Miami Daily News,* Vic Ziegel of the *New York Post,* and George Vecsey, Steve Jacobson, and Bob Sales of *Newsday*. Maury Allen of the *Post* proclaimed himself a chipmunk, though Shecter felt Maury did not cast a critical-enough eye on the sports landscape to rate inclusion in this amorphous fraternity.

We regarded Dick Young of the *Daily News* as an original chipmunk even though he disliked us. Young and Cannon were among the harshest critics of the early Muhammad Ali; the chipmunks enjoyed and defended Ali. I felt Bob Lipsyte of the *New York Times* was one of us, too, even though he shrank from any label.

The chipmunk business was a subtle subplot of Billy Crystal's HBO movie, *61**, about the pursuit of Babe Ruth's home run record by Mickey Mantle and Roger Maris. The script included a character who was a nasty reporter named Artie Green. According to Crystal, he was based on Shecter. He even claimed that Shecter was taken off the Yankee beat by his editor because of the movie.

This was poppycock. Shecter—and I—liked Maris. We rather enjoyed his grumpy persona before he became the central figure in the pursuit of Ruth's record of 60 homers. We rooted for Maris early because he was something of the anti-Yankee, making it a point to declare himself above Yankee tradition. The veteran reporters on the beat such as Joe Trimble, Til Ferdenzi, and Jim Ogle rooted for Mantle. So did most Yankee fans, until injuries forced Mantle out of the lineup and out of the chase. They thought Maris wasn't the kind of larger-than-life character who should break such a hallowed record. Meanwhile, the chipmunks tried to detail the heroic quest and humanity of an ordinary guy.

When Mantle was incapacitated and Maris became the main man, he suffered the mental tension of chasing the record. But there was little of the contentiousness that is part of the myth of 1961. In actuality, Maris's problems stemmed mostly from events of the next season. In the offseason Maris, prodded by his brother Rudy, came to the conclusion that he had not made enough money from his feat. He resented Shecter writing a paperback book about him (*Roger Maris, Home Run Hero*), for which Shecter got all of $1,000.

Maris came to spring training in 1962 with a chip on his shoulder. He blew off UPI reporter Oscar Fraley and columnist Jimmy Cannon. They ripped him in print, and that escalated the controversy about him. Those of us who had long covered him recognized that he was a likable grouch. But as a celebrity, he didn't know how to be gracious, at least on the surface.

Anyway, the chipmunks appreciated a rebellious spirit. At the 1960 World Series between the Yankees and Pittsburgh Pirates, I approached Shecter and Merchant with an impish scheme meant to entrap reporters who spread false trade stories at the World Series. The prime culprit was Joe Reichler of the Associated Press. He would conjure trade deals that alerted sports editors to harass their own baseball writers to track them down. No matter that the majority of would-be trades never panned out; seeking out nonexistent trade deals became a cottage industry at the World Series.

I suggested we make up a trade rumor, as outlandish as possible, spread it around, and hope that Reichler, in particular, would fall for it. We agreed that a story naming a new manager would be fertile ground. The group came up with the man, who, at that time, was considered the least likely to be a manager: Yogi Berra. We concocted the story of Berra going to the San Francisco Giants, who would then send pitcher Johnny Antonelli to the Yankees.

We passed the word around to several of the reporters gathered at World Series press headquarters in Pittsburgh. In a short time, word of the rumor had spread and appeared in some papers. I felt guilt pangs about Jack Lang of the *Long Island Press* using the story because the Press was the rival to *Newsday* on Long Island. When I told Lang the story was a hoax, he said, "I'm using it anyway because it is being talked about."

I was sly enough to go over to Berra and ask him about the rumor. The beloved Yogi was noncommittal about everything, and it didn't surprise me when he neither admitted nor denied that the Giants had been in touch with him. The story made the United Press wire. It did not, however, fool Joe Reichler. He smelled it out. Perhaps he had a fine nose for detecting a false story.

The kicker was that in 1964, Berra became manager of the Yankees. My fake rumor was no longer so outlandish.

2

Chipmunkery

In June 1961, I had been on the road with the Yankees for more than a week. I tended to get restless at about this time, particularly if we were winding up in Kansas City, where my room at the Muehlebach Hotel was too small to swing a dead cat in.

At this time, Athletics owner Charlie Finley was trying to create buzz in Kansas City with Bill Veeck–like stunts. One of them was to station sheep out on a grass terrace behind the right field fence within the outer fence that ringed the ballpark. I decided to vary my routine by sitting out in right field with a sheep's eye view of the game.

My lead on the 8–3 Yankee victory read: "As any of the five sheep out on the hill behind right field can testify, Whitey Ford did a nifty job of pulling the wool over the Kansas City batters' eyes most of last night." The story ran with the headline, "A Sheepish Report of Yanks' Victory" and a picture of me sitting among the sheep.

The twelve-year-old boy, Mike Quigley, assigned to return balls hit out there, greeted me with, "Didn't they have enough room for you in the press box?" Whitey Ford asked, "Is this story going to appear in the *Livestock News?*" Mickey Mantle wanted to know how many blades of grass were out there, his way of poking fun at some of the questions asked by reporters.

In the second inning of the game, Roger Maris's three-run homer had landed a few feet away from me. I ambled over, picked up the ball, and pocketed it for a while. It was home run number 27 on the way to Maris's record 61-homer year. I did not save the ball.

• • •

Chipmunkery wasn't all tomfoolery. We were serious young men intent on covering sports as an adult activity with an underside of warts and imperfections like any big business. We pursued stories good and bad, with an appreciation of the great feats on the playing fields.

After Merchant came to the *New York Post,* he lacerated the hapless football Giants' management of those days with astute analysis. He was among the keenest of football observers, no doubt the result of his once having been the eighth-string quarterback on one of Bud Wilkinson's powerhouse football teams at the University of Oklahoma in the late 1940s. Merchant angered the great Jim Brown by being one of the first to point out Brown's aversion to the unglamorous craft of blocking.

Like others, I had run-ins with athletes who seemed to think publicity and admiration was their constant due. Mickey Mantle was a toughie. He was not comfortable with reporters. Much of it had to do with his being a small-town yokel from Commerce, Oklahoma, thrust into the glare of the big-city spotlight. He was special because he was a phenom from the first day he came to Yankee camp in St. Petersburg. He had great speed and power, hitting prodigious blasts over distant fences.

Reporters flocked to him. The Yankee management could have helped the rube by explaining the needs of a press only too willing to lionize the young man. These were the days of the arrogant Yankee dynasty, though, and they made no such overtures to the press. Worse, I heard that a Yankee publicity man told Mantle, "You don't have to talk to these pricks."

Mantle had a way of looking through a reporter asking a question. This was galling and frustrating, knowing that behind that façade was a likable young man. He was tremendously popular with his teammates because there was little of the big star about him. He had a self-deprecatory sense of humor and told outrageously bawdy jokes. When he came to the Yankees, the big star Joe DiMaggio, a shy, reclusive man in his own right, did not reach out to Mantle. Mickey did not forget that, and he was always quick to befriend Yankee rookies. He was a terrific team player with an intense will to win.

Yet he could be maddeningly difficult at times. One Friday night he hit a home run in extra innings to seal a Yankee victory. In the dressing room afterward, he made himself unavailable to reporters; he hung out in the trainer's room, which was barred to reporters. There were deadlines to meet, and after a while the other reporters cursed him and left. I felt there was no way I could write a story about Mantle winning the game for the Yankee without a comment from him. I determined to wait him out.

When Mantle came out to his locker, he was with a friend, a loud-mouthed lamp salesman. He answered my questions by playing off the toadying lamp salesman to ridicule me. I hung in to get some insipid quotes and wrote the story. I did not mention the difficulties because I felt the readers would not be interested in my problems. But when I returned to the press room to write and was asked by the other reporters what Mantle had told me, I said, "Sorry guys, I waited him out and took his abuse; I'm not sharing."

Mantle was ever the small-town guy. When the Yankees were getting on a bus after a game in Kansas City, up the road from his Oklahoma birthplace, Mantle would smile at an admiring assemblage of fans, sometimes getting out of the bus to sign autographs. Yet, when the Yankees were in a similar situation in Boston, surrounded by taunting fans, he would plop himself deep in the bus. Whitey Ford, who grew up in Queens, took on the Boston street rats. They liked Ford, even as they tried to smoke out Mantle from the bowels of the bus.

Mantle's hard drinking and carousing shortened his career. A young outfielder, Roger Repoz, came to be known as Mantle's caddy because he replaced Mickey in late innings to preserve Mantle's fragile legs. Once, as Mantle went up to his hotel room for an assignation with a tart, he told Repoz, "Stick around kid, maybe my legs will give out."

Mindful of the bone disease that had taken his father's life, he often said after he retired, "If I had known I would live this long I would have taken better care of myself." He died at sixty-three.

When he retired from baseball, I wrote, "He could, when his legs were right, run down to first base as fast as anybody who ever played baseball. He could hit the ball farther than anybody, and he could do it hitting either lefty or righty. There were few young baseball players who excited the imagination the way Mickey Mantle did when he first came down the spring training pike in 1951."

After he retired, somewhat fueled by liquor, he expressed regrets about not enjoying his fame. He wished that he had reached out more to the public via the press. Mantle became almost garrulous in interviews. The price you had to pay was to listen at times to some of the most godawful tasteless stories. Sometimes it was hard to believe that this was the guy who once froze us with a laser-beam stare.

• • •

Willie Mays came up as a phenom the same year as Mantle. Mays was treated as something of a child of nature with the New York Giants. He was enjoyed more than he was probed. Leo Durocher, the manager who adored him, spoke for him.

When the Giants moved to San Francisco in 1958, the press and fans were slow to take Mays to their hearts. Orlando Cepeda and Willie McCovey were the immediate favorites. Mays resented this and had cool relations with the press. He became suspicious of people's motives. Once, when I was in San Francisco and tried to talk to him, he was difficult. When he said, "You guys . . ." I cut him off. I scolded him, reminding him that he had never been treated badly by New Yorkers like me. I resented being lumped in with "you guys."

Whereas Mantle became expansive and friendly when he retired, Mays sulked. He became a cranky, suspicious man, ever resentful that the money he had made as a player and was making in postcareer appearances was not enough. This saddened me, because as an old Giant fan, I gloried in him when he lit up the Polo Grounds.

He thrilled me with his all-around play, especially his sensational fielding. It seemed during the Giants' stirring run to a pennant in 1951 that Mays made a remarkable play in the outfield every day. I talked with people like Chub Feeney, the Giants' longtime official, and chronicled Mays's greatest catches. They were:

The Billy Cox Play: Late in the 1951 season, the Dodgers' Cox was on third base and Carl Furillo hit a fly to short right-center field in the Polo Grounds. Mays had a long run, cutting in to his left to snare the ball. Catching the ball was an outstanding play in itself. Mays then whirled in a 360-degree turn and unleashed a strong, accurate throw to home plate that arrived in plenty of time to nab the surprised Cox. Because of the two components of the play, it is unlikely ever to be repeated. I regard it as Mays's greatest play.

The Bobby Morgan Catch: In a 1952 game, the Dodgers' Bobby Morgan hit a line drive up the left-center field alley at Ebbets Field. The ball appeared to be past Mays. As he raced back to his right, it seemed that he caught up with the ball as he leaped and clutched it in his glove. He then hit the ground and bounced off the base of the concrete wall. Mays lay stunned for a few moments but held the ball. He regarded this as his greatest catch.

The Bob Skinner Catch: The Pirates' slugger hit a tremendous drive to deep center field in the Polo Grounds in a 1954 game. At that time a wire screen on the right-center field bleachers protruded out into the runway leading to the clubhouse steps. Mays raced back and caught the drive over his right shoulder, then ducked in time to run under the screen.

The Vic Wertz Catch: This is his most celebrated catch, more for the setting than the play. It was in the first game of the 1954 World Series at the Polo Grounds. Cleveland's Wertz hit a long drive to dead center. Mays raced back and caught the ball over his head with his back to the infield, like a wide receiver taking a long pass. He then turned and threw back to the infield to hold a runner. This sequence is shown almost as often as Bobby Thomson's game-winning home in 1951.

The Barehanded Catch: In a 1951 game, Rocky Nelson of Pittsburgh hit a wicked drive to left-center. The ball seemed to be going away from Mays, who was unable to reach it with his gloved left hand. So he reached out with his bare right-hand and caught the ball. Ralph Kiner called it, "the greatest catch I ever saw."

• • •

Another aspect of chipmunkery was our dedication to the craft. We liked to talk about sportswriting. It seemed to threaten some of the older reporters.

In the late 1950s, during spring training with the Yankees, the postgame session consisted of Casey Stengel holding court. It was the best show in town. One day, though, Stengel had other business, and none of his coaches showed up, either. That left only a few newspaper men. Shecter and I started a discussion away from baseball. Instead of analyzing the technique of making the double play or the wizardry of the slider, we talked about approaches to writing spring training stories. Tommy Holmes, a veteran of the *Brooklyn Eagle* and *New York Herald Tribune,* chafed and glowered. Others did not join in. The discussion of newspaper craft ended soon enough.

Merchant had some memorable moments. You could almost hear the laughter coming out of his typewriter. Once, he was on the plane typing his story when the Phillies were coming home from a disastrous road trip. Catcher Sammy White, who had swilled more beers than was good for him, came down the aisle and peered over Merchant's shoulder. He read the story, then grabbed the typewriter and hurled it toward the back of the plane. Merchant cracked, "It was the best throw White made all season."

Shecter was probably the most talented among us. He was certainly the toughest. He wrote a hard-edged book on the sports establishment called *The Jocks,* which has been on the reading list of many college courses. A notable incident for him was the time Ryne Duren had a fight with Ralph

Houk during a Yankee road trip in 1958. I was not on that trip but heard about it later.

Duren and Houk, then a coach, had an altercation on a train bound for Detroit in the midst of a celebration after the Yankees had clinched the pennant. A drunken Duren mashed Houk's cigar into his face, and Houk retaliated by swiping Duren with his large-diamond-encrusted World Series ring, opening a cut near Duren's eye. Shecter spotted Duren's eye. He checked with a veteran reporter who said he would ignore the incident. Still young on the beat and not sure of himself, Shecter agreed.

But Shecter mentioned the incident in a casual conversation a few days later with his sports editor. The editor passed it on to a managing editor and after the *Post* blew up the controversy, it became a national story. Shecter was mortified by it all. He understood that it would not have been such a big thing if he had written of the incident right away, or if he had forgotten about it entirely. In *The Jocks,* he wrote, "I still squirm when I recall the incident and I question whether I can be objective in writing about it, but I shall try."

The majority of the Yankees stopped talking to him. Casey Stengel was critical, yet sympathetic. He understood that Shecter was only "trying to do his job." For this Shecter was ever grateful, and became one of the legion of reporters who adored the old man. On his next road trip with the Yankees, Shecter sat in a hotel lobby reading a novel by Jerome Weidman called *The Enemy Camp*. "I don't think any of the players got the point," he cracked.

After Shecter left the *Post,* he became sports editor of *Look* magazine, wrote a book on police corruption, and wrote freelance pieces after *Look* folded. His profile in the January 1968 *Esquire* of kingpin football coach Vince Lombardi portrayed Lombardi as a bully and despot. It easily was the toughest and least admiring extended piece ever written about a man revered by so many in what Robert Lipsyte called "Sports World."

There is a tendency in the business to think that what we write really doesn't have as much impact on people as we would like. I certainly have felt that way, having worked for the little-known *Compass* and long-ignored *Newsday*. I would not have expected somebody as exalted as Lombardi to care about any slings and arrows directed at him by any writer. I was surprised, then, to read in David Maraniss's 1999 biography of Lombardi, *When Pride Still Mattered,* about how Shecter's piece influenced Lombardi.

Maraniss wrote, "Shecter had a profound effect on Lombardi. He was a New Yorker and Shecter was a New Yorker, and he had assumed that Shecter would intuitively understand him." Lombardi noted that Shecter was a real New Yorker because he read a broadsheet newspaper by folding it in eighths, the style perfected by subway riders. A Green Bay official said the article "absolutely destroyed Lombardi" and was a factor in his leaving the franchise.

Lombardi was a natural target for Shecter. With a critical eye, Len examined icons who were something less than the paragons that admiring hordes of scribes made of them. When recalling the Houk–Duren incident in *The Jocks,* Shecter made a point of noting that Houk was a captain in the Rangers during World War II and was made a major only on discharge. Yet his sycophantic buddies invariably called him "Major."

3

Family Ties

During my formative years, from ages five to eleven, I lived at 381 Berry Street in Williamsburg, Brooklyn, in the shadow of the Williamsburg Bridge. If we were poor, we didn't think so, though my father could tell of bleaker times when I was an infant and we lived in Coney Island.

My father, Abe Isaacs, was a short man, 5'5" at best. But he was very strong and liked to brag about it. When he died, I had the epitaph read his favorite boast: "The toughest kid on the block." He drove a cab. One day, after he came home without any fares, he dumped the cab. He became a truck driver shortly afterward. My father said that he "always provided for his family," and he did.

I never felt deprived. Yet embarrassment flooded over me when my mother took me on the long trek via subways and the ferry to Hoboken, New Jersey, to a dentist cousin who did not charge us. After a few years of this, I balked. We stopped going.

The five-story dirty-orange brick apartment building on Berry Street was the equivalent of a *shtetl* because so many of my relatives lived nearby. My mother was named Lillian, and some of her relatives lived in our building. Her maiden name was Lax, so you can be sure the family joke was that my mother was an Ex-Lax.

My father's siblings and their progeny lived in a five-story apartment house around the corner at 100 Broadway. His parents and some of his brothers and sisters lived in a two-story wood-shingled building diagonally across from 100 Broadway. My father had lived there as a child, except for when he was shipped off to an orphanage, because his father and stepmother couldn't afford to bring up a brood that swelled to nine. All in all, I thrived in the bower of a family that included five sets of aunts and uncles, seven cousins, and two sets of grandparents.

My uncle Larry Frankel took me to baseball games more than my dad did. He was Italian. He changed his name from Franzone to Frankel for the approval of my grandfather, Nathan Lax. Uncle Larry never told his family of the name change. When he died, his brother Alex Franzone was confused at the funeral. "Larry Frankel?" he said.

Larry married my Aunt Fanny, a chubby blonde. I thought it was a great match because he taught her how to make Italian food. They had me over for spaghetti and meatballs almost every Thursday. She was coming off an annulled marriage to a man who was a drug addict. Uncle Larry was a burly man who chuckled a lot, particularly when Aunt Fanny talked about his hairy chest. Once, at a summer vacation hotel, I walked in on them in the midst of the furies of passion; Uncle Larry jumped up on the bed with a startled "whuh" as I made a hasty retreat. I was ten. On occasion I overheard Aunt Fanny say, "The man is 50 years old and he still won't leave me alone." She was boasting, not complaining.

When Uncle Larry and I went to games at Ebbets Field and headed for the fifty-five-cent seats in the bleachers, we would get there early before the gates opened. We worked out a little ruse to beat the long line that had already formed. Imp that I was, I would sidle into a place near the front of the line, which snaked from Bedford Avenue to Montgomery Street. Uncle Larry would come by and give me a mock scolding, saying he was looking all over for me. The sly dog would then unobtrusively slip into place alongside me.

Once, on a trip to the Polo Grounds for a doubleheader between the Giants and Dodgers, we walked up the long runway in right-center field to where Uncle Larry was ready to sit in the seats behind third base. I told him the upper stands were much better and urged him to go there. He was tired. He didn't want to go any farther. I said I would go upstairs anyway. A kindly man, he permitted me to do that with the understanding I would come down between games to keep in touch with him.

I found a seat in the upper stands behind third base. When the first game ended, I went down to the lower stands to check in with him. While I was chatting with him, it seemed to me that people were looking at me in an odd way. Later I found out why. When I had left him earlier, people nearby had asked why he was sitting downstairs and had permitted me to go to the upper stands. He said he told them I was a little *tetched* in the head and it was best to let me have my way. My family thought this was hilarious. I did not—at the time.

My uncle Teddy Lax was a handsome guy, a ladies' man, though he always regretted that he lost his hair prematurely. According to him, it was because he didn't dry himself after showers when he played ball. He had been a good club basketball player on the team with a fascinating name: the Laramies. He said they liked the name of the city Laramie in Wyoming and adopted it.

In my junior high school graduation autograph book, Uncle Teddy wrote, "Aim high." That was what he always did—to a fault. He didn't always concern himself with such things as legalities. One day in 1940, as Christmas approached, he took me to F.A.O. Schwarz, the world-famous toy store. He said he would be using a credit card from the store that belonged to a friend. I was eleven at the time, not the most worldly of youths, but alert enough to suspect that a credit card from F.A.O. Schwarz was not something any of his friends would have. Nor did I question his instructions when he said I could choose anything I could take with me but could not pick something that had to be shipped home.

I dutifully dressed up in my red and gray mackinaw and off we went, uptown from Brooklyn to tony Fifth Avenue. Before we entered the store, Uncle Teddy, who seemed a bit edgy, told me to remove the Roosevelt button I was wearing. I was a fervent FDR fan, still wearing the button after Roosevelt beat Wendell Willkie in the 1940 presidential election.

The freedom to choose anything I could carry out of the store put me under considerable pressure. As goodies dangled before me, I became a bit frazzled. Under Uncle Teddy's nervous prodding, I made my choices. I picked a baseball glove—a Hutch brand with the signature of Cincinnati outfielder Harry Craft—and a hockey stick and a board football game. I often have second-guessed my choices, as have smirking friends. But it is one thing to analyze my choices afterward and another thing to have been under the gun making the selections. I never heard anything more about the credit card. I knew enough not to ask about it. But when we got home, I put the FDR button back on my mackinaw.

Another relative, Uncle Harry, was a rogue if ever there was one. Harry was a pixie of a man with a mole on his forehead. He behaved like one of the Marx brothers and usually looked as if he were about to do a little jig. Uncle Harry certainly didn't live by the rules. He had two wives at the same time. He could play the piano by ear. He had a knack for detecting when a woman was pregnant, knowing this before she had even told the world. He always seemed to be employed at different jobs.

One of them was as a watchman for the Wolf Publishing Company, which printed the books of major publishers. Uncle Harry worked the night shift, and now that the statute of limitations is long expired, I can reveal that he gave us a knockout wedding present.

At our wedding, Uncle Harry invited us to see him at the warehouse on a late evening. My wife Bobbie, somewhat puzzled by it all, and I were escorted to a floor with stacks of books. He told us to pick out whatever books we could carry. With visions of the FAO Schwarz caper dancing in my head, we proceeded to take the entire Viking Portable series, the complete works of Shakespeare in one volume, and a few other reference books. We still have the Shakespeare book in our library. My wife, who likes to think this is the only shady enterprise she has ever been involved with, says, "I still can't believe we did that."

* * *

I can still hear the strains of the streetcars that ran along Broadway and on South Eighth, and even the echo of the subway trains going across the bridge. Many years later when I was on the baseball beat, I was lying in bed in a hotel in Pittsburgh. There was a streetcar line outside, and the clanking of the streetcar was like a lullaby, taking me back to my time on Berry Street. I fell into a restful sleep.

We lived two blocks from the acclaimed Peter Luger Steak House on Broadway and Driggs Avenue. When word filtered out that a celebrity was eating there, kids rushed over to ogle the famous person. I would teeter on a ledge and look in. We frequently heard that Joe DiMaggio was there. I never saw him. Many years later, when I could afford to eat at Peter Luger, I told the maitre d' about standing on the ledge looking in for DiMaggio. He told me, "Joe always ate upstairs."

Williamsburg in the late 1930s and 1940s was a mix of second-generation Jews, Irish, Poles, and the early waves of Hasidic Jews and Puerto Ricans. The Puerto Ricans were the most put-upon. I recall that our landlord at 381 Berry, a Mr. Cohen, was considered a benevolent man because he would allow Puerto Ricans to rent apartments on the top floor of the building; other landlords wouldn't accept Puerto Ricans at all. My Puerto Rican friend, Jamie, agreed with me that Mr. Cohen was a good man.

There was no elevator, of course. We moved into an apartment on the fourth floor, and we must have struck Mr. Cohen as the right stuff, because he granted us the privilege of moving down to a first-floor apartment when it became available. I proved my mettle as a small-game hunter there. When a mouse cropped up in the apartment, I would wait until dark with a hockey stick. I put myself between the mouse and its refuge under the refrigerator, and I whacked it to kingdom-come when it tried to scoot back home. I invariably was greeted like a conquering hero by my mother.

It was the tail end of the Great Depression, before World War II. I had odd jobs. I helped lug coal to the stove of an old lady across Broadway. This netted me ten cents. I worked after school as a clerk in a grocery store on Bedford Avenue. I couldn't quite manage the challenge of cutting out from a butter tub the exact amount asked for by a customer, and was chagrined when, after a few failures, the owner of the store relieved me of that duty. I was a *shabbes goy,* lighting stoves for old Jewish ladies on the Sabbath; never mind that I was Jewish and this was supposed to be done by a Gentile boy. I thought what the old women didn't know wouldn't hurt them.

We were not religious. My parents probably would not even have bothered to have me bar mitzvahed except that my father's relatives were more observant. My cousins and I received our Hebrew training from an old rabbi who lived around the corner on South Eighth Street. Rabbi Joseph was not a learned man. Far from it. He was unkempt with a dirty, ashen beard. He had a vile temper and was prejudiced against all Gentiles.

Woe to the supplicant who showed up for a lesson at his apartment wearing the little pin with the red cross that was awarded at Public School 37 for contributions to the Red Cross charity. The rabbi would utter a curse in Yiddish and rip the pin from the culprit. Heshy Wasserheit, a *toomler* if ever there was one, would wear the pin when he hadn't prepared his lesson, so he could be sent home.

I submitted to this Hebrew indoctrination for six months. This was looked upon as a *shanda* by my aunts and uncles, whose children attended the rabbi's ministrations for more than a year. I quickly grasped that I would have no trouble learning the appropriate liturgies of a bar mitzvah ritual. I struck up a sub rosa deal with the rabbi. My parents were paying him fifty cents a week for five days of teaching. I told him I would show up only three days and pay him thirty cents. A shrewder man would have immediately reported this to my parents. He did not. He acceded to my chutzpah, and I pocketed twenty cents every week until I hit the big one-three and had my bar mitzvah.

Still, I left something of a mark at that place of Judaica. All who studied with Rabbi Joseph recited the same speech in English, thanking relatives for helping them become a bar mitzvah boy. I rebelled at the idea of repeating the same speech that I had been hearing from my older cousins when they went through the exalted rite. Now, if I were truly creative, I would have composed my own speech. I wasn't that creative. But when the rabbi heard my objections, he pulled out a booklet of speeches in English for the occasion. I leafed through the booklet and selected a speech that most approximated my feelings. I recited that speech at the post–bar mitzvah party. I learned later that *every* boy who came afterward to Rabbi Joseph used my speech. I had left a legacy.

I am not a religious Jew. I am a cultural Jew with a deep appreciation for Jewish history and culture, even though religion is obviously so much a part of the history. Experiences in Williamsburg did not enamor me of religious Jews. In addition to the ignorance of Rabbi Joseph, there was the behavior of some of the Hasidim. One day my mother was walking on Bedford Avenue when a group of Hasidim approached, including one who wore a large brown fur-fringed hat. After my mother passed, one of his acolytes stopped her and scolded her for not stepping into the street when she passed a high holy man.

Just before the United States entered World War II in 1941, we moved five blocks south to 107 Division Avenue, on the corner of Bedford Avenue. There was a candy store in the middle of our block. Unusual for those times, the store did not remain open seven days a week. The owner closed it every Sunday. When the Hasidim established themselves in our section of Williamsburg, they persuaded the Jewish-owned stores to close on Saturday, the Sabbath. The candy store owner, a non-religious Jew, chose to stay open on Saturday and, as ever, close on Sunday. The Hassidim pressured him to close on Saturday. He refused. He said, "I was closed on Sunday when these other *schnorrers* were open seven days a week. I'm not going to change now."

The Hasidim mounted a protest. Bearded men and boys in *pais*—curly ear locks—milled about the store, discouraging people from entering. Finally, the owner called the police. They quietly but firmly told the Hasidim to desist. The incident didn't make for fondness between the Hasidim and second-generation, nonreligious Jews like the candy store owner, or my family.

* * *

My Saturdays were spent listening to the college football broadcasts of Bill Stern and Ted Husing or, outside football season, going to the movies. Sundays were always for the movies. My mother gave me money to buy a salami sandwich, a plate of Heinz baked beans, and a Dr. Brown's cherry soda at the delicatessen on Broadway. I then proceeded to a movie at the Commodore, Marcy, Williamsburg, or an aptly named theater called The Dumps.

I did not pay attention to starting times. I often arrived during the middle of a picture and stayed until the film came around to what was the starting point for me. If I truly liked the movie, I stayed until the end again.

One Sunday afternoon in December 1940, I was coming out of the movie as the Chicago Bears were slaughtering the Washington Redskins in the National Football League championship game. The appliance stores had their radios on, and, as I moved along, I kept hearing the updates of the score. Chicago ahead, 21–0 . . . 28–0 . . . 41–0 . . . 54–0 . . . and finally at home I heard the final moments of the historic 73–0 Bears victory.

A year later, on December 7, 1941, I was listening to the New York Giants–Brooklyn Dodgers football game at the Polo Grounds. The Dodgers' quarterback Ace Parker was having a big day. Then announcer Bill Slater's commentary was interrupted with a report about the Japanese bombing of Pearl Harbor. The common reaction: "Where's Pearl Harbor?"

4

School Daze

During my years at Junior High School 50 in the early 1940s, we mouthed an underground ditty about the Nazis. It was in the tradition of Spike Jones's "Der Fuhrer's Face," an anti-Nazi propaganda film made by Disney. Our song went:

> *Hitler had only one ball,*
> *Goering had two and they were small*
> *Himmler had something simmler*
> *And Goebbels had no balls at all!!!*

The social world of teenage kids in our neighborhood included social athletic clubs (S.A.C.). One club called itself the SWALLOWS—which stood for the Suck Wind and Lob League of Williamsburg. A lob was a derisive gesture of left palm to right arm, sassing an acquaintance or adversary. Some people called it "the Italian salute."

The naming of an S.A.C. was a serious ritual, as important as picking the colors of the club jackets. I still have reverence for a fellow named Raymond. When there was protracted disagreement in his group about naming the club, Raymond settled the issue, saying, "We keep arguing, we have no name for the club. Let's take no name and turn the letters around." Hence the name, "Emanons" was born. For a long time I regarded Raymond as a genius.

I had the same respect for a fellow in my sixth-grade class at P.S. 37 named Alan Beckerman, because he outslicked our teacher, Miss Ennis. One day during an English lesson, she came up with a word none of us had ever heard of, asking if anybody could put the word into a sentence. Nobody had the slightest idea of the meaning of the word; there was a long silence.

Then Alan raised his hand and proceeded to use the designated word in a sentence. He said, "(Designated word) is a difficult word to put into a sentence." The class applauded. Miss Ennis was not amused.

Miss Ennis was the stereotype of the old biddy schoolmistress who disliked the children in her charge. We responded in kind. She was plump, with a formidable rear end and a mottled complexion. She wore pince-nez glasses and purplish dresses that had the shine of long use to them. She was probably in her fifties, though to my eyes she seemed to be about ninety-nine. She was so mean, I think I hated her second only to Hitler.

She drove me crazy when she delayed our exit from school. She took her time putting on her hairnet after the final bell at 3:00 p.m., making ours the last class unleashed out into the free world. On days when the Eastern District High School basketball team was playing a home game, I would race from P.S. 37 to reach the high school twelve blocks away. On the occasion of a particularly important game, I asked Miss Ennis if I could be let out with the sounding of the bell so that I could get to the game in time. She seemed shocked at the boldness of the request. She took more time than ever putting on her hairnet before letting us out. On that day she ranked ahead of Hitler.

School years were divided into two semesters, and our class, the elite "A" class, had the misfortune to draw Miss Ennis for both terms. I was a restless kid, always looking for reasons to get out of my seat, such as volunteering to go outside to bang blackboard erasers together to get the chalk out of them.

We were in a state of undeclared war with Miss Ennis for most of the year. One day Elvira Powell assumed the heroic proportions of Joan of Arc when she put a wad of gum on Miss Ennis's chair. Miss Ennis sat down on the chair. Bullseye! She was horrified. She scurried to the principal's office in tears. It amazed us that she seemed genuinely surprised there were students who did not like her. Despite the attempts of the principal to ferret out the villain, you could be sure nobody ratted out Elvira Powell.

It all led up to what I have come to call "The Green Yarmulke" incident.

Each year's sixth-term graduation at P.S. 37 included an assembly at which the class put on a play. I had appeared in earlier plays, so I was chosen to play Peter Pan. This play's theme involved stressing the importance of play, whereupon classmates would perform activities such as hitting a ball or jumping rope. Rehearsals started months before graduation. All went well until we were to don our costumes the morning of the performance.

I stood on a chair in the front of the class as Miss Ennis attached the green crepe paper which would serve as my costume. I didn't like how I looked in it and cringed at the titters of classmates. I began to have my doubts.

Consider now that an assembly at old P.S. 37 was arrived at by rolling back the doors between rooms so that six classes in all would make up the assembly space. As Miss Ennis fussed over me, I began to think about my friends in the other rooms; they would get a gander at me in a costume that I felt was, well, unmanly. And then Miss Ennis brought forth the topper, the cap to the costume. Imagine a yarmulke, or skull cap, covered with green crepe paper and topped off by a green crepe paper bow. My class broke into laughter when it appeared on my head. I was mortified and dreaded the thought of my pals in the other rooms seeing me wearing it.

I fidgeted. My body language began to tell Miss Ennis I was not happy. She told me to stand still.

Finally, I asked, "Couldn't I be in the play without the hat?"

She would not hear of it. I fidgeted some more.

I said, "I would prefer not to wear the hat."

She said, "You have to wear the hat."

I said nothing and fidgeted some more.

"Stop fidgeting," she said.

I said, "I really don't want to wear the hat."

"Well, you have to wear the hat,"

I fidgeted some more. She adjusted the hat with a jerk.

Finally, I said, almost in tears, "I don't want to be in the play."

She said, "You have to be in the play."

I said, "I don't want to be in the play if I have to wear the hat."

This upset her some more. She tried appealing to my best instincts by telling me that if I weren't in the play, it would mean that my classmates would be out of the play. I knew that nobody cared that much about being in the play—most of them had to be dragooned to be in it in the first place—so I didn't feel any guilt about hurting my classmates. I only could think of my friends laughing at me.

I was taken to the principal. She pleaded with me. She asked me how I could hurt Miss Ennis that way. Hah! I just said I would be happy to be in the play if I didn't have to wear the hat. Miss Ennis said that under no circumstances should I have my way. I was told I might not graduate. Even though I was only eleven years old, I had enough smarts to doubt this, but I couldn't be sure. In any case, I was in too deep to back out now.

I didn't appear in the play. They sent me to the purgatory of a second-grade class. Those little buggers sensed my discomfort and snickered at me. After the assembly, my classmates were given their report cards and sent out into the world. I was sent home without a report card. I was left in limbo.

When I got home, I told my mother what had happened. She asked if the hat was so bad. I said it was. She accepted that. Word spread among her friends and relatives. My Aunt Dora Sher, who lived a floor below us, thought this was serious. She urged my mother to go back to the school with me. "If you don't," she said, "Stanley won't graduate."

My mother, never a confrontational soul, was reluctant about this, but finally was persuaded about the severity of the situation. We went back to school and met with the principal and Miss Ennis. I was given a stern lecture about loyalty and the need to cooperate. I was contrite, thinking only about getting out of there. Finally, the principal asked me if I would cooperate and wear any costume given to me if I were in a play at Junior High School 50, the next stop in my academic odyssey. I said with fervor that I would. But I thought to myself, "I'll never, never be in a play again."

* * *

I had a rich life playing on the tree-less streets of my neighborhood in pre–high school days. As I grew older, I sensed a feeling of Williamsburg being out of the city's mainstream. The *Brooklyn Eagle* seemed to write only about Flatbush.

I began to resent the lack of a sense of history about the neighborhood. At P.S. 37, we were taught about hemp production in Brazil, but little about the neighborhood in which we grew up. I learned later that Berry Street had been a street of some distinction in the late 1800s, and that some famous jockeys lived there. I'm sure that would have stoked my appreciation for learning more than being inculcated with information about hemp production in far-off places.

I went on from Junior High School 50 (the formal name, John D. Welles, was rarely used) to Eastern District High in 1943. I was a good-enough student considering that I didn't study much. In retrospect, I would have been better off if I studied Latin—it would have helped my grammatical sense—but only French and Spanish were offered.

In high school, I learned about limitations on the power of the press.

It had to do with the name Eastern District High School. The name accentuated a have-not feeling about the school. It was trial enough for a post-Depression child to grow up in Williamsburg and labor with a sense of being a second-class citizen in a marginalized neighborhood. On top of that, there was the matter of being at a high school with what seemed like a terribly un-chic name.

The seemingly important high schools in New York, I believed, were named after eminent people: Abraham Lincoln, Thomas Jefferson, DeWitt Clinton, Peter Stuyvesant, even Julia Richmond, whoever she was. Eastern

District, I argued, was a nothing name. It had no grandeur; it did not roll trippingly off the tongue with the sweep of an Alexander Hamilton or Benjamin Franklin. Eastern District, I had been told, was the name of a judicial district of New York at one time, perhaps even now. Try and generate school spirit with such a name, I wrote with passion.

I believed we would think more of our school, more of ourselves, if the school were named after some eminent figure. I was a member of the sports staff, but I felt strongly enough to volunteer to write an editorial about this. In arguing for a new name, I proposed Thomas Paine High. I wasn't adamant about this, though. I would accept the name of any worthy person as long as we could get out from under the oh-so-meaningless Eastern District.

My crusade met with little success. In truth, it hardly raised an eyebrow. Eastern District High it remained.

One of my regrets about Eastern District was that there was no sense of history conveyed to us at the school. At Eastern the only famous graduate I knew of was Red Auerbach, who had played basketball there before going on to his long, successful career as coach of the Boston Celtics. I was told that some eminent local judges had gone there as well. That's all. I didn't learn until later that Mel Brooks, nee Kaminsky, had spent his senior year at Eastern. Even more impressive to me was to learn that the notorious Henry Miller, author of the ribald *Tropic of Capricorn,* had been in the first Eastern District graduating class.

By the early 1980s, the Eastern District building on Marcy Avenue between Rodney and Keap Streets had been condemned and a new building was going up in another section of Williamsburg. With the erection of the new building there was talk of giving the school a new name. The authorities settled on Nelson Rockefeller High School, in honor of the billionaire, high-powered former Republican governor. At least that is what they thought. The students and residents of this area abutting the Bushwick section in northern Brooklyn were now mostly Hispanic and black. They had no liking for the name Rockefeller. Planners decided against it.

So what is the name that is emblazoned on the new building? Not Nelson Rockefeller, not Thomas Paine, neither W. E. B. Du Bois nor Jack Benny. The building is named . . . Eastern District High School. Ah yes.

Despite the appealing new building, the school deteriorated. Violence and scandals by different principals defamed the school. By 1998 authorities decided to break up the one school into four schools, none of them named Eastern District.

Larry Pollack, a social studies teacher who lived on Long Island and read my columns in *Newsday,* invited me to speak at the final Eastern District graduation. I accepted with alacrity. I told stories of the start of my career in journalism; of my futile attempts to have the name of the school changed; of my days as a none-too-dedicated student at Eastern.

But before I did, I opened my talk looking out at an auditorium of essentially blacks and Hispanics by saying, "I was graduated from this school fifty years ago." The fifty years was greeted with gasps—and then after a pause of a few seconds, the students broke out into applause. I guess it was because I lived that long.

Eastern District was no more. Somehow, it didn't seem like such a bad name after all.

5

Sportswriter

I owe my career as a newspaperman to Abe Risikoff, a teacher at Eastern District High School. In my sophomore year, he taught an honors English class that studied the makeup and operation of newspapers. I impressed him enough that he suggested I try out for the school newspaper, the *Gold and White*. I was surprised and resistant. I told him, "I don't like to write compositions."

He said, "You don't have to write compositions on a newspaper. You write what you like. What are you interested in?"

I told him, "I like sports." Sports was just about all I cared about. I was a sports fanatic: I probably knew more about sports statistics at eleven than I knew when I was a professional sports reporter. I did not come from an intellectual background. There were no books in my house. The only books I read were sports juveniles, the "Baseball Joe" series, and novels by Ralph Henry Barbour and John Tunis.

I knew I should be reading more significant books but didn't know how to go about it. At one point I answered an ad in the *Daily News* and subscribed to a one-dollar book club. I read only a succession of romance novels. I had no clue about nonfiction books that I would have found rewarding. In essence, I didn't become a reader of any books other than school texts until I was out of college. I was basically a reader of the sports pages of the *Daily News* and *New York Post*.

Until Mr. Risikoff approached me, I thought I would become an accountant—not because I had any aptitude for accounting but because it was a vocation that promised employment. Uncle Eddie, a stepbrother of my father, was the only rich man in our entire tribe. Edward Isaacs was a big-time accountant with other financial holdings—he owned the Hattie Carnegie department store and, I later found out, had interests in oil. Uncle Eddie, a benevolent man who gave dimes to us when we were tykes, was prepared to hire any of his nephews as accountants. This was no small matter in those post-Depression years; three of my cousins went on to jobs with the Edward Isaacs Company.

I must have had some newspaper instinct. During World War II, when the *Daily News* always headlined war news on its front page, I wondered what the paper would find to put on page one when there was no war. With Risikoff's urging, I joined the school paper and wrote sports for the *Gold and White,* moving up to sports editor as a senior. The editor wrote the sports column. Naming the column required much thought. I knew right away that I couldn't match the effort of Jerry Schwartz, my predecessor. His column name: "Sports with Schwartz." I chose "The Sports Scene." I have winced the few times I have gone back to read those columns.

I read the metropolitan sports pages religiously with the hope that someday I might realize the dream of covering a major league baseball team—and earn the munificent sum of $75 a week. One weekend I landed work selling peanuts and scorecards at Ebbets Field. I became more involved in trying to hawk my wares than caring about the events in the games. I decided that I was being corrupted and quit after that weekend. Baseball, yes. Business, no.

By the time I joined the *Gold and White,* Mr. Risikoff was no longer the faculty adviser to the student scribes; he had gone off to the army. One day, while in fifth-term English, Mr. Marcus stopped the class to announce he had just received word that Mr. Risikoff had been killed in action in Europe. I was stunned. Some of the girls, notably Selma Weitzman, the editor in chief, sobbed. It is one of my profound regrets that I could never thank Abe Risikoff for starting me on what turned out to be my life's work.

I covered the basketball team for the school newspaper. One particular incident became part of Williamsburg lore. Eastern District, usually a weak team, had a preseason scrimmage against Andrew Jackson High, a perennial powerhouse in New York City basketball. Eastern District coach Gyp Shuman started a ragtag lineup for the scrimmage that included Jerry Shamberger, probably the last man on the squad. When the players went out on the floor to start the game, each pointed to a Jackson player he would guard. Sham, as he was called, took a quick look at the four formidable-looking tall guys on Jackson and hurriedly pointed at a not-so-imposing skinny Jackson player, declaring, "He's mine."

The skinny guy turned out to be the star of his team, making brilliant passes, sinking set shots and hook shots on the run. It was Bob Cousy, who would go on to become a basketball immortal at Holy Cross and the Boston Celtics.

When the guys gathered at the delicatessen on Roebling Street, the story about Sham choosing to guard Cousy tickled everybody. There were jokesters galore at the deli. When Williamsburg product Alan King, nee Irving Kniberg, was making it as a professional comic, some of the wags at the deli couldn't understand it; they were sure they were funnier. King, of course, kept working and polishing his style, while the other boys rollicked on at the deli.

I've always had a special fondness for King because his wife, the former Jeanette Sprung, was in my class at Junior High School 50 and with me at Eastern District. She was the class beauty, a fleshy, dark-haired, smooth-skinned girl with a ready smile. We had joked that we were the two dumbest kids in our Rapid Advance class at Junior High 50.

* * *

I went on to Brooklyn College, where I paid more attention to the student newspaper, the *Vanguard,* than I did to my classes. I eventually became co-sports editor with Jack Zanger, who later covered sports for magazines until his untimely death. Jack was such a gentle and friendly soul. You could never get across campus with him because he stopped so often to talk to acquaintances.

I was lucky to get into Brooklyn College; my high school grades were relatively low to qualify for the free municipal institution with high admission standards. One's high school average combined with the mark on the mandatory entrance examination determined acceptance into Brooklyn or any of the city colleges. I had only a 79 average in high school, so I needed a very high score on the multi-subject, multiple-answer entrance exam to qualify. I came through because of what turned out to be a heady gamble in test-taking.

When the test papers were handed out, we were told to answer only the questions about which we were reasonably sure. I decided that the mechanism marking the papers would gather only correct answers and not penalize incorrect answers. Hence, when the proctor announced "time's up" for each section of the five-hour test, I would willy-nilly fill in answers in the No. 1 column, figuring that the law of averages would provide me with more correct answers.

I scored extremely high on the test. I was admitted to Brooklyn College. From what I have learned about such tests since, I believe my strategy was correct. I must have come up with many more correct answers than if I had heeded the instructions to answer only the ones of which I was sure.

I did not fully enjoy Brooklyn College. I rode the Nostrand Avenue trolley line for an hour to reach the Flatbush campus. When the trolley car was delayed because of parked trucks blocking the tracks, I was late for my first class. I think the anxiety of those hairy trolley rides had a lasting effect on me; now I am always early to appointments. It seemed to me that going to college on a trolley car was more like an extension of high school. I felt that only those who went to sleep-away colleges were first-class citizens.

The administration of President Harry Gideonse was a downer. In those cold war days, he was so fearful of a leftist tinge at the school that he often tried to suppress dissent. He constantly harassed the *Vanguard,* disparaging any criticisms as communist. Shortly after I was graduated from Brooklyn, Gideonse finally managed to suppress the paper. The Brooklyn College *Kingsman,* which toadied to Gideonse, was born. Within a few years, when a new set of student journalists dominated that paper, it, too, was at odds with the high-handed president.

I remained a marginal student while in college. I am almost ashamed to acknowledge how limited I was. One day, when I was working as a clerk in the Brooklyn College bookstore, a co-ed asked if we had a copy of *The Idiot* by Dostoyevsky. I had never heard of the author or the book, and the title struck me as hilarious. I said, "We don't have *The Idiot*. But we do have *The Moron* by Pashnaslorov." I still remember the look of disgust that crossed the co-ed's face. Oy.

During my sophomore year, I spent more time betting in the neighborhood pool hall, trying to hit three-team college basketball parlays, than studying. I failed biology and Spanish. I don't think I ever was more disgusted with myself than when I went to summer school to make up those subjects.

In those days, both Brooklyn and City College, the two municipal college rivals, fielded football teams—not very good football teams, though Brooklyn had sent Allie Sherman to the professional ranks. The quality of play didn't matter when they played each other, because this was a hot rivalry. The games were played on Saturday night at Ebbets Field, which made it a perfect date night. I was no Lothario by any means—I identified with the famous line, "If there are so many pretty girls in New York, why do I go home every Saturday night with the *News* and the *Mirror*?" But I managed to secure a date for the City–Brooklyn game. Generally, I was too wrapped up in box scores and too shy to pursue girls.

The 1946 game was a thriller. City College led 8–6 in the waning seconds. City had the ball on its one-yard line and tried to kill the clock in the final two seconds with a quarterback sneak. The City College quarterback, however, fumbled and Brooklyn guard Bernie Friedlund pounced on the ball in City's end zone for a Brooklyn College touchdown and a 12–8 victory. Sweet memories are made of this.

One of the perks for student sportswriters on New York City college newspapers was the plum assignment of campus stringer for the *New York Times* and *Herald Tribune*. You covered events at the college for the big-time newspapers and got paid space rates. We invariably inflated the details of a story to earn more money, and the editors invariably cut the stories back to an inch or two. I eventually became the *Vanguard* correspondent for the *Times*.

While covering a Brooklyn College vs. Wagner football game for the *Times,* I also sent a story via Western Union to the *Star,* the successor to the highly respected but ill-fated *PM*. The *Star* printed the story, and when I called afterward to identify myself, they said I could keep sending them stories.

The next week I wrote what turned out to be one of the most important phrases of my career. Brooklyn College uncharacteristically had a good team in 1948. It beat Hofstra, 40–0. My lead started, "Brooklyn College's minor league powerhouse . . ." The phrase so impressed Jack Orr, a *Star* staffer who copy-read the story, that he praised me to sports editor Jim Russell. That paved the way for me to join the *Star* as a copy boy.

I worked the night shift after attending classes in the morning and early afternoon. One of my assignments was to go uptown from the *Star* offices at Duane and Hudson Streets in lower Manhattan to pick up the copy of columnists Max Lerner and John McNulty, both of whom lived on East 72nd Street. McNulty wrote a humor column laced with Irish wit. As the expression goes, he took a drink. Sober or not, he always greeted me and the other copy boys expansively.

Lerner always seemed to be in deep thought when I arrived. And he almost always was looking through sources, making last-second corrections, sometimes taking the copy back from me to make a change. The copy boys made jokes about that. We didn't hold him in awe as an important political pundit.

PM had struggled from 1940 to 1948. Marshall Field, the Chicago philanthropist who backed the paper, got tired of the red ink. He let Joseph Barnes pick up its left-wing banner with the *Star* at the Duane Street location, hanging on as a minority stockholder. The *Star* lasted little more than a year. On the day it folded, Barnes stood up on a desk in the city room and announced its demise. The veterans on the staff went downstairs to have a drink at one of the bars on Chambers Street before returning to put out the final edition. I felt lost and out of it. I decided to go home. The head copy boy told me I was disloyal and would never amount to much in the newspaper business.

6

The *Daily Compass*

Almost before the corpse of the *Star* was cold, the *Daily Compass* was born. This birth stemmed from a divorce. Ted Thackery had been copublisher of the *New York Post* with his wife, Dorothy Schiff. The divorce was foreshadowed when they wrote editorials supporting different candidates in the 1948 election. Schiff supported Thomas Dewey, Thackery backed Henry Wallace. Harry Truman made losers of them both.

When that marriage broke up, Schiff asserted her majority hold on the paper and Thackery left. He must have been a genius with wealthy women because he persuaded Eleanor McCormick McLean, an heiress of the McCormick reaper millions, to back him in forming the *Compass*. Even before the presses started rolling, McLean fell ill and was declared *non compas mentis,* a cruel pun if ever there was one, by relatives who didn't want her money going to this "communist" enterprise. That left Thackery to scrounge for financial support from various left-wing angels. Corliss Lamont became the biggest benefactor.

There was little chance for a poorly funded left-wing paper to make it in the Joe McCarthy era. The paper's circulation hovered around forty thousand at best. I. F. Stone, the dogged iconoclast, spearheaded the paper's crusades, after which he went on to publish his highly respected and successful newsletter, *I. F. Stone's Weekly*. The *Compass* hung on for about two years, fueled by Lamont's money, plus the contributions of some other leftist moneybaggers. It also made constant, annoying appeals for funds from readers. The *Compass* folded on Election Day 1952, when Dwight Eisenhower defeated Adlai Stevenson.

I had advanced to editorial assistant at the *Star,* but I was happy to drop back to copy boy to land a job at the *Compass*. We had a memorable crew of copy boys. We had the Dlugoff Brothers, Art and Burt. Art went on to become a show-business entrepreneur around New York City; we called him a poor man's Sol Hurok. He put on folk song shows at Town Hall and Greenwich Village and then opened the Village Gate nightclub. Along the way he added an apostrophe to his name—hence D'Lugoff—for a bit of show-biz flash. The Gate became an institution in the city, a showplace for comedians, actors, and musicians. Woody Allen, Dick Gregory, and Richard Pryor played there, as did jazz greats John Coltrane, Miles Davis, Dizzy Gillespie, and Thelonius Monk. Dustin Hoffman was fired as a waiter for being so wrapped up in performances that he neglected customers.

Art's brother Burt D'Lugoff (he also appended the apostrophe) was the silent partner in the family enterprises, a solid anchor to the flamboyant Art. He and Bob Nemeroff, the husband of playwright Lorraine Hansberry, adapted an old folk song that became "Cindy." It climbed the charts, and the royalties paid Burt's way through medical school. He went on to become a force in Baltimore medical precincts while continuing to provide sober advice to Art.

Two copy boys came to be involved in Supreme Court cases. Ralph Ginzburg, whom we regarded as our own Sammy Glick, went from the *Compass* to *Look Magazine* and then published *Eros,* a classy-looking erotic magazine. It was bold for its time, perhaps, but mild by later standards. Ginzburg might have escaped censure from the Court as a pornographer if he hadn't mailed promotional material from the Pennsylvania towns of Intercourse and Blue Ball. The judges jumped on that and handed him a one-year jail term. Ralph went on to become a photographer at the *New York Post*. At a later *Compass* alumni dinner, nobody made more merriment about his early foibles than Ralph himself.

Milt Shapiro, a City College product like Ginzburg, went on to write juvenile sports biographies. He did one on star pitcher Warren Spahn in which he lionized Spahn for his heroic actions as a soldier during the Battle of the Bulge. Spahn was persuaded by a shyster lawyer to sue Shapiro for unauthorized use of his life, or something. The case actually went up to the Supreme Court. The Court ruled for Shapiro.

Stan Cooperman, an NYU grad and the most scholarly of the bunch, became a professor of literature. At a small midwestern college he told his wife, Cookie, that she would have to shape up intellectually in order to be a respected faculty wife. He drafted a graduate student to smarten her up. It worked to some degree. She left him for the graduate student.

The amiable Sid Jacobson, another NYU man, had a long career as an editor at Harvey Comics. He wrote two novels and then made a splash by coauthoring *The 9/11 Report,* an acclaimed graphic history of the September 11 terrorist attack, as well as a graphic biography of Anne Frank.

After a short time as copy boy I moved to editorial assistant and then to the *Compass* sports staff. Thackery had persuaded Stanley Woodward, one of the most respected men in sports journalism, to be his sports editor. Woodward, called "The Coach" because of his fondness for college football, had been the sports editor of the *Herald Tribune.* He had brought Red Smith to New York from Philadelphia. In a celebrated incident when *Tribune* management wanted to retrench, Woodward was asked which members of his sports department were most expendable. Woodward, a fighter, named only himself and his star, Red Smith. Woodward soon left the *Tribune,* working for papers in Miami and Newark before joining the *Compass.*

The first time I was sent out of the office on an assignment, a Knicks game, Woodward told me "Don't forget to get the attendance into your story." Woodward had a classic line to ridicule any exaggeration: "To say that is like blaming the Johnstown flood on a leaky faucet in Altoona."

Jack Orr and Bill Mahoney filled out the staff when I arrived. Shortly after that, in one of Thackery's many ambitious moves to attract readers, he added two solid, respected sports reporters: Barney Nagler, the boxing specialist, and Herb Goren, who had written a popular baseball column called "The Old Scout" for the *New York Sun* when he was all of twenty-four years old. Goren had a unique way of typing that I adopted for a time; he double-spaced between all words. Like this. It made his copy look cleaner.

* * *

I was a brash youth and had a few ups and downs. My worst gaffe was during the 1952 World Series between the Dodgers and Yankees. At the time, I was deep into my relationship with Natalie (Bobbie) Bobrove, whom I would marry the following December. The *Compass* didn't publish on Sunday, so I chose to skip Saturday's game and co-lead with her an American Youth Hostel weekend bicycle trip to Connecticut. I planned to leave the group early Sunday morning and hitchhike down to Yankee Stadium in the Bronx in time to cover the Sunday game with Orr and Mahoney. By that time Woodward, whose salary the *Compass* could not carry anymore, had left, and Mahoney was the sports editor.

One of my rides dropped me off on a rural road in upstate New York. I was stranded for about two hours. By the time a car picked me up, I knew I could not possibly get to Yankee Stadium by game time. I decided the best thing I could do was to head down to the office and prepare some of the background paperwork and page layouts needed to get the Monday paper operation started.

When Mahoney and Orr arrived back at the office and heard my story, they were infuriated. My punishment was humiliating: For two weeks Mahoney let me sit idle at the sports copy desk, not allowing me to write or copy-read a story. I accepted my punishment, and only later realized that Mahoney was a disturbed individual who had spent time in rehabilitation.

The *Compass* was a wonderful training ground. Woodward instilled a fierce sense of independence. He encouraged vigorous questioning and reporting. The professionals on the paper were solid newspapermen. They demonstrated a good skeptical instinct, a wariness of hype, and a respect for good usage.

Orr, a Scotsman who grew up on the West Coast, was a pro-labor liberal. He was a facile writer who helped instill good writing principles in me. Regrettably, he had a drinking problem that dogged him before and after his *Compass* days. One day, he mentioned his glass eye. I did a double-take.

"What glass eye?" I asked.

"My glass eye," he said.

"You're kidding."

"No, I'm not," he said. "See . . ." He tapped his eye with a pencil. I cringed at the smacking sound. It didn't speak well for my powers of observation that I had never noticed my colleague had a glass eye. (It stemmed from a childhood accident.)

Orr once came home from a night of drinking and put his glass eye in his shirt pocket before going to sleep. He then sent the shirt out to the laundry. When he searched around for the eye and couldn't find it, he suspected it was in his shirt, so he called the laundry.

On the phone he said, "Mr. Lee, this is Jack Orr."

"I've got it, I've got it," came the excited cry from the other end.

Orr served in the South Pacific during World War II. A friend of his was known for booking horse racing bets. He would receive copies of the *Daily Racing Form* in the mail, post the entries on a bulletin board at the base, and take bets on the races. He then would post the results from the next day's papers. Nobody, Orr said, had the smarts to get their own *Daily Racing Form,* learn the results of races, and, in effect, hornswoggle the bookie.

The *Compass* gave me a heightened political awareness. I adopted the left-wing slant of the paper spearheaded by I. F. Stone. My objections to the U.S. involvement in Korea—the so-called police action—motivated a scheme that kept me out of the army. Coached by Stan Harrison, a librarian,

I drew immediate attention to myself in the draft examination on Whitehall Street in Manhattan by writing that I was a bedwetter. That alerted the examining psychiatrist to give me a closer look. I delayed when called and acted in an aggrieved, spacy manner when talking to him. That clinched it. When I completed the examination and moved to the next station, a clerk said, "That's all, son, we don't need you."

I covered the City College sweep of the National Invitation Tournament and National Collegiate Athletic Association tournaments in 1950. I wrote under the name Gary Fiske. Because we had such a small staff, sports editor Woodward invented two fictional by-lines for the staff. Though I had my own byline for some stories, I, like the others, also wrote under the names Bruce Connors and Gary Fiske. The National Invitation Tournament sponsors bestowed monogrammed cigarette lighters on reporters who covered that tournament. Mine was presented to Gary Fiske.

Once, a story bylined with Connors's name contained an egregious error of fact. (I did not write that story). Woodward had a puckish humor about him. He proclaimed a punishment in his column, declaring that the error, which could be traced to an overenthusiastic bit of boozing by Connors, had resulted in a suspension that would see him absent from the sports pages for two weeks.

Gambling on college basketball games was a big activity at the time. Many bettors believed that teams were shaving points to win bets for gamblers. If a team was favored to win by, say, eight points, gamblers would pay the players to win the game by fewer than eight points. This was a seductive way of getting the youths to agree to gamblers' schemes. They could earn money, they felt, but without losing games for the alma mater. Sometimes they couldn't control the game and lost. And in some cases the youths became sophisticated enough at the scheme to suggest games they would dump for the gamblers.

Having grown up in a gambling atmosphere in Williamsburg, I was aware of the swirling talk about "dumped" games. And one night LIU was so flagrant in making sure to win a game by less than the point spread against Bowling Green that I was moved to write a column that "a certain local team was not putting out in the manner of a team trying to win by as many points as possible."

I later wrote that "When the column was shown to a coach of the 'certain team' by another reporter, the coach said, 'You fellows ought not to be writing stuff like that. It's no good for the game.'"

A day later, a dumping scandal broke, involving two Manhattan College basketball players. It wasn't the team I wrote about, but the *Compass* made a big thing of my "scoop." I wasn't sure how to react; I certainly didn't puff out my chest. I went about my business, writing a story noting that the police were investigating another player, and that "there could be many more."

Eventually the LIU players were exposed as dumpers, along with players from NYU, City College, Bradley, and Toledo. Too many people recall City College's involvement, forgetting that non–New York City schools also were involved. When the first scandal broke, the pompous Kentucky coach Adolph (The Baron) Rupp blamed it all on New York. He said, "They couldn't touch my boys with a 10-foot pole." Soon enough, almost the entire Kentucky team was implicated; New York basketball writers sent Rupp a figurative ten-foot pole.

* * *

On September 23, 1952, I went over to the 14th Street Academy of Music in Manhattan to write about Joe Walcott's defense of his heavyweight title against the highly touted Rocky Marciano. The actual bout was in Philadelphia. At the time, closed circuit theater television was the vehicle for viewing big out-of-town fights. The crowd was raucous, full of people perhaps a few steps above the kind you wouldn't want to meet in a dark alley.

At just about the time the fight was to start, the screen went black. There were howls of dismay. Management quickly announced that refunds would be paid; patrons were invited to stay and listen to the audio part of the fight. Otherwise, management might have had a wrecked joint on its hands.

As the fight progressed, we listened to the commentary of announcers who were not aware that we stalwarts in the Academy of Music were not seeing what they were describing. The cheers and jeers rang out in the theater almost as if we were at the live event.

The commentary seemed to indicate that Walcott was winning the fight. Then, in the thirteenth round, after a flurry of punches, the excited announcer suddenly cried, "He's down, he's down." He didn't say who was down. We heard the count by the referee, but without knowing who was on the canvas. The theater echoed with shouts of "who? . . . who? . . . who the hell is down?" Obscenities filled the air. It was only after the referee finished his count that the announcer hailed Marciano as the new heavyweight champion of the world.

* * *

The *Compass* eked out a marginal existence, barely able to hold itself together as its resources withered away. It got to the point that it could not afford wire services, so the paper compiled news by having rewrite men listen to the on-the-hour and half-hour radio news reports on WQXR and WNEW and gather as much information as their speedy fingers could record. The *Compass* was essentially a paper of opinion by this time, so readers did not particularly look to it for news. One afternoon, as the WQXR newsman was giving his report, ace rewriteman Dick Armstrong sat idly, not typing.

"Why aren't you getting that stuff down?" somebody asked Armstrong.

"Oh, I'm on the WNEW reports on the half-hour," he said.

By that time, we couldn't even put fresh photos into the paper, because of the cost of making up the metal plates that imprinted photos onto a page. Whenever we wanted to dress up a story about a winning horse, we illustrated it by using the same piece of metal, a head shot of a horse named Stymie. Our readership was not savvy about horse racing, so nobody noticed.

In the waning months of the *Compass,* the sports staff was reduced to two, Jack Orr and me, with help from copy boys. On August 6, 1952, Orr was ill, so it fell to me to put out the two pages allotted to sports. We had a heavy sports schedule that night, but I think I had a good plan to manage everything because we had refined to an art form the task of covering sports via radio and television.

The events of the night were these: Brooklyn Dodgers, New York Giants, and Yankees baseball games and a boxing bout between Harold Johnson and Bob Satterfield. I handled it this way: a friend in Brooklyn listened to the Dodgers game on radio, kept a box score, and called in with details of the game after five innings. I then wrote a summary of the first half of that game, which was called a "first add." When the game was over, the friend called in the additional details. I wrote a few lead paragraphs that were placed with a headline on top of the first add to complete the Dodgers story. I did the same thing for a Yankee game with the aid of another friend listening on the radio and calling in reports.

In the meantime, I was keeping a box score listening to the Giants game on a radio in the office, sending down a first add after five innings, and then a lead and headline upon completion of that game. That left the fight. I monitored that on the television set in front of me in the office. That should have been enough to occupy me, but I also eavesdropped on a conversation in the adjoining arts department because an interesting visitor, a stage personality, was visiting our critic, Fred Rayfield.

The three baseball games ended and I kept an eye on the television set, noting that Harold Johnson seemed to be doing well, earning a decision. At the time of the decision, I was busy with one of the baseball summaries. In any case, I got the three baseball games and the fight into the paper. I wrapped up and started to make my way out of the building.

When I passed the loading dock downstairs as papers were being bundled to be put on delivery trucks, one of the loaders said to me, "Stan, Satterfield won the fight, not Johnson."

I was stunned. "Are you sure?"

"We were watching the fight on television," he said. "There's no doubt they gave the decision to Satterfield. It's wrong in the paper."

I sprinted back upstairs and called for a replate. I rewrote the story to have Satterfield the winner and sent it downstairs to the composing room floor. I prayed that not too many of the earlier reports had gone out with the trucks. I didn't sleep well that night nor the rest of the weekend.

When I got to work Monday morning, it was with more than a little trepidation that I answered the call of managing editor Tom O'Connor. He asked me to explain what had happened. I did that, emphasizing the difficulties of the task, conveniently not mentioning that I had too much of an ear turned to the conversation in the drama department. He looked at me for a long while, then said with a hint of a smile, "Well, you got three out of four right; that's a .750 batting average. That isn't bad."

I have tried over the years to obtain a copy of the edition with the three baseball results and the wrong boxing result. No success. I have made a few trips to the microfilm section of the 42nd Street branch of the New York Public Library but haven't been able to locate that day's paper. Sometimes I think I was in the twilight zone and made it all up. But I know I did not. I surmise that the replated edition with the correct story went to microfilm.

In those final days of the *Compass,* I was often the last person out of the editorial operation because the sports department closed its pages last. I would occasionally sidle into publisher Ted Thackery's office and check out his mail, monitoring his continuing efforts to raise money to keep the paper afloat. By the end it seemed that Corliss Lamont, the eminent left-wing angel, was his last resort. Lamont kept saying he could give no more, but time and again would accede to Thackery's wheedling.

One time I was sure that the upcoming Friday issue would be the final one. I figured that would be the time to make a personal mark on the paper with the insertion of a one-line short, which was something inserted into a page before it was locked up to fill a small space in a column.

I conspired to insert a one-line short into what I fully expected to be the final edition of the *Compass*. I wrote this one-liner: "Soccer is played in Chile" with the headline, "Chileans Play Soccer." I inserted it at the bottom of one of our two sports pages.

The *Compass* did not fold that day. It limped along for a month or so. I have searched the microfilm of old issues at the New York Public Library but haven't been able to find that, either. But soccer *is* played in Chile.

7

A Wayward Pressman

In August 1952, I met Natalie "Bobbie" Bobrove on an American Youth Hostel camping trip out of Bolton Landing on Lake George in upstate New York. She went by Bobbie because she didn't like being called Nat by her mother.

The first time I saw her, she was laughing at me.

We had been equipped with canoes and camping equipment and started to row out to one of the Mother Bunch Islands on the lake. I settled into the canoe with my pal Burt D'Lugoff and a fellow named Meyer who insisted he sit in the back to steer. Burt sat in the front so, resignedly, I sat in the middle. Meyer was inept; our canoe kept going in circles. Bobbie eased by in another canoe with a guy who knew what he was doing; she couldn't restrain a laugh as she observed our buffoonery. I resented her for thinking I was as incompetent as Meyer.

We became friends during the week. I was particularly impressed with her during a volleyball game when I noted that she had the smarts to pass the ball to set up shots, rather than willy-nilly hitting returns over the net. I was less impressed by her answer to one of my questions. When I learned she had graduated from UCLA, I asked her who was the school's most significant graduate. She said, "Ralph Bunche." I said, "Have you ever heard of Jackie Robinson?" Even though Bunche won the Nobel Prize, she eventually accepted that Robinson was more significant.

She was five-foot three, with beautiful greenish eyes, brown hair, and an ample bosom. As a teenager she had a striking resemblance to Joan Crawford. She had a ready laugh, which immediately endeared her to Burt and me.

About a month after returning to the city from the camping trip, I called her for our first date. She was such a classy dame, I thought it would make a good impression if we went to the opera, my first. We saw *The Barber of Seville* at the City Center. (Decades later we became friends with Edith Frumin, who had been an opera singer and sang in the chorus that night.) We soon agreed that we really wanted to talk more than we wanted to listen to the music. We left at the intermission and spent a few hours gabbing in a coffee shop. Two significant aspects of our relationship emerged: we both were almost obsessive about showing up on time, and we were both political lefties.

I became a frequent visitor to her ground-floor apartment on West 87th Street off Central Park in Manhattan. It was distinctive for lacking a kitchen sink; she washed dishes in the bathroom sink. We spent much time chatting on her sofa.

Bobbie majored in sociology at UCLA. She earned a graduate degree at the New York School of Social Work and went on to a productive career as a psychiatric social worker. She was much admired through the years by her colleagues and her clients. I always enjoyed seeing how people warmed up to her because of her selflessness and sensitivity to people. If I was judgmental, she was understanding. She was of tremendous support to me, the love of my life.

She roomed with her UCLA classmate, Adele Motzkin. After I had been seeing her for a while, I told my mother that Adele's father owned a dry-cleaning factory, while Bobbie's family had a hardware store in Yonkers. "Can't you like the rich one?" asked my mother. After she actually met Bobbie, my mother insisted to her dying day that she had never said that.

One night we ate dinner at an Italian restaurant near Madison Square Garden before going to see a Harlem Globetrotters game. I had seen the Globies' slapstick before, and loved their opening bit, when they adroitly handled a basketball to the infectious tune, "Sweet Georgia Brown." Bobbie usually didn't dominate conversations, but this night she was caught up in a case and went on animatedly describing it to me. I could see the clock moving, the possibility of getting to the Globies' opening act fading with every word from her. She was so enthusiastic with the story and because I didn't know her well enough, I didn't have the nerve to tell her we should hurry up and get to the game.

We blew it. We arrived after the Globies' opening. Whenever I tell the story, she says, "You should have told me about the Globetrotters."

Bobbie has her moments, though. When Tiger Woods was new on the golf scene, I mentioned at breakfast an item about him in the newspaper. I said, "I see where this new, hot golfer has a black father and a mother who is Thai."

Almost immediately she said, "I guess that means he will be invited to a lot of black-Thai affairs."

Bobbie cringes every time I tell this story, certain that no one will find it as amusing as I do. She is wrong.

* * *

I married Bobbie on December 20, 1953, about one year after the *Daily Compass* had folded. By our wedding, my twenty-six weeks of unemployment insurance had run out, and I was relying on some piddling bucks from undistinguished freelance assignments. When people praise Bobbie for her courage in marrying an out-of-work bloke, she answers, "I knew he had potential."

We got our marriage license at New York's City Hall, where we bumped up against an officious, strong-minded clerk. When she asked for my name and I gave it as Stanley Isaacs, she asked for a middle name.

"I don't have one," I said.

"You have to have a middle name."

"I'm sorry. I don't. I'm just Stanley plain Isaacs."

"Okay, that's better,' she said and wrote down Stanley Plain Isaacs as my name on the marriage license. At the wedding ceremony, when the rabbi asked if I, Stanley Plain Isaacs, would take Natalie Lois Bobrove as my wife, she was surprised to hear me addressed that way and could hardly suppress a giggle. On various forms now I am listed as Stanley Plain Isaacs.

We settled into an apartment at 47 West 88th street in Manhattan and enjoyed the environs around Central Park. We played tennis in the park, as well as touch football with some of her old friends from UCLA who had moved to New York.

I wrote some run-of-the-mill pieces as a freelancer after the *Compass* folded, but I was pleased to have one article accepted by *The Nation,* a profile of the right-wing governor of California, Goodwin Knight. In the summer of 1953, my unemployment insurance ran out. I landed a job with the schlock publishing house Magazine Management. It put out men's adventure and tepid pre-*Playboy* girlie magazines.

I wrote picture captions for young women in various stages of *deshabille.* The editor would show me a spread of pictures of young women in different stages of undress and ask which I would select for inclusion. No matter which pictures I chose, the guy picked the other ones. The three others in the department waited for me to catch on to the fact that the editor needed to assert his authority and would always choose pictures other than the ones I selected. After two months, I left. *Fled* would be more like it.

At one point I went down to Charles Town, West Virginia, to work up an article on a jockey, Stanley Palumbo, known as the king of the small racetracks. Palumbo turned out to be uncooperative. No piece. But the trip was interesting. I checked into a rooming house in Charles Town. Up the block was a historical marker attesting that John Brown had been hanged on this site for his 1859 raid on the federal arsenal at Harpers Ferry. He was tried in the Charles Town courthouse in the center of town before being moved to the place of hanging. It inspired a lifelong interest in John Brown.

Joe Goldstein, an indefatigable publicity guy, lobbied for me at *Newsday* with sports editor Bob Zellner. In October 1954, the call came. I had covered the World Series at the *Compass,* and I now covered high school football—and was thrilled to do it. My first assignment was Mineola vs. Hempstead. It struck me that Tord Beck, the assistant coach of the Hempstead team, had a son on the rival Mineola team. I wrote not only a game story, but also a sidebar on the relationship of father and son. When I turned in the stories at the office in Garden City, the editor seemed surprised. Ed Comerford, who ran the desk, said it was a good idea. They held the sidebar out because of lack of space and ran it a few days later.

The *Newsday* sports operation was a backwater affair. The people there were intimidated by the New York City papers. The majority of the staff was Long Island–grown; Comerford was probably the only top-notch professional in the group. I was the first Jew in the department. I did not detect even subtle indications of anti-Semitism. In a way, there was a little bit of awe for me because I had come from the big city. It struck me as more than odd that the conversations in the department revolved mostly around local sports—bowling in particular. Hardly anything was said about the major sports that dominated the conversations of most fans.

My first winter, I worked the evening rewrite shift from 6:00 P.M. to 1:00 A.M. Mostly I waited for late college basketball scores to be compiled for the scoreboard. I was sure we were catering just to bettors, the only ones who might care about a Wichita vs. Louisville score. I grew bored with this. After a while, I spiced up the scoreboard with teams out of my own imagination. I conceived an entire league of teams cavorting on the nightly scoreboard. My undefeated powerhouse was Chelm, which on subsequent nights beat Excelsior, Zenith, Altgeld, and Valhalla. Nobody ever called me on this.

I was emulating my journalistic hero, A. J. Liebling, the great *New Yorker* writer. Early in Liebling's career, when he was a clerk in the *New York Times* sports department, he took scholastic scores over the phone. One night, when the boy reporting the information for a basketball box score did not provide the names of the officials, Liebling made up the name "Ignoto"—Italian for "unknown." When nobody noticed this, Liebling kept inserting "Ignoto" into his box scores. He made the mistake of boasting about it, however. The word came back to the sports editor. He fired Liebling with the word, "Young man, you are not a *Times* man."

Liebling was a hero to would-be newspapermen at all the New York City colleges. In his classic work, *The Wayward Pressman,* he ridiculed the penchant of city newspaper editors to hire kids from the boondocks. He said they had to spend a year just to learn what New York City was all about, when there were street-smart kids at all the New York colleges just panting to get started in the business.

I covered scholastic and college sports my first year. I eked out a few assignments of my own. I wrote about a fox hunt so that I could quote Oscar Wilde's classic line about fox hunting: "the pursuit of the inedible by the unspeakable." I found an eccentric artist named Homer Costello who employed a special system for betting on the horses. He would have his cat, Rusty, jump down from the couch onto a racing scratch sheet. He would then bet on the horses on which the cat's claws had landed. When I went to interview him at his apartment on West 55th Street in Manhattan, he wouldn't open the door until he was assured I wasn't a bookie coming to collect money. I watched his cat in action but resisted any impulse to make a bet.

Costello painted what looked to me like Moroccan street scenes, heavy in browns and oranges, the kind of paintings that wound up in upholstery showrooms on Queens Boulevard. I refused his offer of a free painting because of my high sense of ethics about taking a gift from a subject. I came to regret that I didn't have a memento of that occasion. Luckily, years later I saw a Costello for sale for $10 at a local junk shop. I jumped at the chance.

8

Joining *Newsday*

Newsday, a powerhouse on Long Island, began to spread its wings in the 1950s to cover the rest of the world. The sports department was probably last to emerge out of the Nassau-Suffolk County cocoon. The change came in 1957 with an odd-duck arrangement: a three-man national staff atop the rest of the staff. Jack Mann, a hard-bitten city-side guy, became sports editor, with Ed Comerford and me covering national sports.

One of Mann's first orders of business was to get rid of the Jimmy Cannon column, which ran a day after it had appeared in the *New York Post.* A bit after that, the three of us alternated writing columns. When Mann became editor of the entire sports operation, I became a three-times-a-week columnist. In 1963 I started writing five columns a week.

Mann was a terrific sports editor, one of the best in the country. He added some fine talents and helped develop George Vecsey, Steve Jacobson, Bob Sales, Dave Knickerbocker, and Bob Waters. We soon started making waves as one of the best sports departments in the country—we were probably the best, along with the *Philadelphia Daily News* sports staff, which had Larry Merchant as editor and columnist over Jack McKinney, Stan Hochman, Steve Klessel, Jack Kiser, and others.

There was a time when the *Newsday* sports pages were overloaded with pieces that opened with quotations. This attracted the attention of Lou DeFichy, our racing reporter. He made up for a lack of erudition with intensive legwork. DeFichy, not among the educated elite on the staff, reached for Bartlett's Quotations and led off one of his stories with a quote by John Dryden. He identified the author as "Ibid."

One of Mann's stunts is regarded as a classic among newspaper people. It inspired an adulatory article by Dick Schaap about the *Newsday* sports staff in the press section of *Newsweek*. Mann had long nursed the idea of a story on which he could play off Thomas Paine's "These are the times that try men's souls" with a headline that read, "These are the souls that time men's tries." I told him I could do such a story.

I knew about the rabid track fans who came to track meets at the 168th Street armory in Manhattan with their own stopwatches. They sat in the balcony over the finish line and compared their clockings with that of the official timers. I wrote a straight feature on these colorful gents, thereby setting it up for Mann to affix the headline, "These are the souls that time men's tries." I got my usual byline for the story, and Mann fittingly gave himself a byline under the headline. It was a terrific stunt.

Mann constantly needed praise yet wasn't always quick to share praise. In this case I thought he was less than gracious in taking credit for the headline without at least saying that I had come up with the story that enabled him to launch his long-sought-after headline. Mann's talent was not enough to save him from self-destructive acts that challenged management. He got himself fired from *Newsday* and other choice journalistic positions. I have never known a better pure newspaperman.

* * *

We were serious journalists out to puncture the stuffed shirts in sports, as well as twist the tails of the newspapers in the city. We had fun. I was a leading practitioner of fun and games. Kansas City particularly brought out the puckishness in me. On one trip with the Yankees, when I spotted Leonard Koppett of the *Times* with a novel in the press box, I suggested a challenge: we pick out at random a sentence in his novel and work that sentence into our stories the next day. Koppett agreed. By dint of some strained manipulation of a paragraph, I managed to work the sentence into my story. Koppett didn't even try. "You weren't serious, were you?" said the cherubic one afterward.

I had some columns rejected over the years—"too far out" was the verdict. Not much was made of it by me—or anybody else. We never had the types of brouhahas that the *Times* had after censoring sports columns by Red Smith, Dave Anderson, or Harvey Araton.

Newsday was started by Alicia Patterson, the daughter of *Daily News* publisher Joe Patterson. She had tried many pursuits, with no notable success. She married billionaire Harry Guggenheim. When she launched *Newsday* in 1940 with Guggenheim, it was considered another plaything to keep the little rich woman happy. But she presided over a stunningly successful paper that rode the wave of postwar development of Long Island. Guggenheim owned 51 percent of the stock to Patterson's 49 percent. She was the guiding light of the paper, with little or no input from Guggenheim, until she died in 1963 at age fifty-six.

Newsday became a plaything for Guggenheim. He assumed a somewhat active role as publisher for a time. When I became the five-times-a-week columnist—"*Newsday*'s Red Smith," Guggenheim called me—he must have felt it his obligation to talk to me. I was called into his office for what I gathered was a congratulatory talk. Guggenheim didn't know how to talk to people. Worse, he made you feel as if your fly was open. After an awkward moment or two, he made a stab at conversation. He asked me, "How many teams are there in the National Football League?" I was taken aback; this was almost like being asked how much is two and two. I recovered to say fourteen, which was correct for the time, I think, though I could have said anything and he probably wouldn't have known the correct answer.

There was another awkward pause. This time, I made an attempt. I asked, "How's the horse?"

The horse was Never Bend, the star of Guggenheim's Cain Hoy stable at the time. Though he faded out of contention for the Triple Crown races, he had some success. The Cain Hoy stable had won the Kentucky Derby with Dark Star in 1953, which was the only race the great Native Dancer lost. Guggenheim warmed to my question, and I was home free.

The next spring I was in Florida for baseball spring training and drove over to Hialeah Park to watch Never Bend in the Flamingo Stakes. Steve Jacobson, who was covering the Yankees for *Newsday,* went with me. As we stood in the paddock watching Never Bend being saddled, Guggenheim bent down to feel Never Bend's legs. At this point, Jacobson, not a racetrack-wise gent, asked, "Who's the old geezer over there?" I laughed, informing him it was his boss. He said, "At least I recognized Alicia Patterson."

Guggenheim's family was filthy rich in copper, silver, and finance. The joke around the office was that the Guggenheims owned all of Montana and a good part of Chile. In any case, he was born to the purple and never really had to condescend to learn how to deal with people. Nor was he in awe of anybody.

When Alicia Patterson was alive, she had lunch one day with President Kennedy in the White House. That stuck with Guggenheim. After she died and he took over as publisher, he decided he wanted to have lunch with President Lyndon Johnson. The word went out to Bob Rhodes, the head of

Newsday's small bureau in Washington, to talk to the White House people about arranging the lunch. This was no small order for Rhodes. He had to trade on a lot of goodwill, and after a big effort, passed word up to Bill Woestendiek, Guggenheim's assistant publisher, that it had been arranged for the president to have lunch with Guggenheim at the White House.

When Guggenheim was informed, he told Woestendiek, "I don't want to go down to Washington for lunch. Let's arrange for Johnson to come up to New York." Now this is chutzpah of a colossal nature, but when you consider who Guggenheim was—or who he thought he was—it could be explained. Guggenheim came from one of the country's richest families. He was a presence from the day he was born, a nabob of wealth when Johnson was scheming to make it as a politician in the backwaters of Texas. For Guggenheim it was no big deal to ask a president to come up to New York to have lunch with him rather than for him to go to Washington to see the president.

There was no lunch.

* * *

It seems a bit unusual now that I, or anybody, could write five columns a week. But that was the practice on the sports pages of that time. Red Smith with the *Herald Tribune* and then the *Times;* Arthur Daley with the *Times;* Jimmy Cannon with the *World-Journal-Telegram;* Milton Gross with the *Post;* Frank Graham with the *Journal-American,* and a few others all wrote five columns a week and thought nothing of it. Red Smith said, "If you write two good ones out of five you are doing okay." Smith did better than okay.

Once established as the columnist, I began to develop a style consistent with the name "Out of Left Field," my columnar shingle. I covered the big events and wrote about the pressing issues of the day. In words I first heard from Dodgers first baseman Gil Hodges, I tried to take my work, but not myself, too seriously. I developed some off-beat columns that spiced my output.

The most distinctive recurring columns, and the ones with which readers most came to associate me, were the Isaacs Ratings of Esoteric Distinction (IRED).

The IRED, so titled by Ed Comerford after they had gained a foothold in the section, appeared on or around April 1, as a spoof on ratings in general. In the early 1960s, the only ratings of note were *Ring* magazine's rankings of the top fighters in each division. I lampooned this by rating categories that nobody would have thought of rating. Even into the twenty-first century, when ratings had spread like crabgrass on the land, nobody had rated such categories as Overrated Underrated Athletes; Bridges Over the Seine; and The Four Horsemen of the Apocalypse.

Certainly nobody else in history ever had been so bold as to rate the explorers Lewis and Clark. I rated Clark over Lewis, then a few years later revised that rating and put Clark ahead. My all-time favorite was my rating of the men of the moving company known as The Seven Santini Brothers (1. Pasquale, 2. Rinaldo, 3. Godfrey, 4. August, 5. Paride, 6. Martin, 7. Pietro). Another favorite came in the form of a guest rating from the irrepressible Vic Ziegel. He rated the numbers from one to seven. (Six came in first.)

I said I would revise any rating with any vehement letter of protest but would brook no disagreement in the one category that I took seriously: chocolate ice cream. Only this category appeared every year. Because I declared myself a chocolate ice cream (and only chocolate ice cream) expert, people soon regarded me as such. I was sent suggestions of places to check out—which I did. Before long, I had done so much research that I, too, regarded myself as a chocolate ice cream expert. We solidified the ratings by staging some raucous blind chocolate ice cream tastings at our house. For the majority of the years, Haagen Dazs dominated the ratings.

One year, I dropped Haagen Dazs from first to third, asserting that it had become too sweet. That led to an invitation from Reuben Mattus, founder of the company, to visit the factory. I agreed, checked the phonebook, and noted that Haagen Dazs was manufactured at a less-than-tony address of Southern Boulevard in the Bronx. I arrived at the site of the Ortiz Funeral Company. Somewhat puzzled, I went in, then was escorted down the block to the creamery. The owner seemed a bit abashed that I had gone to the offices over the funeral parlor rather than to the factory.

In any case, Mattus told me his story of Haagen Dazs. He had been in World War II, and he met a Danish soldier who shared a formula for a superb ice cream. He had been in the business of making cheap ice creams for supermarkets and had vowed that if he ever had the chance, he would make this premium ice cream. When that time finally occurred, he did a change-over in his machines, making the premium ice cream twice a week and the supermarket product the rest of the week.

In honor of the Dane, Mattus said, he gave it the Danish name of Haagen Dazs. And he put a map of Scandinavia on the ice cream lid. He also put an umlaut above the first "a" in Haagen, though there is no umlaut in the Danish language, nor any word such as Haagen. Mattus didn't want the secret to get out that he made the ice cream in the Bronx, rather than Scandinavia, because he introduced the ice cream to an upscale trade in fancy groceries. He eventually sold Haagen Dazs to the Pillsbury Company.

I wrote an article on my Haagen Dazs discovery. It was a scoop, if you will.

9

The Early Mets

I came to realize that all the pearls of wisdom I might lay on readers would not necessarily dazzle them. This was brought home to me by a journeyman ballplayer, one of the original Mets: Sherman Jarvis "Roadblock" Jones.

The Mets got going as an expansion team in 1962. There was much excitement the previous winter about the new team. Casey Stengel, a national icon who had been fired by the Yankees, was named manager. George Weiss, who had helped build the Yankee dynasty and then was fired, also came out of retirement as general manager. This occasioned the celebrated comment from his wife: "I married George for better or worse, not for lunch." In the expansion draft, the Mets inherited other teams' leftovers.

I had been covering the Yankees after the Giants and Dodgers deserted New York for the big bucks of the golden West, but as a National League fan in a National League town, I was excited about covering the Mets, the new team in town. In the enthusiastic glow of anticipation, optimistic souls like me actually thought Stengel's wizardry with the Yankees might translate into a golden touch with the Mets.

Not everybody understood that. Les Biederman, a veteran Pittsburgh sports reporter, asked whom I would be covering the next spring. When I said without hesitation that I was looking forward to covering the Mets, he looked at me like he was talking to a fool. He said, "I don't know that that is such a good idea. When you cover a successful team like the Yankees, people associate you with them and their success. That wouldn't be so with a new team that won't be a winner."

I was quite surprised by that. I had always felt I would be judged by my work, not by whom I wrote about. Over the years, I came to realize there was much truth to Biederman's view. People do associate you with your subject, which is one of the reasons so many writers gravitate to the stars, basking in the success of the people they write about. Taking this to its ultimate level, you find the media full of what some call "star fuckers."

The much-awaited first day of the Mets' spring training at Miller Huggins Field in St. Petersburg finally arrived in February 1962. The players heard a speech from Stengel and trotted out to the field for calisthenics and a rag-tag sprint around the baseball field. I must say the desultory trotting style of the not-all-svelte athletes galumphing along wasn't something that inspired visions of grandeur.

The first chance reporters had to meet with the Mets en masse occurred when they came into the clubhouse for their lunch break. With pen and trusty reporter's pad in hand, I approached Sherman "Roadblock" Jones, a six-foot-four light-skinned, freckle-faced black guy from Winton, North Carolina. He *looked* like a real ballplayer, anyway. He had had brief, inconsequential stays with the San Francisco Giants and Cincinnati Reds before the Mets plucked him from the Reds in the draft.

I said, "Hi, I'm Stan Isaacs, from *Newsday*."

He said, "*Newsday*? That's a newspaper, isn't it?"

I said, "Yes, it is."

He said, "I believe only 12 percent of what I read in newspapers."

I was taken aback. "Twelve percent? Why 12 percent?"

He gave me an inscrutable look, shook his head and repeated, "Twelve percent."

Then and there, it dawned on me that no matter what I wrote, it would be wise to remember that astute people like Roadblock Jones would believe only a fraction of what I wrote. That might be something for Journalism 101.

Roadblock Jones played one season with the Mets. His most significant achievement was his appearance as the starting pitcher in the Mets' home-opening game at the Polo Grounds. They lost. He had no victories and four defeats with the Mets before fading into the minor leagues and out of baseball.

I came across his name many years later when I read, with some excitement, that he was running for state House of Representatives in Kansas. A few days later I read that he had won. Rah, rah Roadblock!

A few days after that, I learned that he had run unopposed.

* * *

That first day in the Mets clubhouse was memorable. Familiar faces, has-beens, and never-was or would-be hombres filled out the Mets uniforms.

I was struck by an impish thought. I approached Solly Hemus, a former pepper pot manager of the St. Louis Cardinals who was one of Stengel's coaches. I asked him what he thought about the chances of Walter Plinge.

Hemus said, "Good boy. Has all the tools. Could help the club a lot."

Fine. Except that there was no such person as Walter Plinge. I had invented him to test whether a coach would be familiar with all the strangers in that room.

I hadn't pulled the name of Walter Plinge out of the ether. The name stemmed from the English stage. Plays in London sometimes were not completely cast by the time the programs went to the printers. For those characters who had not been cast, the program read "Walter Plinge." In the old days of horse racing, when a jockey had not yet been assigned to a horse, the appellation "No Boy" appeared in the newspaper listings of the next day's racing card. Walter Plinge, then, was the English theater equivalent of American horse racing's No Boy.

An episode that may have symbolized the wackiness of the Mets' first year was the case of an Everyman named John Pappas. He was a kid from Queens who showed up at the Mets camp asking for a tryout as a pitcher. Fair enough, except that he had little experience; he hadn't even made his high school team. But he was determined.

He said he was a night student at City College, that he had paid $66 to fly down to St. Petersburg, that he had come with $225, and that he had told his parents he had gone away for a few days on vacation. "It would be crazy to tell them I was trying to make the team," he said.

If the Mets had their way, they would have sent him right back to Queens. But Bob Lipsyte of the *Times* and I—Walter Mittys at heart—pressed the John Pappas issue. Johnny Murphy, the Mets general manager, was softhearted. And the Mets, new enough to be wary of bad press relations, agreed to give the twenty-one-year-old a tryout.

It took only a short time for Murphy—and the rest of us—to see that Walter Mitty had struck out. Pappas had little sense of how to throw a baseball. After eighteen minutes, Murphy put his arm on the fellow's shoulder and said, "All you have is guts, son." He told Lipsyte and me, "In my humble opinion, there is nothing there. He's as poor as anybody I have seen—and I have seen thousands."

The ones who made the team that first year—the Joe Ginsbergs and Ken MacKenzies—wound up no higher than they would have if they had a team of John Pappases. I caught up with Pappas a few years later. He had dropped out of City College, joined the army, and hoped to make a career in finance on Wall Street. He said, "I shouldn't have gone down there. My friends told me that if only I had as much talent as I had nerve, I would really have been great."

I later wrote, "There will be many faceless youths at their first training camp this week. For none of them will it be quite like it was for John Pappas, who was not content merely to dream the American dream; he acted on it." He didn't make the team—but in his own way he was truly a Met.

The Mets were the worst team in baseball history, setting a record of 120 losses that still stands. The highlight of the season occurred when they met the Yankees in a spring training game. At the time, it loomed as an important game for the Mets because of what the Yankees represented. They were the powerhouse of baseball, the high and mighty who had long dominated baseball. They were the natural target for New York National League fans who had seen them dominate the Brooklyn Dodgers and New York Giants for so many years. And they had, of course, dumped Stengel.

Stengel was all fired up. He talked it up in his inimitable style. He managed it to the hilt. And the Mets won the game by coming from behind. I knew of the dangers of getting too excited about any spring training game, but by this time I sensed that the Mets would do little in the National League season. A victory over the Yankees under these circumstances would be major.

I tried to persuade the desk editors that this was not just another insignificant exhibition game; I wrote a much longer game story than usual. This did not impress the copyeditors. They ascribed my enthusiasm to a case of being too close to the scene, and the story was cut. I bemoaned that all season, because the Mets had few triumphs that matched the fun-and-games victory over the Yankees.

These are some excerpts from my piece:

St. Petersburg, Fla.—This was a slightly manic Casey Stengel after the Mets beat the Yankees yesterday:

"You can't beat getting' to home plate."

"They [the Mets] were amazin'. If ever it was good to be good this was the time. If you can beat the Yankees, you should know you can beat many clubs in the National League."

"There is some ability in these players if we can get it out of them."

"We looked good in our uniforms. They [the uniforms] are just as good as the other side's."

On Joe Christopher, the man who led off the ninth with a triple that led to the winning run: "I love him, I love him. Tonight I love him. Last night I didn't."

Then he did a little jig and away he went.

If you were with it at Al Lang Field yesterday, you might believe the Mets' 4–3 victory over the Yankees was one of the greatest baseball games ever played. It wasn't of course, but you might have believed it if you were there.

The Yankees led, 2–0, the Mets rallied for a 3–2 lead, and the Yankees tied, 3–3 on some shoddy fielding by the Mets. The story ended with this paragraph:

The finish: Joe Christopher lined a drive to left which was too much for [Hector] Lopez. Christopher made third. Gary Blaylock, the third Yankee pitcher, retired [Don] Zimmer on a foul. Now Stengel was thinking again. Up came Richie Ashburn, pinch-hitting for [Howie] Nunn. Ashburn lined a single to right and Christopher sprinted home. A few of the Mets rushed to shake his hand. The old people in the stands cheered, not the polite claps with which they greet most plays, but with lusty cheers.

"You're the best, Casey," a man behind the dugout yelled, "You're the best."

A *Daily News* headline got that game just right. It said, "Break Up the Mets."

* * *

The Mets lost games and won fans. Symbolic of something or other, there was an incident of passion during the opening game at the Polo Grounds. A couple was hauled into the police station for indecency, namely an act of fellatio in the stands behind home plate. It was learned later that they were married; obviously, the Mets inspired them to such heights of ardor that they couldn't wait to get home to the privacy of their apartment.

The Mets were so inept that after one of their few victories, a slugfest over the Chicago Cubs, a fan called a radio station to get the score. When he was told the Mets scored sixteen runs, he responded, "But did they win?"

During the season the Mets acquired catcher Harry Chiti from the Cleveland Indians for a "player to be named later." After being exposed to the talents of Chiti for a few games, the Mets sent him back to Cleveland as "the player to be named later."

Jimmy Breslin wrote a book called *Can't Anybody Here Play This Game?*, ostensibly basing the title on a comment by Stengel. Nobody around the club ever heard Stengel say that, but that didn't seem to matter. The book was a bestseller.

Much ado was made about the arrival of seventeen-year-old Ed Kranepool, a product of James Monroe High, the school that produced Hall of Famer Hank Greenberg. A wag in the stands raised one of the earliest piquant banners about the teenager. It read: "Is Ed Kranepool Over the Hill?"

Banners caught on early with the Mets at the Polo Grounds, though it took management some time to appreciate them. The Mets tried a ridiculous act of censorship, and it boomeranged on them. After they had moved to Shea Stadium and had solidified themselves as big-time losers, two fans showed up with a sign in right field that read, "Welcome to Grant's Tomb." It was a bow to Mets executive Donald Grant, the former hotel clerk who held owner Joan Payson's hands and had too much say as a spokesman for the Mets.

A security patrol, headed by a man named Matt Burns, was assigned to tear down the offending sign. The sign man, Karl Ehrhardt, and a friend wended their way to the press box to complain. Their cause was taken up by Steve Jacobson and me, and the Mets' Gestapo backed off. The next sign by Ehrardt and Co. read: "We Scribble while Matt Burns."

Ehrhardt, an advertising graphic artist, gained fame as the "Sign Man" of the Mets. He captured the mocking spirit of Mets fandom by coming up with clever, pithy messages, expertly designed, to greet the team's foibles. He agreed later that he went a bit too far when he flashed "The Big Stiff" as an exclamation point underlining inept actions by Kranepool.

The Mets management grudgingly accepted Ehrhardt for the fan-favorite presence he became at Shea Stadium. When the Mets won their first pennant in 1969, it was Mayor John Lindsay—and not the Mets—who invited him to ride in the championship parade down Broadway. I sat in the open car with Ehrhardt. Wearing his comic derby hat and a smile a mile long, he basked in the cheers as he flashed the custom-made signs he worked up for the occasion. I may have had more enjoyable moments related to baseball, but I can't think of any.

The best Mets player—the only one who performed with any kind of distinction that first year—was Richie Ashburn, who eventually was voted into the Hall of Fame for his long, distinguished career with the Philadelphia Phillies. He was a scrapper, a base-stealer, the personification of a lead-off man. Ashburn, who drove in the winning run in that epic spring training victory over the Yankees, was a significant figure for the Mets, and not only because of his play. Ashburn was second only to Casey Stengel in conveying an aura of charm about the Mets.

He was an engaging man. I, a liberal Democrat, enjoyed good-natured jousting with him, a solid Republican from Tilden, Nebraska. He had a dry wit that served him well in his next career as a beloved broadcaster of Phillies games. It was Ashburn who helped nurture the phenomenon that was Marv Throneberry.

Throneberry came over to the Mets early in their first season. He had flopped with the Yankees, failed to impress anyone in Kansas City, and had a brief stint with the Baltimore Orioles. Throneberry idolized Mickey Mantle to the extent that he copied Mantle's mannerisms at bat, but without the same results. A dog-ass ballplayer, he started out badly with the Mets. He became a target of boos.

Yet, somewhere along the line, the fans developed a fondness for Throneberry. He was so bad that it was good. I daresay I was the first to comprehend this. I wrote a column in the midst of the booing, saying that love was the other side of hate, and that a lovefest would emerge from the dislike for him.

That is exactly what happened. Throneberry's screw-ups became the stuff of lovable legend. The most celebrated incident was the time he hit what should have been a triple but was called out by an umpire for failing to touch second base. When Stengel went out to argue, first base coach Cookie Lavagetto told him not to bother: "He missed first base, too."

Throneberry tended to bitch and moan. He lockered next to Ashburn at the Polo Grounds, though, and Ashburn kidded him out of his morose moods. And it was Ashburn who would good-naturedly pass on to reporters Throneberryisms—goofs in language or daily living—that served to endear Throneberry as something of a folk hero. Years later, the Miller Lite Beer people selected Throneberry to appear in one of their commercials. When a limousine picked him up at the airport after he came in from Tennessee, Throneberry sat in front with the driver.

10

The Alvin Dark Controversy

The first time I wrote about an extended conversation with Alvin Dark, it was after we discussed ethics. I posed a situation that I thought would test Dark, the manager of the San Francisco Giants and a devoutly religious man. I asked, "If you slide into third base and are called safe by the umpire and you know you are out because you felt a tag before you hit the base, should you as a moral man tell the umpire that you should have been called out?"

I asked the question after Dark said his philosophy was Christian. When I wondered if there was a conflict between higher ideals and the need to win in baseball, Dark disagreed. He said he saw no conflict between faith in the principles of Christianity and the act of keeping silent in the situation I proposed. He laughed at the question.

I didn't take notes during this conversation, but I wrote about it in a column published on July 14, 1961. It serves as some background for a celebrated incident involving Dark and me three years later.

In 1964 I stopped in on Dark and the Giants in San Francisco on a trip to the West Coast to cover a USA–Soviet Union track meet in Los Angeles. At the time, the Giants were stumbling in the midst of a pennant race, and Dark was beside himself with frustration over some of the misplays of his talent-laden lineup. He was so agitated he vented freely to me in a conversation not unlike the one we had had about ethics a few years earlier. Again, I didn't take notes.

I wrote two columns about the conversation in Dark's office in the Giants' clubhouse. I'll quote freely from them to give the sense of it all:

Alvin Dark, the Giants' embattled manager, agrees the Giants make atrocious mistakes. He is more emphatic than anybody else about his team's bumblings.

That is surprising, because errors of omission by talented athletes often can be blamed on the inability of a manager to keep his team hustling and alert, or on his failure to get the most out of his men.

Normally, Dark would agree. But not in this situation, because he believes it is a special case.

"We have trouble because we have so many Negro and Spanish-speaking players on this team. They are not able to perform up to the white player when it comes to mental alertness." (The Giants lineup usually has at least three Negroes and two Latin Americans on it.)

This is a feeling that exists among other brains of the major league trenches. It is not peculiar to Dark alone. What may set Dark apart is that he discusses his views openly, considering it "a subject which you New York writers and I disagree on."

Dark edged to a seat next to the visitor on the couch in his office, took off his cap, ruffled his wavy black hair in a characteristic motion, and continued in what turned out to be a cordial dialogue despite the strong difference of opinion.

"You can't make most Negro and Spanish players have the pride in their team that you can get from white players," Dark said. "And they just aren't as sharp mentally. They aren't able to adjust to situations because they don't have that mental alertness."

He agreed there were a few exceptions like Jackie Robinson and Willie Mays—but insisted they were the rare exceptions. "You couldn't name three colored players in our league who are always mentally alert to take advantage of situations."

This kind of thinking is, of course, consistent with the traditions Dark grew up with in Louisiana. He insists, however, that it was experiences with the Giants these past three years which have convinced him of the inferior mental capacities of Negro and Latin players.

He pointed out numerous instances of misplays by his Negro and Latin players, adding, "You don't find the pride in them that you get in the white player."

At this point I suggested that Dark himself was at fault for this, that his own prejudices had served to set up a barrier between himself and the players—and that this made them unable to respond as he would like. I argued that black players sensed a condescending attitude, no matter how well-meaning. He disagreed.

He outlined the problems he had with Orlando Cepeda, the man who symbolized his frustrations. Cepeda was the Giants' Baby Bull, an outstanding slugger, though prone to mistakes. Even with his mistakes, he won games for the Giants, but Dark felt he was giving only 40 percent.

The column continued: *"All of sociology, and the ideals that went into fighting the racist theories of the Nazis would make one think a man like Dark—neither unintelligent, nor with malice toward his fellow men—could not think such things. He does. So do others."*

To counter his argument about black athletes not being team players, I cited the Boston Celtics who, I said, were *"a predominantly Negro team . . . and the personification of mental alertness and loyalty to team above self. With a sympathetic coach in Red Auerbach, they dominated pro basketball."*

Dark shrugged. *"I don't know about that . . . I only know what I've seen on this team and other baseball teams. If I am wrong then I have been getting an awful number of the 'slow' ones."*

I followed up with another column the next day which essentially outlined the difficulties he had been having with Cepeda. I asked, "Why don't you trade him?" Dark laughed dismissively. "Why don't you ask the old man that?" he responded, meaning Giants' owner Horace Stoneham. "He won't trade Cepeda or Willie McCovey. They know it and they know they'll get paid well if their averages are good."

* * *

Newsday was not in the mainstream those days, so there was no immediate outcry about Dark's remarks. I was told that our editor, Alan Hathway, tried to have the Associated Press pick up and distribute my column, but that did not happen. The columns made the rounds of the players on the Giants and among other black and Latin American players, though. It bubbled under the surface until the Giants came east for a trip that hit New York on August 4.

I had mixed feelings about what was happening. The effect of the column was quite different from what I had intended. I thought I was raising a sociological issue through Dark's words. Dark articulated what many baseball people felt or said in guarded words, and I thought it would be of service to bring this into the open.

I was naive. The more explosive comments by Dark were highlighted. He had to defend himself against charges as a racist. Others questioned my veracity and raised the question of whether he had ever said such things. In the immediate aftermath, I had second thoughts, because I had not taken notes in front of him. In my mind, at the time, it was no different than the conversation I had had with him three years earlier about ethics.

I felt uneasy enough about that to seek him out in Philadelphia before the Giants arrived in New York. I expressed my regrets to him about the difficulties he was facing, because others were writing that he was in danger of being fired.

Dark met with commissioner Ford Frick before he came to New York. He then held a press conference before a Giants-Mets game. He denied that he had said the things I had quoted. He said he did not consider black or Latin players inferior to white players. "To make statements like that, a man has to be stupid," he said. "I'm not that stupid."

I attended the news conference, but I did not challenge Dark. He was in a pickle, and he may have felt that I should have warned him that I would write about our conversation. I would stand on what I had written. When questioned I said merely, "I think there can be an honest difference about what was said in view of the basic differences in our approach to the matter. I know I didn't distort, but I see where he might think so."

My friend Leonard Shecter of the *New York Post* told me I would be pilloried by the baseball establishment. I didn't think so at first, because many people in baseball knew Dark had said such things, as had some other managers. I was wrong, because many baseball people rushed to Dark's defense.

Joe Reichler, the Associated Press baseball reporter, was particularly incensed by my pieces. He felt it encouraged the racial unrest already prevalent that summer. He met with Dark and, I believe, orchestrated a defense. He elicited comments from none other than Jackie Robinson in support of Dark. Art Rosenbaum of the *San Francisco Chronicle* wrote that because I was married to a social worker, I was overly involved with sociological matters.

Dick Young of the *Daily News,* whom I had long admired for his feisty reporting and writing, peddled the balderdash that I had sold out a friend. Young had never liked Dark, whereas Leonard Koppett of the *New York Times* and I did—and that rankled him. So he laced into me for trading on a friendship. That column resonated with many of his readers, because some of the hate mail I got lambasted me for selling out a friend.

I probably felt worst about my friend Koppett, who, after talking to me at the Dark press conference, wrote in the *Times* that I believed Dark's racial feelings didn't have anything to do with the Giants' problems. He admitted later that he got it completely twisted. Racial matters are precisely what the conversation had been all about.

The letters—many anonymous and laced with anti-Semitic invective—particularly objected to the headline on the first column that read, "Louisiana in Dark Showing Through." Most suspicious of all was a column by Dick O'Connor in the *Palo Alto Times*. He happened into the office while Dark and I were talking; he later wrote an outrageous version of the dialogue between us. He put into my mouth some of the things Dark said. He had me saying, "It seems Cepeda is putting out only 40 per cent," as if I would have seen Cepeda often enough to make such a statement. And there was this:

"Isaacs suggested that perhaps the Giants players—the Negroes—didn't have pride in their team like the Negroes who play for the Boston Celtics."

In view of what has happened since and many other stories where athletes said they were misquoted, I realize I should not have been so defensive at the time. It was not my responsibility to protect Dark because I wasn't taking notes. I knew that my reportage was accurate. I even soft-pedaled some of his comments. For example, though he said Mays was an exception to his remarks about black players, I didn't write that he also said that even Mays wasn't always as alert as he should have been.

Dark hinted that he might sue. I knew that if he did, there were others who could testify to his having said such things. In a later *Sports Illustrated* article that relived the entire incident, he insisted anew that he was misquoted, and he denied that he was a racist. I am sure he felt that in his heart he wasn't a racist. He never understood that however benevolent he felt, his players picked up on his condescending attitude toward blacks.

One of the ironic postscripts to the whole affair was the belief in some quarters that the controversy actually helped save Dark's job. There were those who felt Stoneham was going to fire Dark that weekend—but that he didn't want to fire Dark in the wake of the racial controversy, so he allowed him to finish out the season. The Giants wound up in fourth place in the West and Dark was let go.

Dark later managed for the Kansas City Royals, Cleveland Indians, and Oakland Athletics. I saw him a few times on the ball field. When I attempted to make eye contact, he looked away.

11

Cassius Clay Was a Grand Old Name

If anything marked the difference of approach between the younger and older reporters in the 1960s, it was the reaction to Muhammad Ali when he first arrived on the scene as Cassius Marcellus Clay.

My initial exposure to him came in 1962 at the first Floyd Patterson–Sonny Liston fight in Chicago. I was among the gaggle of reporters in a hotel press suite writing pre-fight stories in the days leading up to the bout. Trainer Angelo Dundee, with a shrewd eye toward getting his warrior some publicity, brought Clay to press headquarters to introduce him. The brash young man lit up the room. He put on his "I Am the Greatest" act, embellishing it with poetry. He was so outlandish, so madcap, it was hard not to laugh with him. Some of the older reporters, though, were offended by him.

He was controversial even in the early days of his career. He knocked out Archie Moore later that year, then knocked out Charlie Powell early in 1963 before fighting Doug Jones at Madison Square Garden that March. As often as not, Clay had accurately predicted the round he would dispose of his opponent. He could not knock out Jones, however. He was bothered by Jones's style and gave one of his less-scintillating performances, but he undoubtedly won the fight. Yet such was the antipathy to him that the crowd booed lustily upon the announcement of the decision.

Clay knocked out England's Henry Cooper in London in June 1963, creating a sensation with his carryings-on there as well. A championship fight with Sonny Liston then was set for February 25, 1964, in Miami Beach. There was considerable doubt that Clay was ready for the vaunted Liston, who had looked so invincible destroying Patterson in two successive fights.

Clay, abetted by the raucous Drew Bundini, his jester in residence, pulled out all his outrageous stops the week of the fight. With the theme that they were going bear hunting, they would actually show up at Liston's training quarters and bait him. They also trumpeted the refrain, "Float like a butterfly, sting like a bee." Bundini gave me a "Float like a butterfly" T-shirt. I kept it for years.

One day at the Fifth Street Gym on Miami Beach where Clay trained, publicity man Harold Conrad had the idea of staging a meeting of two of the hottest young tickets in the world: Clay and the Beatles. Conrad invited the Beatles, who were in Miami for a taping of *The Ed Sullivan Show,* to a Clay training session. When the Beatles arrived, Clay was in a training room getting his fists taped.

I happened to be in the room with him when the door was closed to outsiders in anticipation of the Beatles' arrival. They waited outside for a while, then were ushered into Clay's presence. I was the only reporter there to record the summit meeting. Somehow I contained myself.

They looked at each other quizzically for a few seconds.

Clay said to Ringo Starr, "You play drums?"

Starr said, "You a fighter?" and he shadow-boxed at Clay.

The fighter liked this funning. The others imitated Starr, and Clay flicked punches at them.

Then they went outside and Clay offered one of his standard lines to John Lennon. "You're not as stupid as you look," he said.

Lennon answered, "No, but you are."

It was one of the few times Clay had met his match in tomfoolery.

Clay dominated an uproarious week. He saved his best act for last. He behaved like a madman at the weigh-in, so much so that examining doctors worried about him. They reported that his blood pressure skyrocketed. The veterans in the press chortled that he was scared silly. I was upset by this, afraid the young man was so unstable he didn't stand a chance against Liston. It turned out, of course, that this was all a sham. In his words, he fooled the world.

I liked Clay so much that I had been tempted to go against the 7–1 odds and pick him to beat Liston. But two nights before the fight, I had dinner with Dundee and Bill Faversham, the head of the syndicate that had bankrolled Clay's ring career. They fretted that Clay had pushed them into the fight too soon. "I think he would have been ready for Liston, but in another half-year or so," Faversham said. This conversation steered me off picking Clay to win, evidence that you can be on the inside and know too much.

As it turned out, my *Newsday* colleague Bob Waters was one of the few reporters to buck the tide and pick Clay to win. Prediction doesn't matter much one way or the other, but we do have our vanities, don't we?

Clay floated like a butterfly, stung like a bee, and reduced Liston to a confused hulk. At one point, Clay survived a round in which he couldn't see. A controversy sprung up about whether he was blinded by a substance that had been rubbed into Liston's gloves. Nothing conclusive has been proven. It was astounding to see him bouncing around the ring, doing little more than putting his glove in Liston's face to keep him away while his eyesight cleared. He then peppered Liston into submission. Liston quit on his stool and Clay was awarded a seven-round knockout.

Afterward he was anything but modest. He railed at the press in his locker room, demanding that critics such as Jimmy Cannon and Dick Young chant that he was The Greatest. "You're the greatest," they shouted back, however shamefaced.

Clay became such a controversial figure for political reasons—he refused to join the army because he had no argument with "them Vietcong"—that it is little remembered how vitriolic the press was against him in those early days for no other reason than that he was a braggart. This same business was rich with tales of John L. Sullivan, the first modern heavyweight champion, ostensibly going into bars and declaring, "I can lick any man in the house." Clay was a modern version of John L., yet he was vilified for it. No doubt race had something to do with it, because most in the press were older white men.

I have always had one huge regret about that week in Miami. Dick Schaap had revealed in the *New York Herald Tribune* that Clay was flirting with the Nation of Islam, commonly called the Black Muslims. This was not public knowledge at the time. Though I was reluctant to believe this, I heard at one point that Malcolm X was in Miami with Clay. I decided to check this out.

I went over to Clay's hotel headquarters. I was hesitant because I wasn't sure of myself and sensed hostility among the dour men who seemed to be in the Clay entourage. I didn't see Angelo Dundee or any of his Louisville backers, people I knew. I then saw a man in a corridor who I thought looked like Malcolm X, but I wasn't sure. The Muslims were pictured in such mysterious terms that I was timid. I thought about approaching him, but hesitated. And then he was gone.

Malcolm X was, of course, in Miami with Clay. I wish I had pursued talking to him for what would have been an important story. I blew it.

After the fight, Clay revealed he was a member of the Nation of Islam. He launched his new name, Muhammad Ali. This intensified the dislike for him in many quarters. The older writers for a long time refused to use the name, Ali. I thought Cassius Marcellus Clay, named for an honorable white Kentucky legislator, was such a lovely name. I was reluctant to give it up. Yet I recognized that the man had the right to use whatever name he chose. For a while I solved my dilemma by writing "Muhammad (Cassius Marcellus Clay was a grand old name) Ali." That faded in time as we all became comfortable with Muhammad Ali.

* * *

Nonsense and intrigue surrounded the 1965 rematch between Ali and Liston in Lewiston, Maine. The fight had bounced around, unable to find a city willing to host any endeavor involving Ali, now out in the open as a professed Muslim. When one of the delays was caused by an injury to Liston, Arthur Daley, the *Times* columnist who abhorred boxing, cited it as another reason for banning the brutal exercise. After the fight was forbidden in Boston, it landed in Lewiston.

While reporting the story, we had time to kill. On the afternoon of the fight, the three original Chipmunks played a round of golf, along with Dave Anderson. Leonard Shecter and Anderson were good golfers, while Larry Merchant and I were not. Merchant kept dragging his golf-bag cart across the green when moving to the next hole—this is a no-no. When Shecter spotted Merchant doing it again, he had a near fit, shouting angrily at Merchant that this wasn't done. This amused Larry, who mocked, "Shecter the great iconoclast is suddenly following the rules?" Shecter desisted. He knew he had been had.

Amid all the dark talk about Muslims, José Torres, the former light-heavyweight champion who was covering the fight for a Spanish-language newspaper, joked to publicity man Harold Conrad that he was afraid to sit on press row, where he might be in the line of fire of an assassin trying to kill Ali. Columnist Jimmy Cannon, somewhat overwrought with dislike of Ali, overheard this and seized on it. Conrad, aware that any kind of coverage in Cannon's *Journal American* would help sell closed-circuit tickets in theaters, played the conspirator.

Conrad told Cannon, "Jimmy, please. Do me a favor. Don't print that story." That, of course, was all Cannon needed. The story ran on the first pages of many of the Hearst papers in the country. The story posed two theories: 1) Ali was in danger of assassination by the same Muslims who had killed Malcolm X, because Ali was thinking of joining the Malcolm X camp, or 2) Ali would be murdered by Malcolm X supporters who wanted revenge on the Muslims for killing Malcolm.

This story ballooned to the point that two New York detectives were sent up to Lewiston. The Lewiston police searched the purses of women entering the arena—no men were bothered, even if they were carrying a hidden Gatling gun. Shecter wrote, "They found a lot of lipsticks."

In the first round, Ali knocked out Liston with what seemed like a phantom punch. The shouts of "fix!" arose at ringside almost before the confused referee, Joe Walcott, finished his count of ten over the whipped Liston. Even Joe Louis cried foul at ringside immediately afterward.

I went to the television truck, which had transmitted a closed-circuit telecast to movie outlets. I watched as the producer replayed the action again and again. In that darkened area, aided by slow-motion sequences, one could detect a short right-hand punch on a downward slant of only a few inches that hit Liston. It was, truly, a punch—but not one so devastating that it should have put Liston down for the count. Hence, there was some justification for the cries of fix, however wrong.

No unusual betting money showed up in Las Vegas, so there was no benefit for Liston to throw the fight. I think Larry Merchant was the first to express the valid opinion that Liston was psychologically whipped by Ali. The boasting by Ali had its effect on him. An ex-con accustomed to intimidating people, he didn't know what to make of this outrageous kid who, far from being afraid of him, taunted and baited him before the first fight in Miami and even more boldly before the fight in Maine.

Nothing untoward happened outside the ring. Immediately afterward, when Ali would seem to have been most vulnerable to an attack, the two detectives, having seen the near-fight, trundled back to New York.

The next year, Bud Collins, John Crittenden, and I were with Ali in Houston as he was preparing to defend his title against Cleveland Williams. Courtesy of film historian Jim Jacobs, we sat with Ali as he watched films of past heavyweight champions. Ali had seen these films many times. He sat on a couch throwing punches at the screen as he expressed opinions about some of the past champions. He was unimpressed with Joe Louis ("too slow") and didn't think he would have trouble with Jack Dempsey ("I would jab him silly"). He was more impressed with the power of Rocky Marciano and the skills of Gene Tunney.

Of our group, Crittenden had the closest relationship with Ali because Ali spent so much time training in Miami Beach. One time, Crittenden rode in a bus while Ali drove. He drove the way he fought, ever on the move, darting and weaving in traffic. At one point, as Crittenden cowered against the door, fearful of impending doom, Ali said, "Don't worry, John, Allah is my co-pilot."

* * *

I, like many reporters, defended Ali during his fight to stay out of the Vietnam War. Howard Cosell was also one of his defenders. It irritated us that Cosell, who enjoyed the power of television, conveyed the feeling that he was the only one who defended Ali. Larry Merchant and Jack McKinney of the *Philadelphia News,* Len Shecter of the *New York Post,* Bob Lipsyte of the *New York Times,* Bud Collins of the *Boston Globe,* John Crittenden of the *Miami News,* and I were among those who defended the beleaguered young man at that time.

After his suspension for refusing to serve in the army, Ali resumed fighting on October 26, 1970, in Atlanta. He knocked out Jerry Quarry in three rounds. The activity outside the ring was more exhilarating than the fight itself.

A black Georgia state senator, Leroy Johnson, pulled strings to stage a bout that was turned down elsewhere. Johnson persuaded the racist governor, Lester Maddox, to okay the fight. Maddox said, "I think Clay deserves another chance." Later, after veterans' groups protested, he railed against Ali as a draft dodger, but the local cognoscenti dismissed this as mere talk to mollify the rednecks.

Maddox had first gained national attention when he distributed axe handles at his restaurant to block any blacks who might have wanted to integrate his establishment. Before the fight, I attended one of Governor Maddox's meetings with petitioners at the state capitol. He heard complaints and dispensed favors to constituents in what he called, "Little Peoples' Day." He was a folksy little guy, as attentive to blacks as whites.

He wore a gray suit with three pins in his lapel, one an American flag. At fifty-five, he came across in person taller than he appeared in photos. Maddox had on a mod green shirt with white stripes and an extra-wide print tie in green and yellow. He fondled the tie, wiped his brow with its lining, and said, "I'm so busy, I don't always get the chance to use a handkerchief."

A woman who wanted the governor to get her son into a school for mentally disabled children beamed as Maddox said, "There's 1,800 people trying to get their kids in there, but we'll do what we can." The woman said, "I say if there's any man who can do it, Lester Maddox can do it."

A woman asked, "How are you?" Maddox replied, "If I get any better I couldn't stand it."

He issued a proclamation declaring the day of the fight a day of mourning because of Ali's refusal to join the army, but admitted that he had no authority to stop the fight.

The scene before the fight was more memorable than Ali's quick knockout of Quarry. The hours before the fight featured a parade of stunningly dressed fight-goers at the Regency Hyatt in downtown Atlanta. The gathering was dominated by blacks from the North, peacocking in a breathtakingly gaudy display of the hip fashions of the day. The men outdid the women in plumage.

It reminded me of the time I covered the colorful spectacle of the Henley Regatta on the Thames in England. This was as much a social event as a rowing competition. Tea and cakes prevailed. Old alums dressed in blazers with colorful piping, topped by school beanies. They strolled the greensward adjoining the river amid spectacular Carnaby Street dudes. We came across the actor Robert Morley and overheard him say in his puffed-jaw tones, "The boys are more interesting to look at than the girls."

There was a time when this kind of black fashion show—the Regency Hyatt could well have been the Hotel Theresa in Harlem before a Joe Louis fight—would have drawn patronizing snickers. In this day and age, however, the black fashions of today become tomorrow's white fashions. "The onlookers just gasped," I wrote.

* * *

The first Ali–Joe Frazier fight at Madison Square Garden on March 8, 1971, was my last assignment before taking over as sports editor at *Newsday*. In recognition of the magnitude of the event over and above boxing, I channeled Leo Rosten's Hyman Kaplan and called it, tongue in cheek, a T*I*T*A*N*I*C clash. I wrote one column about Ali's clowning at the prefight weigh-in. In another, I polled celebrities. Woody Allen, Bill Moyers, Erma Bombeck, Arthur Ashe, Billie Jean King, and Casey Stengel picked Ali; Walter Matthau, Walt Frazier, Carl Furillo, and Edward Villella picked Frazier. In my own prefight analysis, I picked Ali to knock out Frazier in the eleventh round.

My story about the fight led off with this couplet that aped Ali's poetry:

It could shock and amaze ya
How he got beat by Joe Frazier

Though I scored the fight in favor of Ali, ten rounds to five, I agreed with the unanimous decision for Frazier. While Ali won several rounds by thin margins, the big left hook that floored him in the fifteenth truly earned the decision for Frazier in my mind.

When Ali was still Cassius Clay, he had said he wouldn't end up broke like Joe Louis, and he wouldn't run around with women like other champions. That, of course, changed. Ali had his share of foxes, along with his four wives. And more exposure to Ali didn't necessarily endear him further to me. I was particularly dismayed by the cruelty he displayed in knocking out Floyd Patterson in 1965 because Patterson continued to call him Clay. He taunted the unfortunate and inadequate Patterson, punishing him unmercifully for longer than he needed to, before knocking him out in the twelfth round.

Supreme Court Justice Louis Brandeis said, "Physical courage is the commonest of human virtues, moral courage the rarest." It is ironic that the man who was so hated by such a large portion of the population when he was making a courageous idealistic stand later became an adroitly managed icon and commercial show horse, huckstering products and raking in dollars for personal appearances from anybody who would pay to exploit his eminence.

When he lit the flame at the opening of the 1996 Olympics in Atlanta, it symbolized a full circle for Cassius Marcellus Clay/Muhammad Ali. It was an oft-repeated tale that he became so disenchanted with this country that he took the gold medal he had won at the 1960 Olympics in Rome and threw it off a bridge into a river. When Bob Costas said during a 1996 Olympics telecast that the story was apocryphal, I asked him if he was trying to rewrite history. Costas told me, "I talked to Howard Bingham, Ali's longtime friend and photographer, and Tom Hauser, his biographer. They told me the gold medal story wasn't true. They said Ali was embarrassed by it now, and they wanted to set the record straight."

12

Jim Brown and Me

Jim Brown was so many things that it is hard to catalog him. He was a great football player with a magnificent physique, an actor of sorts, a social activist, a sexual animal. He was shrewd. And he could be a menacing presence. He was hard to get to know, for me and for most people.

Brown grew up in Long Island. Because he was the local boy who made good at Syracuse University and with the Cleveland Browns, I followed him closely. I met him many times and often wrote about him. Few people have gotten close to this not-very-approachable man; I thought I was simpatico with him in so many ways that I should have felt more comfortable with him and he more at ease with me. It didn't happen.

When I joined *Newsday* in 1954, Brown had only recently graduated from Manhasset High School. He was already the stuff of legend. He had been a phenomenal athlete at Manhasset, the star of the football, basketball, and lacrosse teams, a bulwark of the track and field squad, and had shown some flair as a baseball pitcher.

I regard Brown as the greatest American athlete of all time, ahead of Jim Thorpe and Jackie Robinson. In addition to his prowess in football in college and as a pro, he played varsity basketball at Syracuse and is still regarded as perhaps the greatest lacrosse player of all time. He finished tenth in a national decathlon championship competition as a high school senior even though he benefited from hardly any coaching in the skill events, such as pole vaulting and the discus. It is popular to call the Olympic decathlon champion "the world's greatest athlete." Brown could easily have achieved decathlon dominance if he had been so inclined.

When he was at Syracuse, I asked if he was becoming conscious of the increased interest in social issues by black athletes. He had no interest in that. "Jackie Robinson's way is not my way," he said. And he expressed no activist thoughts early in his pro career.

So it was a surprise to me that in his 1964 autobiography, *Off My Chest,* written with Myron Cope, he spoke out unequivocally on social injustice. This earned him the enmity of racists and people who preferred that black jocks confine their commentary to football. Integrationists were impressed. I certainly was. Much later I came to understand that his activism had a harder edge to it than Jackie Robinson's.

I felt a pang that he never expressed feelings like that to me even though he should have guessed that I would have put them in a sympathetic framework. I wondered if he expressed himself so freely partly because he was paid for the book, or because he had grown in awareness since I talked to him at Syracuse. A part of me felt, though, that if I had been more persistent, he might have opened up to me.

I covered him when he came to New York to play the Giants, and I saw games in Cleveland. He ran with power, great balance, and a keen sense of following blockers, smooth and powerful at the same time. After the Browns won the National Football League championship in 1964, I went out to Cleveland to interview him at his home.

This assignment was at the personal request of *Newsday* publisher Harry Guggenheim. Though his main sports interest was horse racing, he liked to bet on pro football, and he won money on Cleveland in the 1964 NFL championship. Guggenheim thought it would be a good idea to capitalize on Brown's local-boy-makes-good angle with Brown. Hence, I went to Cleveland to do a tape-recorded interview with Brown.

Upon arriving at Brown's home in the eastern part of town, Brown sort of waved me in and did not introduce me to his wife. She was there, but it was as if she wasn't there, as far as the visitor was concerned. I felt awkward.

A clerk who came along with me set up the tape recorder, since our editor knew better than to trust me with any machine. Brown hemmed and hawed about getting the interview started. Finally, I comprehended what was on his mind; he wanted to be paid for the interview. I wondered why he hadn't said something about this before agreeing on the phone to my flying out to see him. I also felt there was no way a newspaper would pay a big star like him what he was worth for a tape-recorded interview. I squirmed at being placed in this position; I can't bargain my way out of a paper bag. Finally I called my managing editor.

Bill McIlwain, a smooth-talking, charming southerner, wasn't fazed. "All right, Stan," he said. "Offer him $50."

I felt humiliated. "Fifty dollars!?! He is a big star; he makes $60,000 a year. A guy like this might as well do it for nothing rather than accept a measly $50."

"That's all right, Stan" said McIlwain, soothing me. "Offer the fella the $50 and see what he says."

Muttering, stuttering, excruciatingly tongue-tied, I finally said, "They say you can have $50." And I winced.

"Okay," Brown said without a moment's hesitation.

I was disgusted with him at the moment and for some time afterward, but I came to understand that it was the principle of the thing with him. *Newsday,* hometown paper or not, was a big, rich white man's newspaper, and he felt it should at least pay him something for his cooperation.

* * *

Over the years, I recorded the feats of the man who is still regarded as the best runner, and perhaps the best pro football player, of all time. The numbers don't tell the half of it, because in his time, pro teams played only twelve and fourteen-game schedules. He scored 126 touchdowns in 118 games. On average he gained more than 100 yards once every two games. He gained 220 yards in a game four times.

Most significant of all, he averaged 5.2 yards per carry, still the highest rushing mark of all time. And Brown did this when opponents stacked their defenses to stop him.

Brown retired from football in 1966. Team owner Art Modell refused to allow Brown to come to training camp late so that he could finish making the movie *The Dirty Dozen*. Modell declared he would fine Brown $100 a day for every day he missed training camp. This was a monumental misreading of Brown, a fiercely independent man. He quit football. Years later, when Modell and Brown reconciled, Modell admitted, "I made a mistake."

Brown has been a controversial figure ever since.

He became involved in a number of incidents of violence against women. At various times, he was charged with assault and resisting arrest; he was hit with a paternity suit. Brown frequently claimed the Los Angeles police made him a marked man with trumped-up charges. But it is evident that his violent streak threatened women at times. After admitting he smashed the windows of his wife's car after an argument, he went to jail for six months. Proud hombre that he was, he preferred to go to jail rather than do the community service work of picking up garbage and going to anger management classes.

He was a black stud in movies for some time, gaining the most attention for a hot sex scene with Raquel Welch in *100 Rifles*. In the HBO documentary *Jim Brown, All American,* directed by Spike Lee, Brown chuckles, "I didn't really know what to do, so I put my tongue in her ear." He frequently had this nervous chuckle, particularly when he thought he was being immodest.

A significant aspect of Brown since he left football has been his social activism. He stressed the need of black people to lift themselves economically. He founded the Black Economic Union, a multicity organization helping blacks to set up their own business.

He has gone where few others dare, forming the rehabilitation organization Amer-I-Can, which worked in the prisons and among Los Angeles gang members. It turned some of society's worst toughs into success stories.

Brown has been a critic of black stars like Michael Jordan and Willie Mays. He accused them of turning their backs on their less-fortunate brothers. When O. J. Simpson was running himself into riches, Brown confronted him about being more than a commercial pin-up boy for whites. Simpson said, "You go your way, I'll go mine."

In 1973, when his film career was winding down into "B" movies, I went to see Brown in New York City to ask him about his charges that black films were exploiting sex and violence to the detriment of good filmmaking. We talked as we walked down Lexington Avenue, toward his appointment downtown. People on the street gushed; they rushed to press flesh, or win a smile or a hello or an autograph from the star suddenly in their midst.

He was a commanding presence. Brown had a massive head on a six-foot, two-inch frame that sports reporters once described in awe as "flowing black steel." He would stand out in any crowd. Nobody could miss him that afternoon in his dark blue long coat and blocky, chic blue shoes. To people scurrying to greet him, he said, "How are you, my man?" exchanging soul slaps and signing autographs.

As we chatted, the subject of President Richard Nixon came up; I was not thrilled that Brown was one of the few black personalities in the country who had supported Nixon during the 1972 campaign. Now, during the early revelations about the Watergate scandal, he refused to be needled into expressing any regret about his action.

He said, "My philosophy has always been the system is made up of crooks. The people who first came here weren't of the best stock; they were people who had been rejected in Europe and Africa, so we have never been strangers to crookedness. I dealt with Nixon because he was feeding more money into black businesses and black colleges than the Democrats were. Nixon knew me and admired me as a football player. I could talk with him." Also, Brown's Black Economic Union was in line for money from Nixon's Office of Minority Business Enterprises.

He derided white liberals. He said, "If a black man is hungry, the white liberal will only throw him a fish when the man needs to be taught how to learn to fish."

I argued vigorously but not well and came out second best. I tried to defend the position that the inadequacies of the Kennedy and Johnson administrations in relation to blacks did not justify support of Nixon by blacks. He rejected my contention that most blacks did not support Nixon.

Among those who had backed Nixon was Wilt Chamberlain. In 1968 he said, "I knew him personally. If Nixon won I figured I'd have some input at the White House." Sammy Davis Jr., who was having personal financial difficulties with the government, supported Nixon, as did singer James Brown, who was picketed by black audiences.

Most black people, of course, did not support Nixon. As Lincoln Lynch, a black leader on Long Island, said, "Nixon seemed to get the support of blacks interested in personal gain—as opposed to ethnic gain."

I recalled a passage in the extraordinary book *Jim,* an account by James Toback about his close relationship with Brown. A young black activist tells Toback, "Jim Brown doesn't hold a prayer as the real black hero. He's talented, he's smart, he's generous; but he's involved in old ideas and old solutions—partying, pleasure, competition, work—making a mark in what is always going to be a white man's world. Hip black cats won't ride with that anymore."

Brown, ever his own man, said, "Don't talk to me about movements. It's all personal." He insisted that he had always, whether in football or movies, been not in the blacks' market, but in the general market. Certainly there was in his general image what Toback called a sense of "lurid tales or freak scenes, brutality and in ineluctable erotic flow."

At 59th Street outside Bloomingdale's department store, an attractive young woman asked Brown for his autograph. He complied. Then she offered him her phone number. I had heard of many such shenanigans in more than a decade on the big-time sports scene, but this was the first time I actually was seeing a strange woman offering a celebrity her phone number.

Brown, hesitatingly, refused at first, then accepted and wrote her phone number on the only piece of paper he had, a five-dollar bill. I edged away, embarrassed, trying to suppress a sense of prudery, feeling like an intruder in an assignation—not aware that Brown was taking a different reading on my discomfort.

We talked about his movie career. I said I had seen his latest movie, *I Escaped from Devil's Island,* and thought it pretty poor. I said his movie career, unlike his football career, was descending to second-rate status. This rankled him. Unexpectedly, he turned and asked, "Are you prejudiced?"

I said, "I think so. I couldn't quite tell you who I am prejudiced against, but it's a rare man who has eliminated all his prejudices."

He asked, "How do you feel about black men and white women?"

I was surprised by the question. I said, "I don't think about that much. Why?"

He smiled. That upset me. It was only later, after we had departed, when it dawned upon me: his question stemmed from his interpretation of my prudish discomfort when the young woman outside Bloomingdale's offered him her phone number. She was white.

In actuality, I didn't grasp the intention of his question at the time because I felt the problem of race involved deeper things than black men and white women. His reputation for dating beautiful women of all colors was so established, I almost didn't think of him as any color in relation to women. But I didn't get to say this at the time.

At 49th Street, a well-dressed, light-skinned black man, who looked like a young executive, came up, hand extended. "Jim Brown. I've admired you at Manhasset, at Syracuse, with the Cleveland Browns. Let me shake your hand. I want to go home tonight and tell my son I shook hands with Jim Brown today."

When we parted, I left him presiding over a cluster of autograph seekers.

* * *

Even in his good works, Brown was controversial. *GQ Magazine* later cast a critical eye on his Amer-I-Can program, pointing out that Brown took 40 percent of the participants' wages as a fee. There were charges that he hadn't certified how many gang members and ex-cons he had turned around, that the bulk of the curriculum for self-improvement was little more than an urbanized Dale Carnegie course.

Brown responded angrily that "Every other program is getting millions and they don't have to justify shit. I work 55,000 times harder than any of them. All the contracts we work on are public record. I provide a service, run this business and pay my men."

I saw Jim Brown again in 1989 when he came back to Manhasset for a book signing for *Out of Bounds,* the fourth book about him, written with Steve Delsohn. It seemed incongruous to see some proper, middle-aged, suburban women, alumna of Manhasset High, clutching the book that he said is "Me, all me. Raw me. Take-it-or-leave-it me."

Reading the book, immersed in some of it, made me feel unhip and square. My thoughts went back to the meeting outside Bloomingdale's. He wrote of an orgy, "You might make love to three girls in one night, and you might see others making love around you. But it was never vulgar or done with disrespect."

With all my mixed feelings about Brown, it came as something of a surprise to me when at that book signing he wrote in my copy, "To Stan, a long time history, Your Friend."

13

Race Matters

Vic Power was a colorful Puerto Rican black man who played in the New York Yankees system in the early 1950s. He deserves credit for a famous line. As a minor leaguer in Arkansas, he was told by a waitress that he couldn't eat there because "we don't serve Negroes." Power replied, "That's all right. I don't eat them."

The Yankees' management was racist and among the last to hire a black player. Power could well have been the first black Yankee, but he was too outspoken and flashy for the franchise. The Yankees preferred to let him drift out of the organization.

In the late 1950s, when Power was with the Cleveland Indians, he was a central figure in a remarkable game sequence. A flashy, outstanding first baseman, Power duped two Yankees into getting picked off first base. He snuck behind Mickey Mantle and tagged him out. Then, after Yogi Berra reached first base, he slipped behind Berra, took the pitcher's throw and tagged Berra out, too. Power's flashing smile radiated all over the ballpark.

A burly, infuriated fan came reeling out of a first base box toward Power with the intent of assaulting him. It turned out the inebriated Yankee fan was none other than the famous Ohio State football coach, Woody Hayes. I was the only New York reporter to go down and find out the identity of the drunk. I made it an addendum to my story. *Newsday* pieces did not create much of a stir at that time, and not much was made of it. I thought of it later when an infuriated Hayes punched an opposing player running freely past him. That was the end of Hayes as Ohio State football coach.

After the game, Casey Stengel orated about Power. In his typical fashion, he addressed his players by shouting at reporters within the players' earshot. He said, "Now when the man does that to you once, why wouldn't you lead off the base looking at him and not at the pitcher?" Mantle, Berra, and some of the others looked at Stengel with incredulity, as if the old man was off his rocker. I later told Power what Stengel had said, and he giggled. He thought it was a good idea.

Power was one of the few players ever to write me a thank you about a column I had written about him.

As for the Yankees, they finally integrated their major league team in 1955 with the quiet, acquiescent Elston Howard. I made a few attempts to get Howard to talk about problems he faced as a black person—particularly during the time he had to live away from his teammates during spring training in the South. It was to no avail.

Howard sought me out on a race matter only once, when he complained about not getting as many commercial endorsements as white players. I was not particularly moved to join that crusade.

* * *

I generally was not enamored of big stars. Usually, they are people with huge egos, not the easiest to interview. Too many of them were accustomed to sycophantic questions or were so programmed they recited rote answers.

Many people did not have a good feeling about Bill Russell, the great basketball player, a proud and haughty man. He was aloof and standoffish with most people. For a long time, he would not sign autographs and generally shied from commercials, interviews, and personal appearances.

Yet, for some reason, we hit it off. After starting my once-a-week column beat, I wrote about Russell in my second column. He seemed comfortable with my questions, sensing, I hoped, that I had a reasonable curiosity about black athletes.

In that first column, he told me he disliked all white people until he got out of college because he such bad experiences with them. Russell told me about the adviser at almost all-black McClymonds High School in Oakland who told him not to go to college but to get a blue-collar job. That served only to goad him to attend college.

Russell was the greatest winning force in the history of sports. His University of San Francisco team won two NCAA championships, he earned an Olympic gold medal, and his Boston Celtics won the NBA title eleven of his thirteen seasons. He channeled his rage about racial discrimination into incredible athletic success.

* * *

Among my most satisfying and intriguing experiences came in 1997, when I won the A. J. Liebling Award. The award, given by the Boxing Writers Association, goes to people who have written with distinction about boxing.

Liebling was a hero to many who grew up reading his sparkling prose in the *New Yorker* after World War II. He was the first significant critic of the press. He also wrote splendidly about food, World War II, Paris, horse racing, New York low life—and boxing. His collection of essays on boxing, *The Sweet Science,* is a seminal work about the business. Anybody who hasn't read it has a treat in store. Anything by Liebling is enriching, as nourishing as some of the expansive meals he describes in *Between Meals.*

Liebling once said, "I can write better than anybody who can write faster than me, and I can write faster than anybody who can write better than me." Well, I believe that nobody wrote better than Liebling. I saw him a few times at boxing weigh-ins but was a bit too awed to approach him. Once, I found myself next to him in a group and he was in front of me as I talked. I was a little nonplussed because he constantly seemed to be sidling to my left. No matter how I turned, he seemed to be on my left. I found out later that he was hard of hearing in his right ear and moved like a boxer to his right to get a better listen.

It was with some reverence that I accepted the award. I spoke about Liebling for those who didn't know much about him. And I added what a pleasure it was to receive an award from the boxing writers, because I had always admired boxers so much. I told of a little incident that always stuck with me—and influenced me.

It concerned the time Rubin "Hurricane" Carter fought champion Joey Giardello for the middleweight championship on December 14, 1964, in Philadelphia, Giardello's hometown. To me and other observers at ringside, Carter was the clear winner. But the judges voted for Giardello in what we considered a rank hometown decision.

As I made my way down to the dressing room to interview Carter, the loser, I had more than a little trepidation. Carter, with his Fu Manchu mustache and bald head, was a menacing figure. He had been in and out of a few penal institutions as a kid. He was a militant figure in defense of black rights. I had a foreboding feeling that an injustice like this could have terrible repercussions. I feared it could turn his career around if he saw the unfair decision as part of a conspiracy against him by a hostile society: I feared he could regress into destructive behavior.

I was no stranger to tense confrontations with athletes after a defeat, so I and a few others approached Carter with deference, prepared for the worst. That didn't happen.

Carter took the defeat graciously. He didn't strike out at those of us asking him about the fight. He actually was wry about it. He talked about the danger of a hometown decision, that he could have averted that by knocking Giardello out. He said he should have fought better. He made little jokes at his own expense.

I came away with admiration for the man. The encounter also influenced my reactions in later confrontations with frustrated, angry athletes after losses. I had little sympathy for the pouting of hostile peacocks who couldn't face up to a loss in a baseball or football game after seeing how gallantly Carter dealt with the injustice of a crushing defeat.

Carter had a career record of fifty-one victories, with thirty-six knockouts and five losses. He fought fifteen times following the Giardello fight. He had been a marked man by police in his hometown precincts of northern New Jersey for some time because of his outspoken race talk. It led to his being convicted and jailed for a triple murder—killings that occurred two years after the Giardello fight. His case became a cause célèbre. After several years in prison and many appeals, his conviction was finally overturned in 1985.

After I spoke at the dinner, I was thanked by a man who said he had been a lawyer for Carter during one of his many appeals. A few days later, I received a call from Ron Lipton, a referee of championship bouts. He was a friend of Carter's. He said he was delighted by what I had said because Carter was such a good guy and deserved recognition as such.

And a few days after that, the phone rang again. The voice on the other end was that of Rubin Carter. Lipton had told him about my speech, and he wanted to thank me. He was living in Toronto, working to help correct injustice as the executive director of the International Association in Defense of the Wrongly Convicted. He said he worked to help free people mired in situations not unlike his own.

His story of the Canadians who helped to overturn his conviction was at the core of the 1999 movie *Hurricane,* which made a hero out of Carter. Also in the movie was the Giardello fight. Movies being movies, *Hurricane* emphasized the injustice of the hometown decision for Giardello, but it distorted the action by making Carter much more dominant in the bout than he actually was. This led to a suit by Giardello against the movie studio and producers, claiming his reputation was damaged. The lawyers defending the movie people dug up the column I wrote, in which I declared that I thought Carter had won. They contacted me about testifying at the trial, but they settled with Giardello out of court, and I didn't hear from them again.

14

Hitler, Stalin, and O'Malley

Disillusionment with the movers and shakers of sports seems almost inevitable. The more sports reporters are blessed or damned to see the inside workings of the sports world, the more they are turned off by the hypocrisy, selfishness, and lack of sportsmanship in the world of fun and games.

Many used to think that sports were a harmless escape from the troubles and woes of the real world. Supreme Court Chief Justice Earl Warren said, "I always turn to the sports pages first, which record people's accomplishments. The first page has nothing but man's failures." Few people are so naive to believe that anymore. Sports reports are rife with high-finance trickery, violence against women, criminal actions, drug abuse, and people's inhumane behavior. For Boobus Americanus, to use H. L. Mencken's inelegant phrase, sports were not a diversion and an illusion, but a passion and an obsession. The old sportsman Karl Marx might have said it is sports that is the opiate of the masses.

Sports probably never were a pure, uplifting activity, as the innocents among us would like to think. Sports are big business, a sprawling multi-billion-dollar industry that is, in certain respects, worse than other industries because it makes hypocritical pretense of a love of fun and games to cover up the basic goal of making money. "There is no other business in this country," Leonard Shecter wrote in *The Jocks*, "which operates so cynically to make enormous profits on the one hand, while demanding to be favored as a public service on the other."

Sports barons blackmail cities to build them stadiums paid for by taxes on the general public. They argue that they must have new stadiums with expensive corporate boxes so they can pay the spiraling salaries demanded by athletes who are little more than mercenaries moving from city to city, oblivious of the sanctity of contracts. Millionaires vie with billionaires. The big money and the adulation we heap upon vain men and women in short pants have produced a race of paper lions bursting with hubris. Excess feeds upon itself. We not only overpay them because they have value in the marketplace, but we rush to bestow honors and awards upon them far out of sane proportion to the service they perform for society.

"Indeed it may be doubted whether the modern system of cultivating athletes, namely by a fierce competition stimulated by heavy bribes, does not inflict positive moral injury by developing animal intensity of the will . . . and a hungry greed for more money earned without toil, of all the passions that renders the heart most callous. Nobody is quite so 'hard' as the professional sporting man, quite so incapable of pity, remorse or self-restraint in the pursuit of gain."

That was written not recently, but in 1870 in a British magazine. As a sports reporter, I recognize that even some of my best work has been part of a process of creating false idols. It's an unusual athlete who retains the ability to see himself and his place in society in perspective.

Back before Yogi Berra became a beloved national teddy bear in the American pantheon, he was irritated by a less-than-complimentary article written about him. Berra, who was earning what then was considered a more than respectable $40,000 a year, snorted that he didn't have to pay attention to somebody who was making $150 a week.

When I was on the beat, the association between athletes and reporters was testy at best; it became a war zone in the 1990s. Athletes have come to regard reporters as necessary evils or more often, as just plain evils. It was never a great pleasure for me to cover any group of athletes for a sustained time, because the interaction between reporters and athletes is artificial, unlike one between actual acquaintances. As with the majority of my peers, my conversations with athletes were one-sided. We talked about their craft, what they were interested in. We did not talk about the world around us beyond the outfield fences. There was little curiosity among athletes about the people who wrote about them.

It is an unusual relationship. A beat writer with a baseball team is a presence around the athletes every day for six weeks in spring training and then for a good part of the actual season. The reporter goes to a player to flesh out a story; the player responds with non-speak, ostensibly answering a question but without revealing anything he fears might be detrimental. In a way the reporter has almost no identity to the athlete beyond a pen and pad.

Once, after I covered the Yankees in spring training and through the first few weeks of the season, I took two weeks off for vacation. The first day I returned to the Yankee beat, I walked over to Bobby Richardson in the clubhouse and said, "Hello." I got no particular reaction from Richardson, supposedly one of the more intelligent and aware Yankees.

I believe that in any other regular association between persons, one coming back from a short absence would invariably be greeted with some recognition by the other, an acknowledgement of his absence. Not so with Richardson. He was accustomed only to having me come up and ask him about his batting average, his approach to fielding, or whatever.

When I got home, I did better; my golden retriever gave me a terrific greeting.

Even in middle age, Richardson and his old teammates failed to shine. At the memorial ceremony for Roger Maris the night before he was buried in his hometown of Fargo, North Dakota, Yankee players joined friends and family at a local school, paying tribute to the Yankee slugger who died at fifty-one. Friends, relatives, and a high school coach recounted his career with affection.

It became noticeable after a while that not one Yankee got up to talk about him. Sitting in one of the back pews, I could see locals occasionally looking over at the Yankees, obviously hoping one would stir himself up to the lectern. Richardson, Mickey Mantle, Whitey Ford, and Bill Skowron, among others, were there.

As the evening wore on, the pressure for a Yankee to speak seemed to intensify. It got to the point where I felt that I, as a guy who had covered the Yankees, should speak—as inappropriate as I thought that would be. Finally, Clete Boyer, the Yankee third baseman, one of Maris's friends on the team, spoke. Nothing he said was particularly memorable, but it was heartfelt and badly needed—his effort broke the tension. I had an affection for Boyer after that.

The burial the next day was in snowy, single-digit weather. While the rest of us were freezing our cojones off at the gravesite, Mantle and Ford were back at the motel bar drinking. They gave us a big greeting when we returned from the cemetery.

* * *

In 1959, the Dodgers appeared in the World Series for the first time since deserting Brooklyn in 1957. The Dodgers played in the Los Angeles Coliseum as a stopgap until their own ballpark could be finished. The Coliseum, built for track and field and football, was an abomination for baseball. It had a ridiculously short left-field fence that reportedly measured only 250 feet down the line. This produced so much ridicule that the Dodgers remeasured the distance and came up with the eye-popping figure of 251.6 feet.

It didn't bother Dodgers owner Walter O'Malley that the arena was not fit for baseball. He preferred the Coliseum's 90,000 seat capacity to Wrigley Field, the ballpark in Los Angeles with normal baseball distances but with a seating capacity of fewer than 30,000.

After the first two games in Chicago, the World Series moved to Los Angeles and the maligned Coliseum. I happened to be standing around the batting cage as the White Sox took batting practice before the first game. I heard White Sox left fielder Al Smith declaim rather loudly against the dimensions of the ballpark. He bemoaned that it was a travesty to be playing baseball here. Sharing his feelings, I pounced on the occasion to pose a hypothetical question to him.

I asked, "Would you prefer to be playing in Wrigley Field, which is a legitimate baseball park?" I noted that its smaller seating capacity would mean a smaller World Series share for the players.

I have not forgotten the look of incredulity Smith gave me—as if I was trying to reach into his pocket to pull out his wallet. He obviously preferred the moolah from the 90,000-seat capacity, however much a travesty upon baseball. He turned away and moved into the batting cage, soon to complain anew about the dimensions of this park, I'm sure.

For that first game in the vast Coliseum, I decided to get the view of the game from the seat farthest from the playing field in this cavernous arena. I trekked up to the deepest row in center field. I talked to a man named Deward Milsaps, who came from Yuma, Arizona, to see this historic game. I did a standard interview with him; this produced some good-natured ribbing from my friend and colleague Eddie Comerford, who edited the sports section that day. He said, "Stan, I let it go, but I don't believe for a moment that you actually went all the way up there and that there was a man named Deward Milsaps."

I assured him that I had not faked the whole thing. He scoffed. It became a joke between us during the many years we worked together. He knew me well enough to know that I wouldn't fake such a story, but the name Deward Milsaps always got him. He harrumphed, "Deward Milsaps, bah."

* * *

Frank Crosetti had been with the Yankees as a player and coach since 1932. Until Yogi Berra came along, he picked up more World Series checks than any other player. Whitey Ford joked that Crosetti still had the money from his first World Series check. Crosetti wore the uniform No. 2 for so long that I proclaimed his number was as much retired as the Nos. 3, 4, and 5 for Babe Ruth, Lou Gehrig, and Joe DiMaggio.

I don't know from where it stemmed, but Crosetti disliked and distrusted the press. He never talked to reporters and, worse, warned players about particular reporters if they didn't evidence pin-striped loyalty. As a naive rookie on the beat, I made a few futile runs at talking to Crosetti for a story. After a time, I think he sensed my less-than-awed approach to the Yankees and warned players about how they talked to me.

Years later, after Crosetti was retired, a lawsuit came up in which 384 former players sued baseball owners because they felt they had been cheated out of baseball card royalties. Five players carried the suit. The man who made himself most available to the press, frequently pressing his case, was none other than Frank Crosetti. They lost the case. Boo hoo.

Not all players fit into the Crosetti category. As sweet a man who has ever walked this earth is Stan Musial. Once, when I was writing my "Out of Left Field" column, the promotion director at *Newsday* suggested an advertisement that would have a picture of me standing alongside Musial, the Cardinal left fielder at the time. I had the further inspiration of having the picture taken along the left field foul line at the Polo Grounds when the Cards came to play the Mets. I asked Musial if he would pose that way with me. He agreed without any fuss or bother. In this day of agents milking whatever money they can for their clients, I doubt that there would be many accommodating guys like Musial.

* * *

Two happenings, more than any other, turned off sports fans in New York: the college basketball scandals in the early 1950s and the scuttling of New York by the Dodgers and Giants for the West Coast.

College basketball became a big stage for betting in the 1940s. Schools made big money off these games. In their desire to build winning teams, admission rules were stretched. Even City College, a bastion of academic excellence, admitted some students for no other reason than that they were excellent basketball players. Those who would have expected City College players to have too much loyalty to the school to be involved with point-shaving were bitterly disappointed. The corrupt atmosphere—the "everybody's doing it" syndrome—seduced the City players. I was in Las Vegas many years later to cover a championship fight and got into a conversation with a former New Yorker. He told me, "After I found out that City College was involved with dumping, I lost all interest in sports."

The Dodgers and Giants left New York after the 1957 season. Walter O'Malley played coy with the fans and the officials of New York, while solidifying a deal with Los Angeles officials that gave him the Chavez Ravine area, the near equivalent of New York bestowing Central Park on a private industry mogul. O'Malley had the Dodgers play several games in Jersey City as a prelude to the move. Yet almost to the very end, he had people believing that he would not move the Dodgers out of Brooklyn. "My roots are in Brooklyn," he said.

To take root in Los Angeles, O'Malley needed to have another team on the West Coast. Horace Stoneham, the bumbling owner who had pretty much run the New York Giants into the ground, was exploring a move to Minneapolis when O'Malley sang him the siren song of San Francisco. So they both deserted New York for the golden West.

The shrewd O'Malley prospered in Los Angeles; Stoneham, who saw life through the bottom of a scotch glass, messed up in San Francisco. He was duped into accepting the wind tunnel that was the Hunters Point area as a site for the Giants' ballpark, Candlestick Park. Inevitably, he alienated fans in San Francisco as he had in New York.

Those moves disillusioned a generation of New York baseball fans. It is no coincidence that pro football took wing in New York when the National League was without a team in New York. Harness racing at Roosevelt Field on Long Island and Yonkers Raceway also enjoyed a heyday shortly after the Dodgers and Giants departed.

O'Malley stands now and forever in Brooklyn as one of the villains of history. There's a much-quoted conversation attributed to writers Jack Newfield and Pete Hamill. They listed the three greatest villains in history as Hitler, Stalin—and O'Malley.

I had occasion to do a question-and-answer interview with historian Doris Kearns Goodwin after the publication of her book about growing up on Long Island as a passionate Brooklyn Dodger fan. When I mentioned the line about O'Malley with Hitler and Stalin, she said, "Yes, and have you heard the kicker to that?

"You are in a room with Hitler, Stalin and O'Malley," she said, "and you have a gun with two bullets. What do you do?"

"You shoot the two bullets at O'Malley."

15

The Purloined Pennant

In this long career in fun and games, few things gave me as much pleasure as "The Case of the Purloined Pennant." I not-so-humbly admit that it was one of my finest hours. Many New Yorkers were delighted by it, too.

When Walter O'Malley died in August 1979, flags flew at half-staff at Dodger Stadium and at City Hall in Los Angeles. You can be sure none flew in Brooklyn, which never forgave that deceitful old dog for moving the Dodgers to Los Angeles twenty-one seasons earlier.

The Dodgers skedaddled west in 1958 and won the pennant the very next season. And thereby hangs the tale of "The Case of the Purloined Pennant." This has to do with what some romantics regard as one of the noblest capers in the annals of American skullduggery—the valiant effort of aggrieved pressmen to avenge O'Malley's dastardly act of depriving Brooklyn of its beloved Bums.

The 1959 World Series opened in Chicago. After two games, it moved to Los Angeles for the next three. Press headquarters in Los Angeles was at the Sheraton West Hotel. A symbol of the only World Series the Brooklyn Dodgers had won, the 1955 championship flag, had a prominent spot at press headquarters. The Dodgers chose to decorate the banquet room with that 1955 flag. The huge banner was an all-too-graphic reminder of the glory Brooklyn once knew.

The flag that had streamed so gallantly for the entire 1956 season over the ramparts of Ebbets Field—the right-center field flagpole atop the scoreboard—measured eighteen feet long. With royal blue letters on a white background and a blue border it read:

WORLD CHAMPIONS
1955
DODGERS

That sacred cloth pinned to the drapes high above a row of buffet tables held a particular fascination for at least four of us at press headquarters following the fifth game of the Series; it would be the last one in Los Angeles before the teams returned to Chicago. These men were my colleagues: Jack Mann, sports editor of *Newsday;* Steve Weller, a columnist with the *Buffalo Evening News;* and my friend Charles Sutton, a city-side reporter for the *Los Angeles Times*. Sutton had no huge interest in baseball, but he liked to come along on freeloads, and Brooklyn was his hometown.

The more we looked at the flag, the more it miffed us. It was so far from the mother borough where it belonged. Finally, and inevitably, one of us—I confess it was me—said, "That pennant should be back home where it belongs."

I believe it was the impish Weller who said, "Why don't we take it, then?" I think it important here to emphasize that the heat that burned within us was born of devotion to justice, and not the fire of an overabundance of liquor. It would cheapen the glory with which we were about to cover ourselves to say we acted with anything but high-minded sobriety.

The somewhat fearsome foursome was now confronted with a technical problem. There appeared no way to get at the pennant hanging above us. Sutton took charge. He summoned the headwaiter and boldly announced, "I'm Charles Sutton from the *Herald Tribune* and we must have that pennant right away." You might ask what the *Herald Tribune* had to do with it, but there was an unmistakable ring of authority in Sutton's voice—probably no less so than in O'Malley's when he told Commissioner Ford Frick he had to move to Los Angeles. The headwaiter did not question him.

He scurried to help, apologizing for not having a ladder. He commissioned some assistants to stack rickety tables toward the ceiling so that one of us—I was the smallest—could unpin the pennant. As I clambered up, holding a pair of scissors provided by the headwaiter, he steadied one of the tables. I unhooked the pennant. A few late carousers looked up in puzzlement, but nobody seemed suspicious of our actions. We folded the flag into quarters and pranced out onto Wilshire Boulevard, giggling all the way.

With visions of O'Malley calling out the Los Angeles storm troopers to foil our getaway, we decided to leave the pennant with Sutton—a local, a bloke unknown to the Dodger management or, for that matter, to the

Herald Tribune. Sutton agreed to hide the goods for the night. His brother, who was a dry-goods merchant, wrapped it up. The next morning, Sutton handed the flag to us at our hotel.

Mann and I flew out of Los Angeles looking over our shoulders from hotel to cab to airport to plane. We saw O'Malley and the LAPD lurking behind every pillar. Finally, we were aloft, home free. "Let them find out about it now," Mann said. "No judge within 100 miles of Brooklyn would convict us." We toasted the flag, we toasted Brooklyn. We toasted Sutton and Weller, whose constant prodding, "Go ahead, you can do it," had helped fuel the caper.

When Mann and I got home, we decided that our first reaction to complaints by the Dodgers about the theft would be to raise the standard high over the *Newsday* lawn. But the Dodgers didn't react at all. There were no outraged stories from Los Angeles. The wire services didn't even send out a short item on the missing flag. Nor did Sutton, our man out west, report any murmurs of anger or dismay. I wrote in *Newsday* that "pulling off the perfect crime and getting caught is not nearly as frustrating as pulling off the perfect crime and having nobody care."

* * *

Many years later I asked former Dodgers general manager Buzzy Bavasi why the Dodgers made no efforts to retrieve the flag. He was a likable gent, even if he worked for O'Malley. He said, "To tell you the truth, I thought it belonged in New York. We decided it was just as well."

In 1963, when the Dodgers won another pennant, they again decorated their World Series press headquarters with past championship flags. They had their 1959 flag and—surprise, surprise—a 1955 world championship flag, too. "We just had another flag made up," Bavasi said. "It cost us about 96 bucks."

We stashed the flag in my basement in Roslyn Heights. The idea was to break it out with a flourish on an appropriate occasion, perhaps with trumpets of the beloved Dodger "Sym-phony," a strolling five-piece madcap band that played in the stands at Ebbets Field. Somehow, no worthy occasion arose.

Nor did there seem to be a proper depository for the flag, all glorious eighteen feet of it. We considered and rejected Borough Hall, the Brooklyn Museum, and the flagpole atop Grand Army Plaza. There was, of course, no longer any Ebbets Field scoreboard from which to wave it on high. A plea to the public in *Newsday* to find a proper resting place produced no acceptable nomination, either, so the flag languished ignominiously in plastic wrapping in my basement.

Wanting the flag to be seen, I donated it to the Baseball Hall of Fame at Cooperstown. The Hall's Ken Smith, a former longtime baseball writer for the *Daily Mirror,* accepted the flag with the proviso that he would never give it to O'Malley—and he would return it to us if ever there were a place in Brooklyn that seemed a rightful resting place for it. Smith promised that the flag would be part of an upcoming display dedicated to Ebbets Field. He left the Hall not long afterward, however, and when I went to Cooperstown sometime later, I was chagrined to see that the gaudy exhibit on old ballparks didn't include the purloined pennant.

An official said, "It's so large, it's difficult to fit it into the display." When I said politely that I wanted to see the flag anyway, just for old times' sake, he took me down to the basement. There it was wrapped in plastic: the flag that flew over Ebbets Field, that was pinned to the drapes of the hotel banquet room in Los Angeles, that we swiped, that lay in my basement for a few years. I told him that if it was not to be seen, it could just as easily have remained in my basement.

A few years later, the Brooklyn Dodgers Baseball Fan Club came into existence. The club was spearheaded by Marty Adler, an assistant principal at Jackie Robinson Junior High School, the school on McKeever Place across from the old Ebbets Field site. (A housing development stands on the site of what once was Ebbets Field. One day a newspaperman who had been a Dodger fan took his ten-year-old son to the street across from the old site, pointed up at the housing development and said, "The Brooklyn Dodgers used to play there." His son said, "On what floor?")

I thought the Brooklyn Dodgers Fan Club deserved to possess the flag. I wrote to the Baseball Hall of Fame asking for the return of the flag, as agreed upon by Ken Smith. To my dismay, the Hall people asked if I had a paper attesting to the agreement between Smith and me. I told them that we were honorable men who had shaken hands on it. I was informed that Smith suffered from Alzheimer's and was no longer at the museum. Some correspondence went back and forth, but to no avail. Museums don't give up anything once they get their mitts on it.

I wrote columns about the flag, wailing about the injustice of it all. I said that Cooperstown was shafting Brooklyn just as Walter O'Malley had. Dave Anderson wrote a column of support in the *New York Times.* Some readers responded they would be willing to join a raiding party to go up to Cooperstown to retrieve the flag once again.

That planted a seed. In 1991, when I went up to Cooperstown for the induction of Bill Veeck, I cased the joint. By this time the Hall had found a place for the flag. I studied it in its niche looking down over a stairway leading to one of the exhibits. My quick analysis was that this would not be as easy a heist as at the Los Angeles hotel. The only way to retrieve the flag would be to have a janitor spirit it away in the dark of night. I mentioned this in a column, but nobody came forth with word they knew any janitors at Cooperstown.

Then Peter O'Malley, the son of Walter O'Malley, entered the story. I would call Peter "a good son of a bad man." He was upset that his father was regarded as such an ogre in Brooklyn. To atone for his father's misdeed, Peter formed an association with the Brooklyn Historical Society, providing them with some Dodger mementos. In 1995 the Historical Society had its annual fund-raising dinner and honored the fortieth anniversary of the Dodgers championship season. It asked O'Malley if it could receive the 1955 World Championship flag.

Now, then, it is one thing for me, a mere scrivener, to ask that the Hall of Fame be honorable and return the flag. It is another thing for the owner of a baseball team to make that request. A baseball franchise owner has clout, considering the Hall is beholden to the goodwill of baseball people. O'Malley made the request. "It really belongs in Brooklyn," he said. The flag was returned. It now hangs at the Brooklyn Historical Society on Pierrepont Street in downtown Brooklyn.

* * *

During the fourth Madison Square Garden's construction in 1968, it occurred to me that it would be appropriate for the new Garden to house an artifact associated with one of its predecessors. A statue of Diana, created by Augustus Saint-Gaudens, had stood atop the second Madison Square Garden, which was designed by famed architect Stanford White and completed in 1890. The nude Diana was a controversial piece, inflaming the passions of too-proper folk embarrassed by the nakedness aloft.

One of O. Henry's short stories referred to the statue. In the story, "The Lady Higher Up," he wrote: "The statue of Diana on the tower of the Garden—its constancy shown by its weathercock ways, its innocence by the coating of gold that it has acquired, its devotion to style by its single, graceful flying scarf, its candor and artlessness by its habit of ever drawing the long bow, its metropolitanism by its posture of swift flight to catch a Harlem train—remained poised with its arrow pointed across the upper bay."

When the second Garden was torn down, the statue went to a warehouse. Diana lay there in anonymity for a long time. Then the Philadelphia Museum acquired it and placed it in a prominent spot over a grand staircase at the museum.

Garden president Mike Burke, urged on by me, offered to buy it for the new Garden. No deal. Instead, he had a replica of Diana created and placed it in the lobby of the new Garden. It stood there for a few years until the building underwent a makeover. It wound up in a storage cellar somewhere. On several occasions, I offered to buy it but received polite denials.

That was not the first time I asked to buy a storied piece of art. When I covered the Yankees, an oil portrait of Abner Doubleday hung in the working press room, adjoining the drinking press room at Yankee Stadium. It occupied an undistinguished place behind a door, hardly noticed by anyone. Doubleday was resplendent in his Union general's uniform as the centerpiece of a tableau, which included scenes marking aspects of his career. There was a Fort Sumter battle scene, as well as the outline of a baseball diamond attesting to Doubleday's invention of baseball. Of course, it is a myth that he invented baseball, but a convenient one, because it justifies the Hall of Fame's place in Doubleday's hometown of Cooperstown, New York.

Every so often I asked to buy the painting, because it was almost an unseen item in the press room. I was met with amused rejections. But when Yankee Stadium underwent a renovation, the press room was remodeled. There was no place for the Abner Doubleday painting. Bob Fishel, the Yankee public relations man, mentioned my request to Michael Burke, then president of the Yankees. Burke said, "Give it to him." Abner Doubleday, resplendent in Union blue, came to my house in Roslyn Heights.

Doubleday, alas, did not enjoy much peace at 2 Overlook Terrace. My wife did not like the painting. She said it was dark and ugly. "Gold, blue, red. Ugh," she said. A painting tug-of-war ensued. I would put Abner Doubleday up in the room where I worked. After a while, she would take it down. It would take me some time to notice its absence. I would put it up again.

Finally, we reached a compromise. It was given in a place in my X-rated closet. There was nothing pornographic about the X-rated closet. It was just the place for paintings that had no other place to hang or that offended my wife's aesthetic sense.

It occurred to me to find out if the Abner Doubleday painting had any value. Did the name on the back, Walsh, mean anything? I sent it to Bill Goff, who ran the Spectrum sports art gallery on West 57th Street in Manhattan. Goff held it for a long time. Finally, after my prodding, he said, "I am afraid it has no particular value, Stan." I also showed it to my friend Len Bernstein, a serious art collector. He agreed with Bobbie that it belonged in the X-rated closet.

Sometime later, I mentioned the Abner Doubleday painting to my friend Stan Marx, whose son Evan ran a used book, baseball card, and collectible shop nearby in Roslyn Heights. I wondered if it had any value. He said, "Let me look at it." When I got it out of the closet for him, he shrugged. "You never know. We have a customer who likes sports paintings. Tell me what you want for it and I'll ask him if he's interested."

I decided to name a ridiculous figure: one thousand dollars. Marx said, "I'll ask my guy, you never know."

A few days later Marx greeted me with a check. His man bought the painting. Marx said, "You know, he likes the painting, but he is still a little hesitant about telling his wife what he paid for it."

A few years after that, Bobbie and I were at our annual wedding anniversary dinner, which we enjoy each year with our friends Len and Elise Elman and Peter and Rita Nord. We all were married on the same day: December 20, 1953. The other couples met on their honeymoons, and we met them through a mutual friend a little while later. We have dined out almost every year on or about that date to celebrate our marriages.

On this night, we were dining at Café Nicholson in Manhattan. Len Elman mentioned they had been to an art gallery that afternoon. He said, "There was a painting I particularly liked and would have liked to buy for my son-in-law because it combined two of his big interests: baseball and the civil war." He proceeded to limn a portrait of Abner Doubleday in his Union uniform.

"Did it have little scenes depicting baseball and the civil war in the corner?" I asked. Elman said it did. He said it was unfortunate that it cost so much. How much? "Ten thousand dollars," he said. I looked at my wife. Her face was ashen.

We let it linger for a while. Then Elman let my wife off the hook. His speech was a hoax; we had cooked it up beforehand as a joke on Bobbie for her lack of appreciation for the noble Abner Doubleday. But in my heart I feel that Doubleday will turn up some day and be worth even more than $10,000.

16

Baseball Characters

I had an interesting relationship with Jackie Robinson. At first, I was awed by him, but that evolved into the usual reporter-athlete relationship. Robinson represented someone above and beyond baseball. When he first played in a Brooklyn uniform in a weekend series in 1947, I was a student at Brooklyn College, a few miles down Bedford Avenue from Ebbets Field. I made a point of going to Ebbets Field to see him even though it was just a Dodgers-Yankees exhibition game.

I had been a Giants fan since the age of seven, but because of Robinson, I couldn't root against the Dodgers with the fervor of old. I made a pact with myself: I would root for the Giants until they were out of the race—which usually was about late June in those days—and then root for the Dodgers.

The *Daily Compass* did not cover the Dodgers on the road, so I was something of an outsider when I started covering the team. I approached Robinson somewhat hesitantly. After a while, I became comfortable with him because he was a significant and approachable presence. His high-pitched voice invariably rose above the chatter of the clubhouse. Dodger manager Charley Dressen was such an "I-me" guy that I didn't find him fruitful as a postgame source. I would make a courtesy call to his office, listen to him a minute or so, and then migrate to the clubhouse to mine Robinson and Pee Wee Reese for the most incisive postgame comments.

Robinson was a fiery guy. I sometimes wondered how he could carry the social burden of being the first black player in organized baseball, as well as being a team leader. One afternoon's action illustrates that. Robinson was playing second base. An opposing hitter drove a ball into an outfield gap and sprinted around second base toward third. The play at third was close. The umpire called the runner safe. This drew an immediate protest from Dodger third baseman Billy Cox and manager Dressen. Within a few seconds, Cox and Dressen had retreated and the man in the middle carrying the argument was Robinson, who had sprinted over from second base. He argued loud and long and to no avail.

I approached him about this in the clubhouse after the game. I said, "Jack, you have so much else to be concerned with—all the abuse you take from fans and players as a Negro in baseball—why would you want to get involved with the umpire in a play that didn't involve you?"

Robinson looked at me with a mixture of surprise and, I believe, disgust. "But he was out, he was out," he said. I walked away shaking my head.

As the seasons progressed, I found that the best way to interview Robinson was to argue with him. He was contentious, challenging. I might ask, "Why did you try to hit to right field in the second inning?" He would answer, "If you'd think about it a little, you would know why." I could come back: "I did think about it and I didn't realize why. That's why I am asking you."

Ironically, the other person with whom I argued to elicit comments was Leo Durocher, whom Robinson detested. Durocher would say to me, "Stupid question," and I would have the confidence to retort, "There are no stupid questions, only stupid answers." Somehow the chemistry between Durocher/Robinson and me was such that we got along—at the top of our voices.

Things were much calmer for me with Pee Wee Reese. The gifted Roger Kahn immortalized the post–World War II Dodgers as the "Boys of Summer." The heart and soul of those boys of summer was Reese, the gentleman from Louisville, as sweet a man as ever walked onto a baseball field. Reese was the captain, the glue, the man who, in his own quiet, droll way, set the tone on that ball club. He sat in an armchair in a corner of the Ebbets Field clubhouse and presided over postgame conferences in a casual, low-key, friendly way. Others took their cue from him.

He lingered after games. "Rush out of the clubhouse and you are rushing out of baseball," he advised teammates. He was a calming influence on the often-petulant Duke Snider. When fans booed Snider after he blasted Dodger fans in a magazine article, Reese made it a point to play catch with his hot-headed teammate in pregame warm-ups. He was so much the leader of the team that Snider was embarrassed to be voted into the Hall of Fame when Reese was not. Snider carried an attaché case on which he put the sticker, "Pee Wee should be in the Hall!"

One of the two years I was up at Cooperstown for the Hall of Fame ceremonies, I met Reese with his son Mark, a documentary filmmaker. He was making a film about his father and the Dodgers. I approached Mark.

Hesitantly, I said, "We all love your dad. Sometimes, though, a man who is loved by the outside world isn't quite as beloved within his family. Is your dad the same for the family as he is with us?"

Mark Reese paused a moment and then said, "More so."

* * *

My longstanding esteem for Robinson and Reese inspired my suggestion in 1999 for a statue commemorating the revered moment when Reese, the gentleman white southerner, placed an arm around Robinson, his black teammate, as an answer to the bigots in the stands and Cincinnati dugout who were spewing racial epithets at Robinson.

Mayor Rudolph Giuliani picked up the idea, but as I wrote earlier, the committee meeting to choose a sculptor was held at City Hall on the morning of September 11, 2001. The 9-11 attack stalled plans for the statue's erection. There were several missteps along the way, as well. For a time, it looked as if the statue project would founder, lost in the red tape of a mayoralty change and the sensitivities of some people involved in the project. In 2003, though, Mayor Michael Bloomberg got on board, and the fundraising accelerated. A total of $1.2 million was raised by sports and civic figures, though we also accepted the pennies of schoolchildren.

The statue exhibit includes a slab of stone on which is inscribed the names of all the people who contributed money to the statue project, including those schoolkids. One of the names was that of Leo Seligsohn. He was a colleague at *Newsday* who cared nothing about sports but was moved by one of my columns to contribute. And now Seligsohn, the non-sports fan, is inscribed in stone outside the ballpark in Coney Island.

And so it was that the Reese-Robinson statue was unveiled amid fanfare and merriment on the lovely, crisp morning of November 11, 2005, outside the ballpark of the Brooklyn Cyclones, the Mets farm team in Coney Island. The statue, designed by William Behrends, is about eight feet high. It stands atop a pedestal that traces Robinson's history as the first black man in modern baseball; it features the incident on May 13, 1947, when Reese put his arm around Robinson to silence vicious heckling.

The wives of the players, Dottie Reese and Rachel Robinson, were on hand along with their children. Mayor Bloomberg presided. The colorful Brooklyn Borough president, Marty Moskowitz, spoke. The ragtag, beloved "Brooklyn Sym-Phony" made noise for the crowd of some three hundred kids and old Dodger fans.

Mark Reese spoke eloquently. He said, "My father had done his own soul searching. He knew that some fans, teammates, and, yes, family members didn't want him to play with a black man. But my father listened to his heart, and not to the chorus."

I regretted that Jack Newfield was not there. He died in 2004. He was represented by his widow, Janie. Jack's spirited column in the *New York Post* had first attracted Mayor Giuliani's support. Along with union activist John Turciano, I did some behind-the-scenes needling of the mayors' staffs to keep the project alive. Newspaper pieces by Vic Ziegel in the *Daily News,* Joe Gergen and Bob Keeler in *Newsday,* and Bob Lipsyte and Frank Clines in the *New York Times* helped.

The mayor's people were generous in giving Newfield and me our due. Friends were lavish in their praise. I treasure the comments of Marty Appel: "You left a fantastic legacy." Larry Merchant said, "It's a monument to you for a lifetime of good work."

* * *

Over the years, readers and friends have often asked me about the famous personalities I have covered. They want to know: "What is so and so like?" In most cases I said, honestly, "I don't know." I could only say what they seemed to be like in public; I didn't know what they were like in private.

For better or worse, though, I met some grand characters who charmed, angered, thrilled, and inspired me. I like to believe that I never lost my skeptical view of my world, but I admit that I did feel at times that it was a privilege and a joy to be in the company of Casey Stengel and Bill Veeck.

First, Stengel. What a grand, old, irascible charmer he was. Stengel started his career in Kankakee, Illinois, in 1910 at the age of twenty. He moved on to Maysville, Kentucky, and Aurora, Illinois, and within two years was playing for the Brooklyn Dodgers. Stengel went down to Montgomery, Alabama, for a season and then came back to the big leagues for good in 1913. He moved from the Dodgers to the Pittsburgh Pirates to the Philadelphia Phillies and then to the New York Giants.

Stengel provided the punch in the only two games won by the Giants against the Yankees in the 1923 World Series. His inside-the-park home run with two out in the ninth inning gave the Giants a 5–4 victory in the first game. I do believe that he thumbed his nose at the Yankees while scoring on that home run. Or was it when he hit the homer in the seventh inning that won the third game for the Giants, 1–0? Either way, it was Stengelian to the core.

Stengel was a continuous force in baseball until 1965, when he retired from the New York Mets at age seventy-five. For all his rough-hewn image and his Stengelese language, he was a shrewd, enormously bright man with a remarkable memory. He seemed able to recall almost anything and anywhere he had been. Listening to him roll off the names of little towns far and wide, you could almost believe he had been everywhere. Those of us covering him when he managed the Yankees from 1949 through 1960 and then the Mets from 1962 to 1965 never stopped being amazed at his recall and knowledge of past events.

Stengel first started managing as a player in the Eastern League in Worcester, Massachusetts, in 1925. He played and managed for the Toledo Mud Hens of the American Association from 1926 through 1931 and then had his first managerial job with the Dodgers in 1934. He had no particular success in his three years in Brooklyn. He called it "the borough of churches and bad ball clubs, many of which I had." Nor did he do any better in six years with the Boston Braves (also called the Bees for one year) from 1938 through 1943. Once, he got run over by a taxi, and such was his popularity in some quarters of Beantown that one columnist nominated the taxi driver as "the man who did most for Boston baseball."

His odyssey through the minor leagues continued with Milwaukee and Kansas City of the American Association and Oakland of the Pacific Coast League before he came back to the majors with the Yankees in 1949. Critics who thought he was a clown found out otherwise, as he led outstanding talent to five straight pennants and ten in all. He won seven World Series in twelve years.

Stengel was an inspiration. He had a face of knots and crevices, a nose of aristocratic curve, a raspy voice. He talked in circles, ambling, rambling, but he almost always got back to the point, even if he took you on a verbal trip around the world en route. He charmed almost everybody—even those who didn't want to be charmed.

One night, in the lobby of the Hotel Muehlebach in Kansas City, I sat with him for a short while and then edged away to listen as the guests and locals gathered around him. Several fans, who indulged in the good American pastime of hating the Yankees, started out by baiting Stengel. He accepted it graciously, nodding at any comment and continuing to talk. Little by little you could see him win over even the most die-hard anti-Yankee fans. It was in their eyes or by the shake of their head as they walked away. I hung around for at least two hours and watched people come and go, happy at first just to be with this celebrated man and then awed and delighted by him.

I left to have a light dinner in the hotel coffee shop; when I came back about a half-hour later, Stengel was still on the couch, talking to a new group of listeners. As John Lardner once wrote, "He can talk all day and all night, and on any kind of track, wet or dry."

Being around Stengel was invariably entertaining. He said of an undistinguished young player, "He's 20 years old; in 10 years he's got a chance to be 30." When reporters gathered around a young winning pitcher in a postgame session, hitting him with a barrage of questions, Stengel sneaked to the outer edges of the circle, pretending to be a weird journalist, and asked, "Vas you born in Poland?"

He said, "The secret of managing is to keep the five guys who hate you away from the guys who are undecided." When the Mets made Hobie Landrith their first pick in the expansion draft, he explained, "You've got to have a catcher because if you don't, you're likely to have a lot of passed balls." He preferred married players because "It ain't the screwin' that wears 'em down, it's the chasin'." At age seventy-five, he said, "Most people my age are dead at the present time."

One night, when the Mets were playing some preseason games in Mexico City, the wealthy owner of the Mexico City team threw a party for the Mets. Stengel and his wife, Edna, drove me and my wife out to the party in the suburbs. Edna kept badgering him. He responded heatedly. In the rear seats, my wife and I suppressed giggles. It was as if we were in the company of two bickering teenagers.

Stengel and Leo Durocher were successful managers because they were probably the first to not see color when managing ballplayers. The black ballplayers sensed this and hustled for them at a time when they sensed dislike or condescension from other managers. I once asked Stengel about his views on race and he said, "I've been around so long I can dislike anybody," his reverse way of saying he treated everybody the same.

Howard Cosell, who could be insufferable, frequently trumpeted the charge that Stengel was a bigot because he used the word "jig" and because he once said about Elston Howard, "How come if they all can run so fast, I've got the one who can't?" Early in his career as a radio guy at Shea Stadium, Cosell had been snubbed by Stengel, partly because he put his arm around people in a proprietary manner when interviewing; Stengel didn't like that and shook him off. Stengel also had a good nose for insincerity, and he sized Cosell up as a man of dubious merit.

I disdained Cosell's opinion. Unfortunately, it was accepted by Jackie Robinson, who was a Connecticut neighbor of Cosell's. Certainly, Cosell was a liberal and he and Robinson could be sympatico on many things. But Jackie was wrong, not only to accept Cosell's label of Stengel, but also to parrot it publicly, citing Stengel's use of the word "jig."

I was on a television show with Robinson and we had it out about this. Stengel grew up in Kansas City in the early 1900s. It reflected his past and his lack of sensitivity to the nuances of racial pride to use the word, but it hardly mattered against the bigger issue of the way Stengel related to his black players. I told Jackie that as much as I admired him—worshipped him in a way—I was impressed by the fact that two of the men he disparaged, Stengel and Leo Durocher, with whom he had many run-ins on the field, were two of the most colorblind managers in handling their players.

* * *

It is regrettable that Stengel and Bill Veeck never hooked up on a big-league team, though they were associated with Milwaukee in the minor leagues. Actually, it took some time for Veeck to appreciate Stengel. As Bob Creamer related in his invaluable book, *Stengel: His Life and Times,* Veeck was away in the Marines in 1944 when Charlie Grimm, who had been general manager and manager of the Milwaukee Brewers, was called up to manage the Cubs. Grimm hired Stengel to replace him. Veeck ripped the choice from afar because of Casey's reputation as a clown who had had no success in the big leagues. Stengel's contract was ironclad so Veeck, much to his later satisfaction, had to accept him.

They both were zanies, but inordinately talented zanies. It is no coincidence that in the eighteen years the Yankees dominated the American League from 1949 to 1964, winning the pennant fourteen times, the only other teams to break through and beat them were the 1954 Cleveland Indians and the 1959 Chicago White Sox, both run by the ever-smiling, ever-shrewd Bill Veeck. He brought Larry Doby to the Cleveland Indians in 1947 as the first black player in the American League, and he gave Satchel Paige the chance for some glory in the major leagues in the waning days of his fabled career.

The last words of Veeck's book, *The Hustler's Handbook,* written with the talented Ed Linn, convey the irreverent essence of Veeck. He wrote: "Victita volup! (which means Have Fun) and Ne unquam aliquid raptes quod tibi non ferat superblam rapatando (which means, Never Steal Anything You Will Not Be Proud of Having)."

Among other zings, Veeck leveled at the baseball establishment, he said, "The automatic turnstile was the last innovation greeted with approval by baseball moguls."

Veeck was literate, pixieish, sly, Falstaffian, a debunker of stuffiness, and always fun to be with. On a trip to Chicago with the Yankees, I sought out Veeck at his downtown hotel in the afternoon before a night game. I called from the lobby and was told to come right up. I saw him in the bathroom, where he was soaking his leg. Veeck had been injured in the Marines in

World War II. His right leg was shattered by a recoiling anti-aircraft gun. Eventually, a part of his leg was amputated. He was constantly undergoing operations to remove parts of his leg that were gangrenous.

He welcomed me with his cigarette-husky laugh while lounging in the bathtub water with his good leg, holding the prosthesis of his other leg outside the tub. Without any self-consciousness, he flicked the ashes of his cigarette into the socket of the prosthesis. Veeck was never embarrassed by his deformity. He always said, "I am not handicapped, I am a cripple."

His driver took us through the south side of Chicago to Comiskey Park. Veeck was a pied piper of good cheer. Every time we stopped at a light, people recognized him and chatted with him and exhorted him and the White Sox to beat the Yankees that night. He acknowledged their good tidings with a wave and a laugh.

Veeck, the ultimate showman and innovator of baseball, dared to tweak diehards in the face of tradition. He put the names of his players on the backs of their uniforms. When that irritated opposing owners, claiming it would cut down on scorecard sales in their ballpark, Veeck laughed. He loved their way of getting back at him, by putting the names of their players on the backs of uniforms to cut down on scorecard sales at *his* ballpark. This helped all fans, which was Veeck's intention in the first place.

The New York Yankees were among those who held out against this fan-friendly innovation. Veeck once said, "The Yankees always took the attitude that they were doing you a favor in permitting you to watch them perform."

His most famous stunt, of course, was the outrageous act of signing the 3'7" Eddie Gaedel and having him pinch-hit and draw a walk for the St. Louis Browns in 1951. Veeck, a prolific reader, revealed he had gotten the idea from the James Thurber short story, "You Could Look It Up," about the little person Pearl du Monville, who actually swings at the ball and costs his team the game. Veeck said he warned Gaedel about any such foolishness. There is a classic picture of Gaedel at bat with catcher Bob Swift on his haunches behind him, waiting to accept a pitch from Bob Cain. When Gaedel died, there was one baseball person at his funeral: Bob Cain.

Another of Veeck's innovations was the exploding scoreboard. It flipped its lid when a White Sox player hit a home run, shooting off fireworks, exploding bombs with music and a glowing display of lights. Veeck was one-upped on this one by none other than the hated Yankees on a visit to Comiskey Park. Bob Fishel, the Yankee publicity man who once worked for Veeck in Cleveland, had some sparklers smuggled into the Yankee dugout. When a Yankee hit a home run, the Yankee players in the dugout jumped up with lit sparklers. Stengel led the group, gleefully parading around on his gimpy legs, waving the sparklers. Veeck was in the press box when it happened. He chortled. Nobody appreciated what he called "a brilliant satire" more than he did.

When illness forced him to sell the White Sox, Veeck entered a period of retirement. He had lived in the Midwest most of his life, but his health demanded a more temperate climate. In deciding where to live, he wanted an area that wasn't far from a major city or an airport. In effect, he had all of the United States to choose from. He wound up in a rambling, wood-shingled house on Chesapeake Bay outside the town of Easton on Maryland's Eastern Shore. It had a temperate climate, the airport in Easton was nearby, and it was within an hour's driving distance of Baltimore and Washington.

While on assignment in Washington one weekend, I drove over to Easton to see him. He was his old ruddy self, laughing, twinkly eyed, drinking beer, and smoking. After dinner, we sat and talked about baseball and cabbages and kings into the night. His wife, Mary Frances, smiled and said, "I can see you boys won't be going to bed." She was right.

I didn't drink beer with Veeck, but he had me, a nonsmoker, puffing on a Schimmelpenninck, a small Dutch cigar, almost until dawn. He talked about the people he liked to tweak, none more than Yankee general manager George Weiss, his "most unfavorite man." He often said, "If baseball owners ran Congress, Kansas and Nebraska would still be trying to get into the Union."

We were brothers in mechanical ineptitude, so I loved his story about a Christmas toy. Once, he ordered a wooden rocking horse from a mail-order house for one of his young sons. The toy didn't arrive until the day before Christmas. Much to Veeck's dismay, it had to be assembled. So Veeck spent the night before Christmas and into the early hours of the morning fussing and fuming and finally getting the rocking horse put together and placed under the Christmas tree. His boy loved it.

Veeck wrote out a check to the toy company. He then tore the check into little pieces and put it in an envelope with a note. He told the toy people, "I put your horse together; you put my check together." The company did; sometime later, the check came back from the bank all pasted together.

Veeck ran the Suffolk Downs racetrack in Boston for a time. I went up there for his opening. I saw Veeck in all his glory making things glow. The first thing he did was take down the barbed wire fence surrounding the racetrack plant. "A barbed wire fence," he said, "is not exactly a welcoming sight." As we walked around the track in the few hectic hours before the opening, he greeted workers and attended to a myriad of details.

He didn't like the artificial flowers around the track. "Let's get fresh ones," he said, ordering the artificial plants removed. At just about this point, a sweet old lady came up to Veeck and said how much she enjoyed the artificial flowers. Without batting an eye, Veeck picked up some of the flowers that were to be discarded. With a flourish, he handed the lady the flowers. She was thrilled.

In 1991 Veeck was elected to the Baseball Hall of Fame. I am not a big fan of ceremonies honoring sports figures—there are far too many of them, and too often the honorees are far from worthy. But Veeck was different. I made it a point to trek to Cooperstown to be there. His wife Mary Frances and writing collaborator Ed Linn were among those at the ceremonies.

"My epitaph is inescapable," he said. "It will read, 'He sent a midget up to bat.'"

From the ages of five to eleven, Stan lived in the apartment building at the corner of Berry Street and Broadway in the Williamsburg neighborhood of Brooklyn.

A Stan Isaacs column was sometimes light and whimsical, but it could also be hard-hitting. He prided himself on his reporting.

In the press box at Yankee Stadium. Isaacs is in the first row, seventh from the front.

With the legendary columnist Jimmy Cannon, whose cutting remark christened "The Chipmunks."

"Stanley, Is It Really Ewe?" was the caption on this June 1961 photo, when Isaacs reported on a baseball game in Kansas City from the hilly pasture in right field.

Isaacs was among the legion of reporters who loved Casey Stengel because Casey Stengel loved reporters.

Isaacs always appreciated Stan Musial, one of the nicer, more generous sports stars of his era.

Muhammad Ali knocked out Sonny Liston during their rematch in Lewiston, Maine, in 1965. Isaacs is in the top left, third from the corner. Leonard Schecter is on the far right, standing and wearing glasses. Isaacs and Shecter were among the young reporters who delighted in Ali's rise.

Above: Isaacs first wrote about football star Jim Brown as a Long Island high schooler. He considered Brown the most enigmatic figure that he consistently covered.

Hobnobbing with Billie Jean King, the tennis star and feminist icon.

With Jack Nicklaus, a superb golfer who also appreciated a bargain on sweaters.

Isaacs loved both lower-tier college football and marching bands. One year, he was a guest of the Columbia University band, playing a unique instrument called a lengthopipe.

With his friend and fellow columnist Larry Merchant and Stan's beloved wife, Bobbie Isaacs.

Isaacs was so ambivalent about shaking hands with Richard Nixon that he resolved not to smile, and then he displayed the photograph only after adding snarky captions that referenced the Watergate scandal.

With New York Knicks legend Walt Frazier.

"TV Sports," the groundbreaking column that Isaacs wrote in his last fifteen years at *Newsday,* often featured John Madden, one of his favorite television broadcasters.

For one contribution to *Sports Illustrated,* Isaacs wrote about watching twenty-four consecutive hours of the new all-sports cable network ESPN.

One of Isaacs's favorite stories was the "tale of the purloined pennant," when he and his friends pilfered the 1955 championship flag after Walter O'Malley moved the Dodgers from Brooklyn to Los Angeles. Here he poses with Bobbie in front of the pennant while it was on display at the Baseball Hall of Fame.

Isaacs conceived of the idea and enthusiastically lobbied for the statue of Jackie Robinson and Pee Wee Reese, which the Brooklyn Cyclones unveiled on November 11, 2005. Larry Merchant told Isaacs: "It's a monument to you for a lifetime of good work."

17

Olympic Hypocrisy

The Olympics are a huge distortion of "sport for sport's sake." The Olympics were established by the French baron, Pierre de Coubertin, with a credo that now seems stunningly naive. De Coubertin said: "The most important thing in the Olympic games is not to win, but to take part. Just as the most important thing in life is not the triumph but the struggle. The essential thing is not to have conquered, but to have fought well."

Hah.

The Olympics have become the gigantic supermarket of sport. It is the most fertile of all sporting grounds for big bucksters. Sponsors, TV stations, and marketing people all look to cash in on the Games. The emphasis on winning is all-consuming for many of the athletes in the sports that dominate TV.

Participation in sports used to be the hallmark of a healthy youth. Today, athletes use drugs to prevail. The revelations at the Sydney Games that American shot putter C. J. Hunter had tested positive for drugs a few times raised charges that American officials had been covering up drug failures by other athletes. Allegations about drugs at the Olympics inspired Bob Verdi of the *Chicago Tribune* to say the Olympic motto should be "Citius, Altius, Fortius, Urinalysis."

In his excellent book about the East German doping machine, *Faust's Gold,* Steve Ungerleider wrote, "It is astonishing that the most horrific chapter in sports history has remained a minor story." He chronicled East German teenage girls transmogrified into hirsute, sex-crazed Amazons because of the little blue "vitamin" pills their trainers gave them. He wrote of steroid-boosted male athletes growing breasts and watching their testes shrink. And yet Manafred Ewald, the East German bureaucrat who oversaw the doping program, was awarded a medal from International Olympic president Juan Antonio Samaranch in 1985 for upholding "the perfect ideal of sports and humanity."

Probably the most disheartening poll I ever heard about asked prospective Olympic athletes if they would be willing to use a drug that would enable them to win a gold medal—but killed them a year later. Almost 60 percent responded they would take the drug to win the gold medal.

The Olympics have evolved into the preserve of millionaires and officials of third-world countries on the make. The three Ps—politics, profiteering, and professionalism—mark the Olympics. Bribery is one of the participant sports for cities vying to host the Olympics. This broke out into the open with the scandalous revelations about payoffs by Salt Lake City officials to bring the 2002 Winter Games to Utah. The International Olympic Committee did some housecleaning, but the Olympics remain an overblown commercial extravaganza.

Samaranch, who oversaw the expansion of the Olympics into a bloated monstrosity, survived the assaults on his regime. Despite the frequent revelations about the bribery involved in awarding the Games to various cities, not enough was made of one particular set of shenanigans: the Japanese fat cat who led the successful effort to land the 1998 Winter Games in Nagano made a multi-million-dollar contribution to help build the Olympic Museum in Lausanne, Switzerland, one of the projects dearest to Samaranch. When is a bribe not a bribe?

The most lasting impression of the 2002 Games in Salt Lake was the scandal involving the long-suspect judging of ice skating, when a deal between the French and Russian judges was exposed. The French judge was reprimanded and suspended, with promises of reform. A month later, Lithuanian skaters made accusations of skullduggery in the judging of pairs ice skating. There seems to be no end of controversy whenever subjective judging is involved.

The gigantism of the Olympics moved Marty Glickman, a longtime Olympic booster who was on the 1936 American sprint team, to conclude that "there's no point to the Games anymore except to sell products. I predict they will last for only a few more Olympics and die out." Glickman was probably wrong because as John Hoberman, a University of Texas professor, said, "The Olympic Games is one of the greatest marketing vehicles of all time."

One of the most uplifting and rewarding aspects of the Games is the Olympic Village site that houses all the athletes. At the Olympic Village at the Mexico City Games in 1968, Al Oerter, the great American discus thrower, told me that he had more in common with, say, a Czechoslovakian discus thrower than with an American sprinter on his own track squad. Athletes of all shapes and sizes from all over the world rub shoulders in the Olympic Village. Yet big-time millionaire basketball and tennis players often eschew the camaraderie of the Village for posh accommodations in hotels.

I used to think that the Olympics had been perverted only in the years I covered them or followed them closely. I came to know better after some correspondence about the 1936 Games in Berlin with Bud Greenspan, the Olympic film man. I first became an ardent adherent of the Olympics when I saw *Olympia,* the much-acclaimed, two-part documentary of the 1936 Games by Leni Reifenstahl, the celebrated German filmmaker.

I was about twenty when I saw *Olympia* as part of a film series at the Museum of Modern Art in New York. It is a remarkable film, capturing the pageantry of the Olympics and the skill and artistry of the athletes. Riefenstahl trained her cameras on Jesse Owens; this played no small part in glorifying his achievement of winning four gold medals. I was captivated by the film and saw it a few more times over the years.

When I became the TV sports critic at *Newsday,* I came to criticize Greenspan as an Olympic propagandist. His films glorified the Olympics, virtually ignoring negative developments, particularly steering clear to a great degree of the commercialism, the gigantism, and the drug scandals. I ridiculed Greenspan's view that he "deals 100 percent with the 95 percent of the Olympics that are positive, unlike the journalists and the networks that deal 100 percent with the five percent that is negative."

I cited the great work by Leni Riefenstahl to the extent that an exasperated Greenspan responded with a letter that jolted my entire approach to the Olympics. He wrote: "I share your feeling that Riefenstahl's film is an artistic triumph against which all other Olympic films must ultimately be measured. But Riefenstahl surely was not concerned with telling the story of the 1936 Olympics from a journalistic standpoint, as I believe your column implied. Had you been reviewing *Olympia* in 1948 when it was first shown in the United States, I would assume you might have addressed some of the following questions to her:

> Why did she ignore the fact that in January 1936, seven months before the Berlin Games, the AAU voted not to send a team to the Olympics that year? This decision was reversed only after Avery Brundage, whose anti-Semitism was notorious, made a quick trip to Berlin to receive assurances that all athletes would be treated equally.

Why did she fake the torch relay from Mt. Olympus so that only young blond German actors and actresses were seen carrying the Olympic flame?

Why did she ignore the feature stories in Nazi newspapers that the United States was "being aided by members of the Black Legion," along with reports that compared Jesse Owens' physical structure with that of an ape?

Why did she choose to disregard the announcement that Jewish citizens of Germany would be permitted to remove the Star of David from their clothes during the course of the Olympic Games, and that they were ordered to replace the insignia immediately after the closing ceremonies?

Why was the soundtrack of the film altered so as to disguise the boos and jeers that greeted the United States team when it did not dip the flag to Hitler during the opening ceremonies?

Why did she not mention that three token Jewish athletes were placed on the German team, when it was common knowledge that they had been selected precisely because they would not cause embarrassment by winning a medal?

Greenspan's letter was a revelation for me, but not in a way he may have intended. It only punctured the idealized view I had about earlier Olympics. It persuaded me that my early reverence for the Olympic Games film was misplaced. This episode underscored the need for truth, not illusion.

* * *

The worst event I ever covered was the 1972 Olympic Games in Munich, at which eleven Israeli athletes were murdered by Arab terrorists. The murders stand out as a permanent blot on what Germans had hoped would be "The Games of Joy."

On Tuesday, September 5, the terrorists scaled a fence into the Olympic Village, rushed the Israeli compound, killed two of the Israeli contingent of forty-three athletes and officials, and held nine hostages. They later escorted the hostages to the airport in a helicopter, where they hoped to move on to an airplane that would take them out of Munich. The ostensible Israeli policy, though, was never to negotiate with terrorists; we learned that they advised the German authorities not to allow the Arabs to leave. The plan was to intercept the Arabs on a plane filled with German security men, but the Germans were inept in their execution. The Arabs, sensing a trap, blew up the helicopter. Several died with the Israelis.

During the afternoon, stark television pictures showed the shadowy head of a terrorist on a balcony, darting in and out of a window in the building where the Palestinians were holding the hostages. I waited outside one of the athletes' gates with other reporters and some Israeli tourists. The strains of the song from the movie *Exodus* sounded from a portable radio. I winced at some of the racist remarks about Arabs shouted by Israelis. On German television there was the vignette of an Israeli TV man and a German announcer.

The Israeli said, "It is a real shock."

The German said, "It is a real shock for me, too."

The Israeli said, "But it is an Israeli who is dead."

A few days earlier, I had been in the Olympic Village and had a few brief conversations with Israeli athletes. I believe one of them was a wrestler later killed by the terrorists. The world reacted with horror to the event. So did I.

But I could not comprehend the actions of the Israeli government. I felt it should have allowed the Arabs to escape if it meant saving the Israeli lives. The Israeli authorities' claim that giving in to terrorists encouraged more terrorists seemed ridiculous. Terrorists are fanatics who cannot be dissuaded from their mission. I felt the Israelis could let the terrorists go, save their people, and attend to tracking down the terrorists afterward. That is precisely what happened. Some of those who escaped from Munich were captured by the Germans and later let go in exchange for a German hostage. They were then hunted down and killed by the Israelis. I was repelled by an Israeli policy that worked against their own people.

There were many cries to call off the Olympics. I had mixed feelings about this. On the one hand, games didn't seem very important in the wake of the tragedy. On the other hand, to call off the Olympics was to give the terrorists a final victory. I was not particularly happy that in this one instance, I was in agreement with American Olympics head Avery Brundage, who worshiped at the shrine of the Olympic Games *uber alles*. Yet even Brundage realized it was outrageous to allow competitions to continue at the very moment the Arabs were holding Israelis hostage in the Olympic Village only hundreds of yards from the arenas. He called off that Tuesday's evening events.

The Olympic heads decided the Games would go on after a memorial service to the Israelis. That service left a bad taste. It was more of a show-business tribute staged like a Hollywood Bowl spectacular than a solemn coming together. The grief-stricken Israelis were front and center, but more like extras in a cast of thousands. They straggled out of the stadium to search for a bus; they had to avoid being knocked over by attendants officiously marshaling limousines for the VIPs.

Brundage, who somebody once said, "looked like Oliver Cromwell's ideal of God," hit a low point. He showed barely a shred of concern for the Israelis. Brundage was more dismayed that people had dared interfere with his precious Olympic Games. He hurled himself at the microphone and, with Olympian gall, paired the struggle to keep Rhodesia out of the Games (a pre-Olympic controversy) with the murder of the Israelis. Ever one to inflame troubled situations, he babbled on with a *pronunciamento* dripping with hypocrisy. He said, "The Games must go on and we must continue our efforts to keep them clean, pure, and honest and try to extend the sportsmanship of the athletic field into other arenas."

He said this amid the petty wrangling and lack of sportsmanship that inevitably is a part of the Olympics. Athletes in several sports were disqualified for using drugs. Shooters did not deny an indictment that many of them used tranquilizers to steady their nerves. The Russian weightlifters were called home in disgrace because they suffered upsets. Judges were dismissed as incompetent or biased in a few sports. A Munich woman lodged a civil suit against the coach of the Japanese women's volleyball team because she saw him kick and punch his players during a five-hour training session. A North Korean gold medal shooter said he had won because he had heeded Premier Kim Il Sung's advice "to aim as though shooting at your enemies."

I did not stay for the final ceremonies, partly because of what a press release said was planned for the finale. It would include a farewell to Brundage, speaking the traditional words closing the Olympics, after which "as Mr. Brundage retires to the VIP stand, the words, 'Thank you, Mr. Brundage' will appear on the scoreboards and the Armed Forces band will play, 'For He's a Jolly Good Fellow.'"

The $650 billion "Games of Joy" had turned into one of the greatest sports debacles of all time. I wrote that the Olympic rings stood for Terrorism, Fanaticism, Hypocrisy, Incompetence, and Arrogance.

* * *

Swimmer Mark Spitz was the dominant American at Munich, winning a record seven gold medals. He did not thrill me. Handlers hovered around him, keeping him away from the press for fear he would say something stupid. He reminded me of Ken the Barbie doll. The press conference that had been scheduled for him after he won the seven gold medals took place in the midst of the Israeli hostage situation. As a Jew, it was a time for him to show a real face, to talk with some feeling about what was happening to the Israelis. When asked how aware his American teammates, only a few hundred yards from the terrorists, were of the situation, he said, "No comment." More than a few of us looked at him with some disgust. He was spirited out of the press conference.

Even before the Israeli tragedy, I was dismayed with the stupidity, boorishness, and downright sore-headedness of American losers. This started with the debacle of the American sprinters who did not show up in time for their trial heat race. Eddie Hart, Reynaud Robinson, and Robert Taylor won early heats in the 100-meter sprint and were scheduled to participate in the quarterfinals. Their coach, Stan Wright, was working off an inoperative early Olympics sprint schedule and got them to the track too late for Hart and Robinson to compete. It was just in time for Taylor's race, and he qualified for the final.

Everybody but the American track coaches and athletes seemed to know the correct time for the race. It had been printed in the *Track & Field News* two weeks earlier and in the *International Herald Tribune* and *Stars and Stripes* that were posted outside the track dormitory in the morning.

The American officials refused to admit they were at fault. They gave out this line of gobbledygook: "The USA track and field staff has conscientiously made every effort to obtain all information from the proper source—the Village information center. However, for some inexplicable reason, information pertaining to the second round of heats in the 100 meters was not received and disseminated to the coaching staff and an erroneous schedule was followed." And what pray tell could those "inexplicable reasons" be, *dummkopfs?*

The "erroneous schedule" was a year-and-a-half old. As liable as the coaches were, the athletes deserved little sympathy for not paying attention to the time for the most important race of their lives. A distraught Stan Wright said, "I am deeply grieved for these boys." He took the mistake to the grave with him. Hart said, "I don't blame anybody. . . . I'll be afraid to face my father."

Valeriy Borzov, the rapid Ukrainian, won the 100-meter event easily. The absence of Hart and Robinson tainted the victory, of course, but Borzov had the logical answer: "I beat the men who were there." It is the custom in track parlance to label the winner of the Olympic 100-meters "The Fastest Man in the World." The Americans wouldn't concede that to Borzov because of the freak absence of two top Americans.

The Americans had another crack at Borzov in the 200-meter race, which was not regarded as his best event. No matter. Borzov repeated his 100-meter efforts, winning all the heats easily and then beating the Americans in the final. He was surely "The Pluperfect Fastest Man in the World."

The Americans wouldn't admit that. Larry Black, who finished second, said the Americans in the event all were affected by the 100-meter incident and weren't at their best in the 200-meter. He said Borzov hadn't set world records in his finals and had looked back while winning those races. "What world-class runner would do that?" he bleated. He called Borzov a clown.

On hand was the legendary Jesse Owens, who had won both the 100- and 200-meters at Berlin in 1936. He had a different view of Borzov. "Sensational," he said. And which runner did Borzov remind him of? "Me," said Owens.

I was dismayed by a black-white thing at these Games. This was a far cry from the idealism of the Black Power protests at Mexico City four years earlier. American blacks at Munich rooted for Kenya's Kipchoge Keino over Jim Ryun, the white American in the 1,500 meters. There was some resentment by blacks against white heavyweight Duane Bobick because he was getting so much attention in the press—but it was the same attention that heavyweights like Floyd Patterson, Joe Frazier, and George Foreman, all black, had gotten in their time. And there was glee, as well, by some white track people when American black sprinters failed to win early events, inspiring petty talk that finally this would be a white Olympics.

It was also depressing that in the wake of the Israeli tragedy, few Americans showed up at the memorial ceremony in the Olympic Stadium, and only one black athlete, triple jumper Art Walker, was present.

* * *

In basketball, the United States suffered its first-ever Olympic defeat, falling to the Soviet Union, 51–50, amid game-ending chaos. The United States, which had dominated basketball since Professor James Naismith supposedly put up a couple of peach baskets in a gym in Springfield, Massachusetts, had won every previous gold medal in basketball. The loss snapped a sixty-two-game winning streak.

Though the highly favored U.S. team clearly was superior, it let the Soviets set a slow pace. The U.S.A. played badly, making only 19 of 57 shots. The Soviets led through most of the game. Late in the game, the Americans went to a full-court press. This befuddled the Soviets and the U.S. team finally closed the gap. The Americans took a 50–49 lead on two clutch foul shots by Doug Collins with only three seconds remaining.

Madness ensued. The Soviets were given three chances to throw the ball downcourt.

Immediately after Collins made his foul shots, a referee handed the ball to a Soviet player. He made a long, futile pass downcourt and time seemingly ran out. It turned out that the Soviet coach had asked for a timeout when Collins went to the line. That should have been given to the USSR after Collins made his first foul shot. But the referees did not hear the Soviet signal and let Collins shoot his second foul shot. Here, William Jones, the Secretary General of the International Basketball Federation, interceded. He came down on the court and ruled that the Soviets should have been given their time out. This negated the resumption of play after Collins's heroics.

A Soviet threw the ball in again. Another long pass downcourt was futile; time seemed to run out again. Nope. It turned out that the referees allowed play to resume too soon. They did not hear a timekeeper's horn, because the clock had not yet been set back to three seconds. So the second resumption of play and the second Soviet pass was negated.

Play resumed again, another chance for the Soviets amid excruciating feelings by Americans. This time the long pass was caught by Russian star Alexander Belov. Two Americans guarding him fell down. He turned and put in a lay-up, which gave the Soviets a 51–50 victory.

Pandemonium. Bedlam. Tears. Cries of Foul. Robbery. %$%#@*^%.

American coach Henry Iba stormed at the referees, at the timekeepers, at the officials. American coach Henry Iba contemplated taking his team off the floor. American coach Henry Iba had his watch pickpocketed.

There is little doubt the two officials, one from Hungary and the other from Brazil, lost control of the game. The Americans deserved to win. But basketball is an impossible game to officiate. Frailty by basketball officials is almost an integral part of the game. Just about everybody who has played the game knows that. The Americans became vulnerable to officials' incompetence when they allowed the game to remain so close.

The cold war between the U.S.A. and the Soviet Union was the dominant undercurrent of the Olympics at that time. American Olympians saw Communist conspiracy rather than the pitfalls of basketball officiating. They did not accept their misfortune with any grace. They wailed, they cried. And of course, they made an official protest of the game.

The press was barred from the American dressing room for an extended period. When allowed in, we were met with rage and tears. An American official said immediately that the U.S.A. would not accept the second-place silver medal. There have been many screw-ups and injustices by officials judging in the Olympics through the years, yet no individual or team had ever refused a medal. But the Americans did. And Doug Collins and Kenny

Davis put in their wills the stipulations that the silver medals should never be accepted for them.

The Americans' protest was rejected. This was seen as a Communist plot because three of the five judges on the appeal panel were from Communist countries. Cuba, Poland, and Hungary voted against the Americans, while Italy and Puerto Rico of the western bloc voted to uphold the protest.

An international official responded to the charge of a Communist plot by revealing that the Hungarian official was a man who hated the Russians. His family had been killed by the Russians and there had been such hostility between Hungary and the Soviet Union that they bloodied each other in an Olympic water polo game in 1956. And William Jones, the man who had turned back the clock on the Americans, was an Australian who had fought with the Poles against Russia in World War II and had no particular reason to favor the Soviets.

It was a travesty for sure, and the outrage of the American boys was understandable to a point. But there was no plot against the Americans. Among other things, the loss inspired the idiotic statement by U.S. Olympic Committee head Clifford Brock that the United States would suspend indefinitely any further participation in Olympic basketball.

Americans back home raged as well. But to no avail. If ever any group earned a gold medal for sore losing, it was the entire U.S. basketball contingent. The postscript to it all that infuriated the cold-war chauvinists was the final standings: Soviets 50 gold medals, U.S. 33—and a 226–191 Soviet advantage in the unofficial scoring of the overall medal count.

* * *

Before the Israeli tragedy, I was slated to write a long cover piece about the Olympics for the Sunday sports section of *Newsday*. I chose to write about the dreary atmosphere, the general disgust and malaise around the Olympics. To my dismay, one of the managing editors overseeing the sports operation ordered a piece about Mark Spitz. It didn't matter that I was the sports editor at the time. It was a case of editors in the office overruling a man on the scene who possessed the truest feel for the happenings. They went for the cliché approach of featuring the upbeat American hero, rather than the downer of gloom and doom that I was feeling.

I wrote the Spitz story; my atmosphere piece was truncated and relegated to the back of the sports section. I was disgusted.

Thanks to the ABC telecasts in the United States, the star of the 1972 Olympics was the petite Russian gymnast Olga Korbut. ABC, in addition to picking up German television's gymnastics feed, placed one of its own cameras near the balance beam exercises. American viewers saw close-up views of the charming, diminutive Ms. Korbut, and took her into their hearts. ABC knew it had a good thing in Korbut and milked her appearances. So much so that most people came to think that she won the overall gold medal. Actually, she won her gold medals in the balance beam and floor exercises. Her countrywoman, Lyudmila Tourischeva, who did not have the ABC cameras trained on her, won the overall gold medal.

Like most American reporters on the ground, I had little awareness of the impact gymnastics was having back home. Gymnastics? Who paid attention to gymnastics when track and field, swimming, boxing, and basketball had always been the heart of the Olympics?

This was the beginning of television determining the essence of the Olympics. Sports that appealed to television and women viewers have become dominant. In the drive for higher ratings on the tube, the Olympics have become what television has made of them. Gymnastics and figure skating have become the big-ticket items of Olympic telecasts.

Gymnastics flourishes, even though they are a form of child abuse for young women. Girls are taken from their families at a young age to train in distant cities under professional coaches. They are starved in training. One elite gymnast died in 1984 from complications of anorexia. Another discovered twenty-seven stress fractures in her spine from the pounding her still-growing body took every day. Another trained for three years with a fractured wrist, too fearful to take any time off from her Olympic quest. Young women figure skaters also become anorexic in response to coaches' instructions to slim down.

Events such as rhythmic gymnastics, synchronized swimming, and synchronized diving bear little resemblance to the Olympic motto of "Citius, Altius, Fortius"—swifter, higher, stronger. No matter. Women like to watch them, so they have TV appeal. Ice dancing is lovely to look at, but it is dancing, by golly, not a sport. So it is no surprise that the ballroom dancing people want a place on the Olympic stage. And why not? Can bridge and scrabble competitions be far behind? Tiddlywinks, anyone?

18

Perfect Games

Some events stand out in my memory for different reasons: the happenings were dramatic in themselves, or I had a special window on some aspect of them, or I found myself in unusual circumstances.

One of the greatest games ever pitched was the perfect game Don Larsen threw at the Brooklyn Dodgers for the Yankees in the fifth game of the 1956 World Series. That day, I sat in the auxiliary press box behind home plate in the mezzanine at Yankee Stadium. The tension grew as Larsen inched closer and closer to the shutout, the no-hitter, the perfect game. The Series was tied at 2–2 and the Dodgers were behind only 2–0 when they came to bat in the ninth. So, for all the drama surrounding Larsen, it was right and proper for the impish Dodgers publicity man, Irving Rudd, to stand up and shout from an aisle, "The hell with history, guys, let's get some runs."

Rudd, a publicity guy, a tub thumper of the old school, started out as a boxing guy. I loved him for his shout at Yankee Stadium that day, as well as for one particular remark. When somebody said, "Howard Cosell is his own worst enemy." Rudd said, "Not while I am alive."

* * *

During the waning days of the 1960 season, I covered the Pittsburgh Pirates on their way toward winning the pennant. As the Pirates' bus readied to leave for Candlestick Park in San Francisco one late afternoon, Roberto Clemente and Alvin McBean, a rookie, were late. When Clemente got on the bus, he explained to his impatient teammates that McBean, his roommate, hadn't been feeling well, but that he would be down in a few moments. After a while, many of the Pirates urged the bus driver to get started. Clemente asked them to wait. Finally, egged on by the players, the driver began to take off without McBean. Clemente, agitated, got off the bus cursing. McBean came down a few moments later and he and Clemente took a taxi to the ballpark. That night Clemente won the game for the Pirates, beating the Giants with a home run.

I liked Clemente. I liked talking to him or hearing him complain about things. There was an endearing eccentricity to him. I believe many reporters of the day were put off talking to him because he tended to be somewhat hyper, sometimes difficult to understand because of his Puerto Rican accent.

He was a hypochondriac. Manager Danny Murtaugh used to laugh when he heard that Clemente was complaining that he wasn't feeling well. "That means," Murtaugh said with a smile, "that he'll go three-for-four and make a terrific throw to nail somebody."

Clemente was underrated because he played in the shadow of Willie Mays and Henry Aaron. Clemente was a better hitter for average than Mays, though not his or Aaron's equal as a power hitter. He was a better fielder than Aaron. His death in a plane crash when flying food to needy people in the Caribbean gave him the belated recognition he deserved. He is as important to Latin culture as Jackie Robinson is to black culture.

Clemente's Pirates won the World Series that October. It was special for several reasons. The Yankees won the runaway games, by scores of 16–3, 10–0, and 12–0, while the Pirates won the close games, by 6–4, 3–2, 5–2 and the final game, 10–9. Hal Smith hit a three-run homer in the eighth to tie the final game at 7–7. The Pirates added two more to go ahead, 9–7. The Yankees scored two to tie at 9–9, and then Bill Mazeroski won the Series for the Pirates with a home run in the Pirate ninth.

In the midst of that series, I spent a remarkable night on the town. Dick Schaap, the renaissance media man of newspapers, magazines, and the airwaves, had struck up an acquaintanceship with comedian Lenny Bruce. He commandeered a group of us to see Bruce performing at a club outside Pittsburgh. The club was virtually empty for Bruce's gig, except for us and a guy named Kalish and his date. Bruce was brilliant, incisive, iconoclastic. He paradiddled his outrageous view of life, breaking down taboos about sex and patriotism, assaulting the hypocrisy within himself and within us. He played to us, using Kalish as a patsy, because Kalish was foolish enough to try to parry with him.

I went to see Bruce a few times after that at different theaters and clubs, hoping he would match that night outside Pittsburgh, but I was disappointed. He became obsessed with drugs and his fight against the police. He was a shell of himself in the end. I choose to remember his cackling laugh as he wowed us in that darkened near-empty nightclub outside Pittsburgh.

* * *

Texas Western's 72–65 victory over Kentucky in the NCAA basketball championship game on March 19, 1966, is regarded as a watershed game in college sports history because it marked the first time an all-black team played—and won—an NCAA final. At the time, I didn't even mention the all-black angle in my column, probably because I didn't want to make too much of it. I had shown an awareness of the race angle, however, in a column the previous night on the semifinal victory of Texas Western over Utah. I wrote:

All of the first seven [on Texas Western] are Negroes. That shouldn't be significant one way or another except that many people make it noteworthy with snickers about the racial makeup of the team.

In the press row for example, a reporter from Virginia noted at one point in the game that Texas Western had five Negroes on the court and that Utah had three. "I'll say one thing," this snotty observer noted, "whoever wins this game will be the dark-horse team tomorrow night [in the final]"

His neighbor, also a Virginian, said, "What do you mean?"

"It's eight to two on the court," the first noted.

"Eight to two?" the second repeated with puzzlement. Then he grasped the meaning. "Eight to two, oh."

The point here is that the second fellow was seeing the game for what it was: a battle of two teams. His neighbor was blinded by the color of skin. Perhaps there is a bigger point there. Who would have thought, say 10 years ago, that two schools—not City College or NYU or UCLA—but such outlanders as Texas Western and Utah would be involved in a game with such representation. Democracy, it's wonderful.

Oddly, the insignificant consolation game for third place stuck with me. In the closing seconds of the game between Utah and Duke, Utah had a chance to tie at the end, when one of its substitutes went to the foul line for a one-and-one attempt. At that point, Duke coach Vic Bubas, hoping to unnerve the foul shooter, called a timeout. Then after the timeout elapsed and the youth went back to the line, Bubas called *another* timeout.

Back then it was a new tactic to call successive timeouts. It was the first time Bubas tried it, and it was the first time I had seen it. It could be an effective psychological ploy because it gave the foul shooter more time to think.

It bothered me, though. It was only a consolation game, I thought. Was it necessary to try such a tactic in this game? I read in the Utah press guide that the youth on the line was a senior. He was a substitute, probably not accustomed to this kind of pressure. I fretted about the impact it might have on him if he missed the first shot as the final act of his college athletic career. I wondered if third place in the tournament was worth resorting to such psychological manipulation of a college kid.

The youth went to the foul line. He bounced the ball and shot. He missed. Duke won the game, 79–77.

In the midst of the winners' celebration, I looked across the floor at the dejected young man. Attention turned to the championship game, so there was no time to get to the Utah youth. Given space limitations in *Newsday* and the need to focus on the Texas Western upset of Kentucky, my thoughts about the Utah player did not get into the paper.

I understood that I could be accused of a sob-sister angle. The Duke coach operated within the rules, after all, and we hold up athletics as an endeavor that can teach kids to react to pressure. You could argue the experience might toughen the kid to cope with the vicissitudes he would face in later life.

But my doubts lingered. Given the cruel instincts that underscore so much of big-time athletics, I could see unthinking people branding the kid a "loser" to the point of it affecting his psyche beyond his athletic career. Through the years, I wondered about the young man and what happened to him. Some twenty years later I was moved to make phone calls to find out about him and write a follow-up column.

By then most of the people at Utah were not old enough to remember the occurrence. I then got lucky. I was put in contact with the coach, Jack Gardner, who had retired to California. "The boy's name was Leonard Black," Gardner told me. "He was a nervous type. What Bubas did was relatively new at the time. He was wise, I think, to do this because it put pressure on the boy."

Gardner thought my objections to Bubas's strategy were "naive." He said, "Competition is tough. One of the lessons a person learns in competition is how to be cool under pressure. That is one of the realities of life and the game of basketball."

He gave me Black's number in a Utah town called Bountiful. Black was cheerful.

"Oh, I remember it all right," he said. "I was excited at the time. It was only a consolation game, but winning is winning. During the first timeout I recall the coach told me to go through with my shot without interruption.

During the second timeout he told me, 'Don't worry, I know you'll make it.' And then he turned to the other guys and said, 'If Black misses, I want you to do this . . .'"

He felt awful at the time, he said, but he was heartened by the reaction from people. "I got letters from one of the local editors and from people all over the state that I still have in a scrapbook. They told me I had a good season and that it shouldn't bother me. My fraternity brothers were encouraging and even made a joking thing of it. A few years later I saw Coach Gardner try the same tactic. Even now I meet people who say, 'Aren't you the Leonard Black who missed that shot?' It's always said in a nice vein. I often wonder now if anybody would recall anything about it if I had made the shot."

There was no lasting trauma. A business major, Black went on to a successful career, first in the Air Force, then as an instructor of economics at the Air Force Academy. He owned real estate and gold mining operations in Utah. He was married, with three boys, and coached and played recreational basketball. He even had a videotape of the end of that game and showed it to his boys.

"My sister was at the game and she was angry about it," he recalled. "She says she's always hated Dick Butkus for what he did to me." Butkus, Bubas, you get the picture.

Black said he could understand the Duke coach's tactic. On the other hand, he said, if he were a coach in recreation or high school ball, he didn't think he would employ it.

How about as a college coach? "I don't know."

I also called Bubas, then commissioner of the Sun Belt Conference. "It was the idea of the assistant coach," he said. "I didn't think about it in terms of what effect it might have on the boy. There is always some kind of pressure to make a shot in basketball. That is what competition is all about. You are the first person ever to raise this point with me, but I am not offended by your asking it."

Would he use this tactic if he were coaching a high school team? "I don't know."

* * *

A college football game of no particular importance to anybody but the schools—and me—was the Alcorn A&M–Prairie View game outside Houston on November 12, 1966. I was in Houston to cover the Muhammad Ali–Cleveland Williams heavyweight championship fight. Because *Newsday* didn't publish on Sunday, I didn't have to write a piece on Saturday. I forsook the fight camps for an afternoon and drove over to the Prairie View campus specifically to see for the first time a game between two primarily black schools.

I was received cordially and given press box credentials on a campus laid out on prairie land outside Houston. I seemed to be the only white person walking to the stadium, and I did not see any white people in the stands. It felt unusual, but people were friendly. In many ways it was like being at any college football game.

Alcorn A&M, a Mississippi school, won a high-scoring game. Two aspects of the afternoon stood out. The spirited bands from each school played on and on. They played almost constantly, even while play was in progress. I enjoyed this because I was as interested in the scene as I was in the game.

The setting provided an apt backdrop for a cross-country race run in conjunction with the football game. Just before the opening kickoff, the cross-country field lined up on the track in front of the stands and a starter's gun sent the runners out from the stadium out into the flatlands surrounding the college. From the high vantage point in the press box, we could see the thin-clad harriers disappearing into the distance. Then, at just about halftime, the leaders appeared at the horizon and sprinted into the stadium, making one lap around the track to the finish, to encouraging cheers. Memorable.

* * *

I recall the 1967 Kentucky Derby as much for Martin Luther King Jr. as the race itself. Martin Luther King Jr.? Yes.

Three days before the Derby, King spoke at a protest at the St. James African Methodist Episcopalian Church in the West End section of Louisville. Local activists were threatening to interfere with the running of the Derby after aldermen voted down an open-housing proposal. The previous day, five black boys had run out on the track during a race. King's appearance at the rally was an inspiration to the activists, whom he called, "the creative minority who carry on the fight." His magnificent voice ringing out in support of the protestors sent tingles down my spine.

The church resounded with civil rights anthems adapted to the Derby situation. I heard, "Go tell Bill Hartack . . . we shall not be moved," a reference to the leading jockey, and "No more Derbies . . . no more Derbies over me."

King provided some valuable historical perspective in response to the charge that the majority of black people in Louisville did not support this protest. He said, "There is real apathy in any ethnic minority. We didn't have 10 percent of the people in Selma or in Birmingham, either, but the majority was eager to accept the benefits. The history of the civil rights movement has shown that Negroes don't make any strides in civil rights without insistent civil protest."

There was talk of one novel stunt at Churchill Downs on Derby Day: a "bet-in" tactic of lining up in mobs at the mutual windows to delay betting. King told the press, "Any demonstrations taken against the Derby would be up to the leaders of this community. I wouldn't tell if I knew."

With King counseling moderation, there was no protest at the Derby. Proud Clarion, ridden by Bobby Ussery, won the race on Saturday at a whopping return of $62.20. The favored Damascus ran one of his bad races.

King left after the protest and before the race. At the church, I asked him a particular question. And Martin Luther King Jr.—clergyman, militant, Nobel Peace Prize winner, great disturber of the public conscience—added a tiny footnote to history. He answered, "No, I have never been to a racetrack."

* * *

A game storied in college football annals was, of course, the epic battle of undefeated Harvard vs. undefeated Yale at Harvard in 1968. Harvard, behind 29–13, scored 16 points in the last 42 seconds and gained a 29–29 tie. It led to the immortal headline in the *Crimson,* Harvard's student newspaper: "Harvard Beats Yale, 29–29."

I included the game as a chapter in my book, *Ten Moments That Shook the Sports World,* a chronicle of outstanding events that I covered. It was interesting to me that when I did radio interviews plugging the book, many interviewers in college football bastions like Alabama and Nebraska wondered why I would include an Ivy League game as one of the epics. I would try to enlighten them about the richness of Ivy League football and a time when it dominated college football.

The 1968 game ranks with the all-time thrillers because Harvard came back from these deficits: 22–0 in the first quarter; 29–13 with only three-and-a-half minutes remaining in the game; and 29–21 with only 42 seconds left. It scored a tying touchdown from the eight-yard line on the last play, then completed a two-point conversion on a pass.

Harvard surged behind its second-string quarterback, Frank Chiampi, a 5-foot, 11-inch junior from Everett, Massachusetts. He was a balding, dumpy-looking figure. He came in late in the first half when Yale led 22–0. Yale's star runner Calvin Hill would later marry a Wellesley roommate of Hillary Clinton and they would produce basketball standout Grant

Hill. Yale's star quarterback, Brian Dowling, was the inspiration for Gary Trudeau's character B.D. in his *Doonesbury* strip. And an All-Ivy guard on the Harvard squad was Tommy Lee Jones, who would go on to Hollywood stardom. His roommate was Al Gore. Jones seconded the nomination of Gore for president at the 2000 Democratic Convention.

The legendary columnist Red Smith left the press box in the middle of the fourth quarter, before the Harvard heroics began. At the time, Smith, whose *Herald Tribune* had folded in 1966, was writing a syndicated column seen in New York only in the *Women's Wear Daily* and the *Long Island Press*. He had yet to join the *New York Times*. During that miraculous comeback, Smith was probably driving on the Merritt Parkway.

19

Fighters and Writers

Super Bowls are big and gaudy, and the Olympics are so gigantic that one can hardly think of them as a single event. But major heavyweight championship fights—robust, vulgar, flush with scoundrels, abounding in plots and schemes—topped them all for sheer drama, tension, and raucousness.

I have been a press-pass witness to some of these spectacles: among others, Floyd Patterson knocking out Archie Moore in Chicago; Patterson being knocked out by Ingemar Johansson in Yankee Stadium, then coming back to knock out Johansson in Miami; the then–Cassius Clay beating Sonny Liston in a tumultuous scene in Miami Beach; then, as Muhammad Ali, taking out Liston in a controversial first-round knockout in Lewiston, Maine; Ali losing to Joe Frazier at Madison Square Garden after his return from suspension.

The first Patterson-Liston fight in Chicago stands out because the scene surrounding the fight was so gaudy, so bawdy, so rich. Boxing came together with literature, politics, and farce in late September 1962 for the bout at Comiskey Park. The scene at the Sheraton Chicago fight headquarters throbbed all week with gabbing, boozing, lying, and carousing.

There were reporters, boxing beat writers, and columnists from all over the country. There were boxing luminaries: former champions Rocky Marciano, Barney Ross, Archie Moore, Ezzard Charles, Joe Louis, and even Jim Braddock, whom Louis knocked out to win the heavyweight title in 1937.

Playboy publisher Hugh Hefner was rarely seen by anybody and, as far as anybody knew, wasn't at the fight. But he was a presence nonetheless. He put up some of the celebrities at the famed Playboy mansion on the near north side.

And there were the writers: Norman Mailer, James Baldwin, Budd Schulberg, and a man named Gerald Kersh, a novelist I had never heard of before and haven't heard of since. He was there to write a piece for *Playboy*. Schulberg wrote for the *New York Post,* Baldwin for a magazine called *Nugget,* and most notably, as it turned out, Mailer for *Esquire*.

The writers were a rousing presence at press headquarters. Some of the buzzards among the reporters resented them; I, like many of the other young newspaper guys, including Larry Merchant and Pete Hamill, was delighted and a bit awed by their presence. We were happy to be regarded as equals and engaged in banter with them. Mailer was pleased that we took his opinions about boxing seriously. He seemed more brilliant in conversation than in print. Aphorisms dripped from his lips.

A dynamic aspect of the week was a debate scheduled for Saturday night between Mailer and William F. Buckley on the subject, "The American Right Wing." Amid all the fight talk, there was much revelry about the debate. One wag put up a "bulletin" from Las Vegas. It read, "Battling Bill Buckley (Brown Shirt) is a 2½-1 favorite over Norman (Ex-Boy Wonder) Mailer in the Great Debate."

I, naturally, rooted for Mailer, the liberal, over Buckley, billed as the conservative. To my mind, though, Buckley was a reactionary. I worried for Mailer, as did his friends.

Schulberg said, "Sometimes Norman is brilliant; sometimes he's very erratic. He could get hurt badly." I recalled a debate between Buckley and Murray Kempton about ten years earlier on the upper west side of Manhattan in which Buckley, it pains me to say, wiped the podium with Kempton. He did it with cheap debaters' tricks, even insinuating at one point that Kempton was something less than manly. This infuriated me a lot more than it did Kempton, because they seemed to maintain a friendship through the years.

I was so caught up in it, I had a stronger rooting interest in Mailer beating Buckley than in Patterson beating Liston. And Patterson seemed like a better bet than Mailer.

Some 3,600 people, right- and left-wingers galore, showed up for the debate at the Medinah Temple. Mailer later said, "We grossed over $8,000."

As I saw it at the time:

Buckley came out talking first. In cutting tones he started to work on Mailer's weaknesses, turning against him much of what Mailer had written. It was a workmanlike, if undistinguished job, and whispers of overconfidence began to stir through the Buckley sections. Mailer came out with a stunning ploy, walking past his opponent to the lectern with an ape-like, arms-swinging gait that brought laughter from friend and foe. He responded to Buckley in kind. In the direct question and answer session, Buckley was unable to cope with Mailer's strategy of talking about international tactics in boxing lingo.

Essentially, Mailer won the debate because he took a radical rather than a liberal position. Buckley was used to beating up on liberals, as he had with Kempton many years earlier. Mailer was just as critical as Buckley was of liberals and that won the day for him. He outpointed Buckley in the eyes of any fair-minded observer.

But not in the *New York Times*. The multitalented Gay Talese chose on this occasion to play it safe. He called the debate a draw. This infuriated Mailer. The moment he read Talese's piece, he went on a drunken toot. He was stewed during the fight and, most embarrassingly, the morning afterward.

I met Buckley at a postdebate party at fight headquarters. I like to think I was being quite the shrewd politico when I told Buckley I had great hopes for him as a future liberal. When he looked puzzled, I explained that many conservatives had been liberals early in their career and then backslid to become conservative or reactionary. Considering that Buckley had been a conservative as a youth, I predicted he had a great career as a liberal when he grew older. He responded to all that with a puzzled look.

I thought of the encounter in the ensuing years. How wrong I was. The conservatives gained as the liberals waned. And Buckley was one of the leaders riding the conservative tide. A sap was I.

* * *

The fight itself was a shocker. Liston knocked out Patterson at 2:06 of the first round. At the time, it seemed Liston didn't hit Patterson often, but that the punches he landed were so devastating they demolished Patterson. Subsequent events changed my thinking. Liston later hit Ali with better shots than he unloaded on Patterson, but without terrible effect. Patterson, sad to say, had a glass jaw. He had been knocked down by the less-than-potent Ingemar Johansson and he folded again in the first round against Liston six months later.

A first-round knockout brings the usual cries of fix. This time, there was hardly any basis to it; there were no funny odds changes or late betting moves in Las Vegas.

Patterson did not face the press. We learned later that he waited until everybody had left, donned a disguise, and snuck back to New York. Humiliation overcame him. The poor guy had such low self-esteem you couldn't help but feel his pain.

That evening's escapades didn't end with the fight. After we transmitted pieces to our newspapers, we heard about a party at the Playboy mansion. We promptly joined a horde of celebrities and hangers-on at the mansion. Visions of orgies danced in our heads.

The mansion was extraordinary. People ate and danced almost until dawn in a large living room above a swimming pool and a grotto. Bathing suits were available to anybody who wanted them, but I don't think the water tempted any of the fight crowd. It was enough to look through a trap door in the living room down into the pool at curvaceous beauties. If there were any in the buff, I didn't see them. Nor did I see anything but some smooching on the couches in the near darkness. It was a source of satisfaction to a few of us that Joe DiMaggio, considered something of a ladies' man, wasn't hitting any sexual home runs.

The strangest one of all was the host, pajama man Hefner; he never came out from behind the closed door to his bedroom off the living room. "He does that all the time," one of his many servants said.

We munched on food, hung around, and gabbed just as we would have back at fight press headquarters, smirking a little about having crashed the party. The sun was just coming up when I walked out onto the sidewalk with Budd Schulberg. Not much of a drinker, I was more sure-footed than he was. We had become acquainted during the week. He seemed embarrassed and stuttered a bit before asking if I could lend him $10 for cab fare. I gave him the money happily.

A few years later, I saw Schulberg at a fight weigh-in, when I had long forgotten about the loan. He came over and handed me the $10, with apologies.

* * *

Mailer was a guest at the Playboy mansion. In what he later would call "a mind half-gorged with juice," he conceived an outrageous idea that it was up to him to defend Patterson's performance and to personally beat the drums for a return bout between the two. He told people, "I am the only man in this country who can build the second Patterson-Liston fight into a $2,000,000 gate instead of a $200,000 dog."

Mailer crashed Liston's postfight press conference that morning. He took a chair on the stage before Liston arrived and wouldn't leave. Reporters shouted, "Throw the bum out." He sat there with a goofy smile as the gendarmes picked him up in the chair and carried him out.

Mailer returned and, incredibly, imposed himself on the scene again and carried on a dialogue with Liston. The fighter called him a bum. Mailer told him that Patterson could beat him. The unlettered goon started to patronize the famous man of letters. Liston said he was beginning to like Mailer, and he shook his hand.

The rest of us were aghast. I cringed at the spectacle Mailer was making of himself. Finally, mercifully, he was dragged off the stage. Last seen he was flashing a loopy smile. If he wasn't embarrassed by it all, I and others were embarrassed for him. I thought, "How in the world could the man ever show his face in public again?"

At the time, I was a beat reporter who covered events and wrote a column once a week. The Mailer farce didn't lend itself to sports-page coverage and I wasn't scheduled to write a column for at least a few days. I should have asked to write an extra column about the scene, but I was not confident enough as a columnist at that point to venture into writing about what was an adjunct to the fight. A mistake.

Mailer did not sink into obscurity even for a short time. To my amazement, he actually wrote a piece for *Esquire* entitled "10,000 Words a Minute," in which he described the entire week. As stewed to the gills as he was, he recalled just about everything that happened. He described better than anybody else what a fool he had made of himself.

Mailer set it all in mystical trappings. He wrote, "I began in the plot-ridden romantic dungeons of my mind, all subterranean rhythms stirred by the beat of this party, to see myself as some sort of center about which all that had been lost must now rally. It was not simple egomania nor simple drunkenness, it was not even simple insanity: it was a kind of metaphorical leap across a gap."

There was more of this. Anytime that Norman—or anybody—starts talking about existentialism my eyes glaze over, yet he was chillingly accurate in re-creating the scene with Liston.

Mailer's drunken buffoonery came back to haunt him. He was on probation at the time for knifing his wife, and when authorities read Red Smith's column about the incident, they tightened the screws on him. The way Mailer handled this was to write that some people "kept taking little bites at me. First it was a red jaybird named Mr. Smith and then A.J. Liebling, a loverly owl." Liebling, whose book *The Sweet Science* is a bible of boxing, didn't take kindly to Mailer, either and, most deservedly, excoriated him in one of his eloquent New Yorker pieces.

About thirteen years later, I interviewed Mailer for the *Newsday* magazine in connection with the publication of his book, *The Fight,* an account of

Muhammad Ali's victory over George Foreman in Zaire. I told him, "I was amazed by the essay you did in *Esquire* on your public exhibition making a fool of yourself at the Liston-Patterson fight, and then writing about it." His response: "Well, I didn't do it on purpose. You know how it happened. I was half out of my head."

Back in the press room in Chicago, I had been bold enough to exclaim that his novels were not as significant as his journalism and that he should stick to journalism. He dismissed me then, but I repeated the comment in this interview. He said, "I think it's a legitimate criticism. You see, I don't take journalism as seriously as a novel for one reason. Which is why I've always found journalism easy. And I have terrible trouble with a novel's story."

I don't know if anybody ever showed more chutzpah than the alcohol-sotted Mailer who confronted Liston in that public forum. And I am still in awe of the man for the way he addressed his own behavior in the *Esquire* piece.

Chicago, as it turned out, was just a preview for the antiwar march on the Pentagon five years later. Mailer drank himself bourbon-silly, and two nights before the march, he laced the air with a scatological tirade at a fund-raising affair for antiwar protestors. He then put himself front-and-center in his brilliant third-person account of the march in *Armies of the Night,* which won him a Pulitzer Prize.

The man was a congenital exhibitionist. He was incorrigible, in certain ways a charlatan and a mountebank. I could abhor him. I don't. I was in awe of him and his nonfiction. He may be the most memorable individual I have ever met.

20

The Sporting Hemingway

Norman Mailer frequently referred to Ernest Hemingway as the greatest American writer of the twentieth century. Over the years, Hemingway popped up in some of my "Out Of Left Field" columns. There were stories of his run-in with a photographer and reminiscences of him by baseball players. In one column, the son of one of those ballplayers reacted to my earlier column about his father and Hemingway.

My first piece on Hemingway dovetailed with the firing of Dick Sisler as manager of the Cincinnati Reds at the end of the 1965 season. I grew interested in Sisler when I read the following passage in Hemingway's novel *The Old Man and the Sea*.

> "Tell me about the baseball," the boy asked him.
>
> "In the American League it is the Yankees, as I said," the old man said happily.
>
> "They lost today," the boy told him.
>
> "That means nothing. The great DiMaggio is himself again."
>
> "They have other men on the team."
>
> "Naturally, but he makes the difference. In the other league, between Brooklyn and Philadelphia, I must take Brooklyn. But then I think of Dick Sisler and those great drives in the old park."
>
> "There was nothing ever like them. He hits the longest ball I have ever seen."
>
> "Do you remember when he used to come to the Terrace? I wanted to take him fishing but I was too timid to ask him. Then I asked you to ask him and you were too timid."

"I know. It was a great mistake. He might have gone with us. Then we would have that for all our lives."

"I would like to take the great DiMaggio fishing," the old man said. "They say his father was a fisherman. Maybe he was as poor as we are and would understand."

"The great Sisler's father was never poor and he, the father, was playing in the big leagues when he was my age."

My remembrance of *The Old Man and the Sea* had centered on the old man's poignant comment about "the great DiMaggio." I was surprised by the reference to Dick Sisler. I hadn't remembered Sisler because he was never as significant a ballplayer as DiMaggio. So I wondered about the validity of Hemingway pairing Sisler with DiMaggio. We are always ready to trap the great ones in factual goofs, aren't we?

The novel was published in 1952. Sisler hit a dramatic pennant-winning home run for the Phillies over the Dodgers on the final day of the 1950 season. Hemingway was writing the novel at about that time. I wondered if he reached for Sisler's name because it was prominent at that moment.

If he did, I felt Hemingway wasn't being good and true to the old man. Surely the old man, who obviously knew his baseball, wouldn't have talked of Sisler and DiMaggio in the same breath, would he?

Not long after reading the novel, I broached Sisler about his presence in the book. He knew about it. And he revealed that he had played ball in Cuba during the winter of 1945–1946.

Sisler was a mild, soft-spoken man, a bit of a stutterer, the son of Hall of Famer George Sisler. Dick played eight years in the big leagues, with a career batting average of .276 with two teams, the St. Louis Cardinals and the Philadelphia Phillies. Though a power hitter, he never hit more than thirteen home runs in a season. The pennant-winning home run on the last day of the 1950 season was his shining moment.

"You probably don't know it," he said, "but I was a national hero in Cuba at that time. I led the league in home runs. One day I hit three homers in a game. The next day I hit a tremendous home run over the back wall at Tropical Stadium. The stadium was named after Tropical Beer, which owned the stadium. Before the war the owner of the beer company had offered $1,000 to anybody who hit a ball over that wall. Now that I had done it, the *fanaticos* felt that I should get the money."

"The owner said no, that the offer was off. But he gave me a solid gold watch. I still have it somewhere at home. It says that I, Dick Sisler, hit the only ball ever hit out of the park at that spot. It must have gone about 450 feet."

"You might think it immodest of me to say so," Sisler said, "but people idolized me down there. They waited around outside my apartment. When I walked out, they followed me. Store owners came out and begged me to pose with them so they could put the picture in their store windows. Actually, I was just a kid, then. I hadn't even come to the big leagues, yet. The Cards sent me there to learn to play first base."

Sisler said, "Tropical Stadium must have been the 'old park' the old man mentioned. It was torn down." He did not know what "The Terrace" was. I found out later that it was the bar in a fishing village outside Havana where Hemingway hung out.

Sisler said, "I think Hemingway sent me a copy or had somebody send me a copy of the book. Yes, I am quite pleased to be mentioned by him. It's an honor. He was a great writer."

Sisler said he met Hemingway that winter. "We were at a bar with some people and we were introduced. He was quite a guy. He'd like to trade punches with people, one-for-one. You hit him and he hit you. The fellow could drink, you know."

Sisler never went fishing with Hemingway.

I wrote in my column that "Sisler *did* hit 'those great drives in the old park.' He was indeed 'the great Sisler.' And Hemingway, the old literary slugger, has been good and true to the character of the old man."

* * *

A year later, I picked up on Sisler's comment about Hemingway liking to trade punches with people. I approached another former player, Billy Herman, because A. E. Hotchner mentioned him in his book, *Papa Hemingway*. In that book, Hemingway is quoted saying: "You can't ask for better shoots than when the Dodgers are training and we have matchups with Hugh Casey, Billy Herman, Augie Galan, Curt Davis and some of the others who are all crack shots."

Herman was managing the Boston Red Sox when I talked to him. Recalling the days with Hemingway, he said, "This was during the spring of 1942 when the Dodgers were training in Havana. Hemingway was a baseball fan. He used to come out to the park every day to watch us train. We got friendly and he invited us out to a gun club to shoot with him. They had live pigeons and clay pigeons."

"He was a good shot, better than any of us. We shot with him every day for a week or 10 days until we had this safari to his home. We had dinner and we sat around and talked. He wanted to talk baseball. We were more interested in hunting. Larry French was an avid game hunter. He was interested in seeing pictures of a lion hunt—there were about a thousand of them—that Hemingway had been on."

"He was a very interesting man, one of the most interesting men I ever talked to. The war was on in Burma then. He had covered that whole area as a newspaper man once, and he told me what would happen. He said how far the Japanese would go and where they would be stopped. He was pretty much right as I recall."

Hemingway had recently written *For Whom the Bell Tolls*. Herman said, "He gave us each an autographed copy. I guess I've lost it in all the moving around I've done since then. His wife made a nice meal. After dinner we talked about the war, and we drank and sat around. She went to bed. Hemingway was a pretty good drinker. He could hold more liquor than the average person. He was a good guy but he became a tough guy—real mean—when he was drunk. He wanted to fight. Anybody. He was a pretty good-sized man, about six-feet, two, 235 pounds."

"Hugh Casey was the closest to his build so he challenged Casey to a fight. Casey wasn't very anxious to fight, but Hemingway insisted. So they put on the gloves. He went right after Casey. He tried to hit him anywhere. He tried to kick him in the groin, he was a dirty fighter. Finally, Casey knocked him into the bookcase. It was knocked over with a loud crash onto the terrazzo. It woke up his wife and she came downstairs. He told her, 'Oh, we are just playing.'"

"After that," Herman said, "it seemed like a good time to end the fight. We were getting a little bit uneasy and wanted to get out of there. He insisted we stay. He tried to persuade Casey to stay overnight. He said, 'We're drunk now, but tomorrow we'll be sober, and we can fight again. We can have a duel, any weapons you want.'"

"Well, we got the hell out of there after that. He was the nicest guy in the world sober, but when he was drunk he was like an animal. We didn't go back after that, but we kept seeing him at the ball park."

In the Hotchner book, Hemingway says about writer John O'Hara: "When I first read him, it looked like he could hit: *Appointment in Samarra*. Then, instead of swinging away, for no reason he started beating out bunts. He was fast and he had a pretty good ear but he had the terrible inferiority complex of the half-lace-curtain Irish and he never learned that it doesn't matter a damn where you come from socially; it is where you go. So he kept beating out bunts instead of trying to learn to hit, and I lost interest."

Hemingway, of course, was driven to keep knocking them over the fence. When he couldn't write anymore, he committed suicide with a gun.

"That's the funny thing," Herman said. "Casey also shot himself."

Many years later, I got an e-mail from an interested party who had read the Hemingway piece. It was from Hugh Casey's son, Mike. He noted that a "spectator to the ball-playing in Cuba was a young unknown by the name of Fidel Castro. He loved baseball and watched the practices when he could."

Hemingway came up in connection with a longtime Associated Press photographer I knew. Harry Harris, a rough-hewn, amiable man, was modest about the fact that he once had a run-in with Hemingway. It took some coaxing to get him to relate the incident.

"The Hemingway thing wasn't anything," he said. "I was a pool photographer with the First Army in World War II. We got into a hotel outside Paris, Don Whitehead, Ernie Pyle, William S. White and others. When we went to check in, the clerk told us we'd have to get clearance from Ernest Hemingway. That made us angry.

"We took a look around and saw the stables, which were nice, so we decided to sleep there. Along comes Hemingway. Bruce Grant of the *Chicago Tribune,* an older guy who was a little drunk, tells Hemingway, 'You chickenshit general, who are you to take over the hotel?'

"Hemingway knocked Grant down. I got sore at that and grabbed him by the shirt and threw a punch at him. I said, 'You're so tough taking on an old man . . . ' But they grabbed us right away."

* * *

My interest in Hemingway inspired two trips to academic conferences. I confess that I went not because of a passion for the writer as much for the location of the conferences. One was in Paris, the second in Cuba.

I joined a group of thirty-five scholars, writers, and Hemingway fans for an eight-day trip to Cuba's second International Hemingway Conference in Havana in August 1997. Hemingway is associated with Paris, Spain, Key West, Oak Park (the Chicago suburb that was his birthplace), and Ketchum, Idaho (where he committed suicide). He lived in Cuba longer than in any other place as an adult. He is a one-man cottage industry of tourism because they are constantly holding conferences or social schmoozes to honor the old tough guy at these way stations.

Aspects of an author's work emerge from papers and discussions at academic conferences. The papers may be significant. Or they may be obtuse, obscure, or just plain silly.

Wolfgang Rudat, a crew-cut, roly-poly, roguish professor from the University of Houston, provided a stir early in Havana by larding explicit sexual references onto a paper about *For Whom the Bell Tolls.* He examined whether Maria was pregnant. He could hardly suppress a giggle as he talked about

Hemingway's explanation of courage in terms of female eggs, *huevos,* and men's testicles, *cojones.* He talked about Hemingway's "antiandrocentric satire," which he chose to call "antiphallocentric satire."

"Wolfgang likes to shock people," a colleague said.

Bill Deibler, a Latin American specialist for the *Pittsburgh Post-Gazette,* delivered a paper about Hemingway's early newspaper work, illustrating that the writer was perfecting his fictional techniques at the expense of accurate reportage.

The group visited Finca Vigia (Lookout Farm), Hemingway's fifteen-acre estate that stands atop a hill twelve miles southeast of Havana, above the dirt-poor town of San Francisco de Paula. The house is a rambling one-story, nine-room, whitewashed Spanish colonial structure with high ceilings, tile floors, and a sixty-foot-long living room. Adjoining the house is a three-story tower that provides a good view of downtown Havana.

A path from the house leads to a large swimming pool. On the former tennis court is the fishing boat *Pilar,* on which Hemingway allegedly hunted for German submarines during World War II. The house is now a Hemingway museum.

There were some nine thousand books on shelves in almost every room. The books reflected Hemingway's eclectic interests in politics, literature, the outdoors, entertainment, biography, and sports. The titles included *Who Struck John,* a collection of Jimmy Cannon columns, as well as *The New Yorker Album of Sports and Games.*

One evening, we rode a bus downtown to the Floridita Restaurant, a Hemingway hangout celebrated for its daiquiris. Tourists gazed at photos of Hemingway with Spencer Tracy and Gary Cooper, along with a bust of Hemingway above the barstool on which he allegedly drank.

Another excursion took us to the nearby village of Cojimar, where Hemingway fished. It was the locale for the Pulitzer Prize–winning *The Old Man and the Sea.* There were more photos of Hemingway, this time in La Terrazza, a restaurant with windows that opened onto an inlet off the bay. The photos included one of Hemingway with Fidel Castro at a fishing tournament, the only time they met.

* * *

When I attended a Hemingway conference in Paris in 1994, I heard a paper read by a young Swiss teacher about the short story, "My Old Man." I was interested to hear the presentation because the story was about horse racing. I had read it and seen it as in the movie, *Under My Skin,* with John Garfield. "My Old Man" was about an old jockey and his son, who adored him.

Listening to the teacher rambling on in academese, I didn't know what in the world he was talking about. He made few if any references to horse racing. I was puzzled enough to stay and ask him what motivated his interest in this story.

I started out by being a phony and telling him I enjoyed his paper. Then I asked, hesitantly, "Have you ever been to a racetrack?" He said he had never been to a track; I believe he said there were no racetracks in Switzerland.

"So why did you find this story of interest?"

He said, "I was interested in Hemingway's use of the color yellow in the story."

The color yellow? Hemingway referred to "a great big yellow horse" and "his yellow coat shining in the sun." That is a reason for a paper?

I thanked the young professor. I told him he might find it of interest to go to a racetrack and said I would be happy to take him out to Belmont Park if he ever came to New York. A few days later, I happened to bump into him again at the conference. He said, "You know, I have been thinking about what you told me. I think it would be helpful for me to go to a racetrack. I will try to go."

The invitation is still open.

21

Naked Romances

In my column, I sometimes told some fanciful yarns, sourcing them to people who had told me their tales—and were now dead. My favorite was the story behind the story of Babe Ruth's fabled called shot in the 1932 World Series.

In the fifth inning of the third game, Ruth made some motion toward Cubs pitcher Charlie Root or to the outfield before hitting a humongous home run in Wrigley Field. It has been a source of great debate whether Ruth was pointing to where he would hit the ball or telling the world that he had one strike left.

I wrote a column claiming I had the true inside story about the incident. I said it was told to me by a good citizen of Chicago before he died a few years ago. I "revealed" that this man told me Ruth was an avid bird watcher. He said Ruth attended a bird watchers' meeting in Chicago the evening of the game in which he hit that homer. He told the bird watchers that he had pointed toward the outfield stands because he had spotted a rare bird, a boat-tailed grackle.

It was, of course, a tongue-in-cheek effort. A month or so later, though, somebody passed on to me a piece by a Tennessee columnist that treated my exclusive seriously. He said, "Stan Isaacs has come up with a new explanation of the Ruth incident" and proceeded to quote my bird watcher explanation. Such is history on the fly.

* * *

Many years later, when I was long past *Newsday,* I wrote a piece for an internet site about an unbelievable romance involving baseball slugger Jimmie Foxx and actress Judy Holliday. This time, I was almost the fool.

Foxx played for twenty seasons, starring with the Philadelphia Athletics and Boston Red Sox. He tacked on two seasons during World War II with the Chicago Cubs and Philadelphia Phillies. He won three Most Valuable Player Awards, hit 534 home runs (second only to Babe Ruth at the time), and was voted into the Hall of Fame as one of the outstanding sluggers of all time. In his later days he managed a woman's baseball team and was the model for the bilious baseball manager portrayed hilariously by Tom Hanks in the movie *A League of Their Own*.

Foxx had grown up on the eastern shore of Maryland. He was an unsophisticated farm boy and a generous spender who liked to take a drink. By contrast, Holliday was not only an acclaimed comedienne, but also a hip, politically liberal woman with a reported IQ of 172.

I was surprised in 1996 when a friend sent me a clip from the *Philadelphia Weekly*, an alternative newspaper, about a little-known romance between the two. It seemed unbelievable that Holliday would have an affair with this brawny, unlettered ballplayer. I checked with friends in Philly. They told me the *Weekly* was a respectable newspaper with a good reputation, so it was surprising to me that more wasn't made of this beyond Philadelphia.

A writer named Tom McGrath wrote about a cache of love letters from 1945 that he discovered between the pair after both had died. In 1945 Foxx was thirty-seven, ending his career with the lowly Phillies during the wartime shortage of bona fide ballplayers. Holliday was twenty-four, drawing rave notices for a supporting role in a Broadway play *Kiss Them For Me*.

The five-page *Philadelphia Weekly* spread included fourteen letters. McGrath said they had come to him from the wife of a friend who had just died. The friend, whose name was Eddie, had been a clubhouse boy for the Phillies in 1945. He had told McGrath he had letters between Foxx and Doris Day.

McGrath wrote that after Eddie died, his wife dropped off the box of letters. They turned out to be correspondence between Foxx and Holliday, not Doris Day ("Eddie was never much for getting names straight," McGrath wrote.)

The letters traced the growing relationship between the unlikely pair. They met in early April 1945 at a bar in New York when Foxx was in town with the Phillies. Foxx noted that the Phillies would be back in New York soon to play the Dodgers and wrote, "How about if me and Merv take you and Bev out for a night on the town? We'll show you a real major league time."

In a letter to Foxx dated May 2, Holliday wrote, "Boy, you sure know how to make a girl's heart race, don't you? Your package arrived this morning, and when I opened it and saw what it was I nearly dropped dead on the floor."

It was a fur coat. McGrath noted that it indicated the pair "must have really hit it off." Later, Holliday wrote, "I did nothing but think of you—your warm eyes, your big safe arms, your easy laugh."

Foxx told her about his failing skills. "Is there a sadder sight on the baseball field than me these days?" He said it wasn't always like this. "Back when I was playing for the A's I could have hit a ball across the Grand Canyon using only one arm and with my eyes closed." He included a P.S. "I've been thinking about you being Jewish and all, and I've decided it doesn't bother me."

McGrath's story continued: "Starting in late May the letters between the two became more frequent and intimate. Indeed, the letters—which Holliday sent from New York and Foxx sent from St. Louis, Chicago, Philadelphia and Cincinnati—are a remarkable account of two people in love."

McGrath explained that one of Holliday's references to a "Lenny" who had an altercation with Foxx at a party probably was Leonard Bernstein, the acclaimed musician, a friend of Holliday's. She told Foxx not to be bothered by what Bernstein said. "You're twice the man he is, no matter how far you went in school or how many books you've read or how many times you've been to a symphony."

Foxx wrote about his plan to ask to pitch a game, because he had been a pretty good pitcher before A's manager Connie Mack converted him to an everyday player. That surprised me, so I looked up Foxx's record in the *Baseball Encyclopedia*. Sure enough, he was credited with one victory as a pitcher in 1945.

In the end, Foxx realized it was time for him to hang it up as a ballplayer and retire to a farm. He wrote, "Why don't me and you buy a little farm down in Maryland or somewhere and just be together there?"

This scared Holliday. She broke off the relationship. She wrote on September 20, "I love you right out of my mind, but I'm afraid right now that I can't have you. . . . I have this feeling that something big is about to happen to me, something that couldn't happen in Maryland or Philadelphia or wherever you and I would be together."

She opened in *Born Yesterday* on Broadway in February. Holliday was a sensation. She gave a knockout, comic performance. Her career took off after that.

A note in the *Weekly* said that McGrath, a Philadelphia writer, was talking to William Morrow about publishing the complete collection of the Foxx-Holliday letters in book form.

I decided to call McGrath to find out how he was faring in getting the letters published. I was unable to reach him. After a few unsuccessful phone calls, I was prepared to relate the Foxx-Holliday saga in the internet column

I was writing for ESPN. Just about then, he finally returned my call. After my greeting, McGrath interrupted before I could ask a question.

He said, "I have to tell you right off that *none of this is true*."

I was stunned. "None of it true? A hoax?"

With some embarrassment, McGrath said, "We thought the whole thing was so improbable, we assumed people wouldn't take it seriously." I told McGrath I had covered baseball for more than three decades and it completely fooled me and other veteran baseball observers.

McGrath, thirty-two, a freelance writer, said the idea originated with *Weekly* editor Tim Whitaker in connection with the 1996 All-Star Game in Philadelphia. "Foxx was a local guy, a great player who had been pretty much forgotten. We thought this was a good way to get his name back in circulation, to honor him. We were sitting around brainstorming, looking at movie stars and Holliday seemed like a good fit with him because it seemed so illogical for them to be a pair."

The piece was cleverly done. The unsuspecting buy the little errors, such as a reference to Harry Truman as vice president when he was already president. Foxx misspells the Bellevue Hotel in Philadelphia. There is a reference to teammate Vince DiMaggio, Joe's brother, which I wondered about. But the *Baseball Encyclopedia* corroborates that Vince indeed had been on the Phillies in 1945.

There was a flap that summer about the questionable ethics of some journalists, particularly Joe Klein, who hid behind "Anonymous" in his novel about Washington. McGrath acknowledged he was culpable. "I would have liked it to have been packaged better with a wink. That would have given people more of a hint that it was all a joke."

I asked the editor, Tim Whitaker, if the *Weekly* had revealed the hoax. It had not. He said, "People who figured out it was a hoax were just delighted that Jimmie Foxx was given some attention."

I then wrote my column, setting up the surprise finish and my amazement at finding out it was a hoax. I sent it to my friend Stan Hochman, the *Philadelphia News* veteran. He passed it on to the editors at that paper.

That started something. Stu Bykofsky, the city-side columnist of the *News* who had frequently been criticized by the *Weekly*, seized on the opportunity to get back at Whitaker. He lambasted the *Weekly* for unethical journalism. *City Paper*, a rival weekly, took up the cry that this kind of tomfoolery was reinforcing the public's lack of trust in newspapers. *City Paper* even called up some libel lawyers to see if descendants of the Holliday and Foxx families could sue. It reached Holliday's son, Jonathan Oppenheim, and, based on what they told him, he called the hoax "an outrage."

I thought it was a funny stunt that hurt nobody. Hoaxes are almost as old as newspapers. Mark Twain pulled off numerous hoaxes. Edgar Allen Poe fooled people with his long story in the *New York Sun* about a hot air balloon that crossed the Atlantic in three days. Hoaxes stir the juices.

This brings me to *Naked Came the Stranger*.

* * *

It all started with Mike McGrady and *Valley of the Dolls*. McGrady was a talented feature columnist for *Newsday*. A redoubtable guy, he respected writers and writing. It offended him that Jacqueline Susanne's novel, *Valley of the Dolls,* which he regarded as trashy soft-core pornography, made the bestseller lists. He thought anybody could do as well and cooked up an ingenious scheme to outdo Susanne's book. He named it *Naked Came the Stranger* because he believed the word "naked" had a salaciously salable ring to it, particularly paired with the word, "came."

He concocted a plot outline and passed it around to many *Newsday* staffers, asking each to contribute a chapter. He invented a couple, radio hosts Billy and Gillian Blake. They were patterned after Tex and Jinx Falkenberg, two well-known Long Islanders who presided over a talk show. Gillian finds out that her mate has been cheating on her. She decides to get even by having affairs with all the neighbors in their Long Island development.

McGrady asked staffers to write chapters reflecting their own expertise. So boxing reporter Bob Waters wrote about her seducing a boxer. Crime reporter Bob Greene had her in bed with a mob boss. Education reporter Marty Buskin paired her with a teacher. All in all, twenty-four people contributed. Some had Gillian as a ravishing redhead, others a sultry blonde; it took some editing by McGrady and feature writer Harvey Aronson to give Gillian some uniformity.

That was only the beginning of McGrady's low genius. He got his attractive sister-in-law to pose as the author, Penelope Ashe, and take the manuscript around to publishers. She hit paydirt with Lyle Stuart, a rogue who frequently published books no other publisher would take. Some were of questionable interest or taste; others were muckraking books that deserved attention. Stuart liked the scheme and agreed to publish *Naked* without even reading it.

It was a wise decision. Stuart earned his inordinately high 50 percent cut of the proceeds by paying for a daily promotional campaign in the *New York Times*. Some of the authors posed as the lovers who had affairs with Gillian. The book jacket featured a provocative, rear-view naked photo of a kneeling model. One reviewer improved our vocabulary by calling it a "callipygian" pose.

The book got a few lukewarm reviews and some poor ones. But it promised enough sleaze to sell twenty thousand copies. When it was revealed that Penelope Ash was a hoax, a front woman for the twenty-four rogues of *Newsday*, the book moved onto the *New York Times* best seller list. It remained there for four months.

The book lacked any redeeming qualities. It wasn't even particularly dirty by the standards of the day and certainly not by what has since passed for literature. The only incident that gave readers value for their filthy minds was John Cummings's ice cube maneuver. He had Gillian pressing an ice cube to her partner's prostate at the moment of climax. His partners in sin heaped praise on Cummings, while speculating whether he was writing from personal experience.

I wrote about a New York Mets catcher named Joe Miracle. I attributed a particular skill to him. I gave him an unerring eye on pop flies. If he went back from home plate for a pop foul, it invariably would come down in play and he would catch the ball. If he did not go back on a pop foul, it was because he knew it was uncatchable—it would fall in the stands out of reach. He never miscalculated. The fans adored Joe Miracle on foul pops. This was one of the few attractions for the hapless Mets of that period.

We had a swimming pool at what I liked to call our "baronial estate" in Roslyn Heights. To jazz up Gillian's pursuit of the ballplayer, I had them both naked in Miracle's pool. Disaster befalls Miracle there. Despite Gillian's stimulation, he is unable to sustain an erection in the pool to consummate the union. Gillian is disgusted. He is shattered. The failure of his manhood is so traumatic that it affects his play on the field. In the very next game, an opposing batter lifts a foul behind home plate. Miracle takes a look and doesn't move. But the ball falls well onto the field. Miracle magic is no more. It affects not only his fielding but his hitting. He becomes a shell of his former self.

I typed the manuscript on our patio adjoining our less-than-Olympic-sized pool. Such was my expectation of the caper that I typed it without carbon paper. It took me about two hours. I sent my epic to McGrady. A few months later, when McGrady was putting the chapters together, he couldn't locate the Joe Miracle chapter. I did not have a duplicate. It became the famous Lost Chapter. I believed this was his way of telling me it wasn't good enough, but he insisted that wasn't so.

Not each of the twenty-four contributions made the finished manuscript. McGrady combined some, rejected others. But he was such a classy gent that when the book came out and the royalties came in, McGrady included as equal partners everybody who had submitted chapters, no matter how much or little their efforts fitted into the final product. He was a class guy.

At just about the time the book came out, the Mets, who had been doormats earlier, won the World Series. I now argued facetiously to McGrady that had he not lost the Joe Miracle chapter, the Mets success would have ensured even more sales for the book and that I should have been awarded two shares. He chuckled.

There was much levity when the book was published, more so when we appeared on radio and television shows and at book signings. There was joy when it made the bestseller lists—and elation when we got royalties. I think each of us netted about $5,400. In 2003 Stuart reissued the book and a few more pennies in royalties tumbled our way.

There was talk of a *Naked Came the Stranger* movie with a legitimate producer. That fell through. It eventually was made into a movie, an xxx-rated production that created a stir in the pornographic world, because this was the first hard-core porn movie made from a bestselling, so-called legitimate literary work. Put the emphasis on so-called.

There actually was a gala first night at the palace of porn, the World Theater on West 49th Street in Manhattan. Spotlights scanned the sky and fans applauded the actors and actresses who starred in the movie. The authors quietly sidled into the theater. The highlight of the evening came during an interminably long fellatio scene when one of the literary lions in the audience shouted, "Author, author!"

* * *

In another literary pursuit, I once played baseball with Jack Kerouac, the Beat Generation writer who became a cult figure. Well, it wasn't real baseball, but rather a baseball card game devised by Kerouac. I had read that Kerouac was living in Northport on Long Island and that he had made up such a baseball game. I called him. We made a date one afternoon in February 1961 to meet at his home, where he lived with his mother.

As I wrote in the column, "The snow was a few feet deep, but the cry of the hot dog vendor and the crack of the warm-up pitch against the catcher's mitt sounded inside writer Jack Kerouac's house in Northport recently . . ."

Kerouac made up a set of cards that included various baseball actions—strike, ball, single, double, groundout, fly out, and the like—which simulated real baseball action. He said he had used it in some of his short stories.

The game took wing, I thought, with Kerouac's invention of player personalities out of his own imagination, based loosely on some actual figures.

There was El Negro of the St. Louis Whites, the leading home run hitter. ("He's a big Negro from Latin America," Kerouac said.) Wino Love of the Detroit Reds was the league's leading hitter. ("He's called Wino because he drinks.") Big Bill Lewis is everybody's favorite. ("I patterned him after Babe Ruth; one day I had him come to bat chewing on a frankfurter.") Pic Jackson, he said, "likes to read the Sunday supplements so his name, 'Pic,' is short for Pictorial Review."

We played all afternoon. I managed the Pittsburgh Browns against Kerouac's Chicago Blues. His mother occasionally stopped by to scold him about making a mess. We sipped Petri wine, and I was a bit woozy by the end. I came away with a 9–2 victory for the Browns. I ended the column saying, "It was a good game."

Kerouac had been a star prep school football player in Lawrence, Massachusetts. He was recruited to Columbia University by coach Lou Little. Kerouac broke his leg as a freshman and never played for Columbia. He felt Little lost all interest in him then, so he did not have fond feelings for the coach. When Kerouac's *On The Road* was on the bestseller list, I ran into Little in the Yankee Stadium press box and mentioned to him that I had been with Kerouac. Little said, "Kerouac, yes, he was a good prospect before he got hurt. What is he doing now?"

* * *

"Out of Left Field" was an apt name for my column because I frequently went off on tangents beyond the playing arena. I did an entire column listing all the personalities with the initials J.D. (Jack Dempsey, Joe DiMaggio, John Doe) and invited readers to come up with a weightier entry. (The J.B.s of Jim Brown, John Brown, Joe Blow were a strong challenger).

When Truman Capote threw a fabulous party inviting most of the glitterati, I was not invited, so I put together an entire column of people I would invite to *my* party. Jack Mann said that probably no other sports editor in the country would allow me the freedom I had. That was probably true, but it was these offbeat columns that were most popular with readers.

"Muted Cries from the Bullpen" was a series of short first-person sketches in which I assumed the identity of various athletes to capture their essence as I saw it. On April 28, 1961, I limned these, among others:

Stan Musial:
When I was going well
I could see the stitches
On the ball

But I couldn't
Read the letters.

Tony Galento:
Joe Louis was a bum
If I coulda kicked
And bitten
And thumbed
I woulda moidered him.
They wouldn't let me.

"Lieberman's Leap" was an annual honor that I bestowed upon a person who best followed in the tradition exemplified by Tony Lieberman, a tennis player. Always a careful reader of the papers, I learned one day that Lieberman had lost to Sidney Schwartz in a tennis match in South Orange, New Jersey, under peculiar circumstances. On match point, Lieberman hit a shot that looked like a winner. He bounded over the net, prepared to shake hands with his opponent. Except that Schwartz somehow returned a winning shot. Schwartz won the point and went on to win the match.

I reached the players by phone. Lieberman, a young man from Philadelphia, was embarrassed. Schwartz of Long Beach couldn't stop chuckling about it. He was happy to provide details. The "Lieberman's Leap" award was born. I gave it every year to anybody who had enriched the Lieberman tradition by messing up gloriously.

One winner was an English soccer player who chased a ball that had gone out of bounds and bounced into a stream. He got into a canoe to chase it down; meanwhile, the game resumed without him and his team lost. There were many Liebermans, but none topped the original.

22

Mea Culpas

When I started working at *Newsday* in 1954, I covered high school sports, bowling tournaments, Jones Beach softball, and summer-league basketball. Boy, did we cover summer-league basketball. We had more of those recreation basketball box scores in the summer than we did during the regular high school season. It moved me to write an anonymous letter to the sports section. Editors pay more attention to readers' complaints than to the wisdom of staffers. The letter accomplished its mission; we cut back on summer-league basketball.

I started covering major league baseball when *Newsday* dipped its toe in big-time coverage. Then, when Jack Mann took over as sports editor, I moved onto a major sports beat, beginning to travel out of town to cover spring training and road trips. I moved to a column, first once a week, then two and three times a week, and later five times a week. I'm not being immodest, I believe, when I say I was one of the popular features in the paper, though far behind Ann Landers and the robust advertising pages. Only the Manhattan telephone book had more heft than *Newsday* on Thursdays, when the paper carried grocery-coupon ads.

When Bill Moyers took over as publisher, I was offered a column in the op-ed pages. I started "Stan Isaacs' Long Island," a general feature column. Then the call came to go back to sports. The department had fallen into disarray when Dick Clemente quit in disgust owing to interference from the top editors. Leadership felt I would be the best person to take over the department.

I warned that I didn't have executive ability and that it would probably be a Marx Brothers regime. Bingo. My first day as sports editor, we couldn't get into the department. Charlie Clark, the man who usually came in early and started the operation, was off that day; nobody else had the key. It seemed like hours before we located a security man to open up the sports department.

An early incident persuaded me the job wasn't for me. I felt that one of the things I could bring to the job was an imaginative flair. I hoped to put out a unique section, in which readers could not quite predict all of our stories. We did that to some extent. And then came Richard Nixon's 1972 trip to China.

This was not a sports story. But I was fascinated by the photo of President Nixon that ran on the front pages of most newspapers. It showed Nixon standing in front of the Great Wall, while a few Chinese leaders were explaining some of the wall's history to him. A devilish thought came to me. I checked with the art department and ordered a cartoon that showed Nixon at the wall, with the leaders looking at a sign in Chinese, and one official explaining to Nixon, "The sign says, 'No handball playing allowed.'"

I thought this was hot stuff, a neat takeoff on the "no handball playing allowed" signs we were accustomed to seeing on walls in New York. My glow of triumph was short-lived. I was notified immediately that we didn't run cartoons or illustrations in the paper unless they accompanied a particular story. We didn't have a Nixon-at-the-wall story in the sports section, so the cartoon was out of place.

I knew then that my tenure as sports editor wasn't going to be a jolly good time. After a year or so of dealing with administrative duties and editors' restrictions and some staffers who had a low opinion of the way I ran things, I asked to be relieved of my exalted status as sports editor. I went back to writing a feature column.

I wrote a column that was a mixture of politics, entertainment, sports, human interest, and oddments. All in all, I thought it was good. I must have been in the minority, because readers would heap some lukewarm praise on me, then say they missed "Out of Left Field." The editors probably thought so, too, because they eventually nudged me back to the sports department.

One city-side column I wrote has lingered with me because I came to regard it as dishonest. It was a column about the 1976 memorial service for Paul Robeson, the great actor-singer-athlete and left-wing activist, the most controversial black man of his time.

The service took place at Mother AME Zion church on West 137th Street in Harlem. Anticipating parking and traffic problems around the church, I parked about ten blocks south of the church off Lenox Avenue and walked up. As mourners hurried through the rain, the haunting words of Robeson singing "Ballad for Americans" rang out from church loudspeakers onto the street. "Paul Robeson," I wrote, "had come home."

Robeson's brother was the pastor at the church from 1936 to 1963. Bishop J. Clinton Hoggard said, "Many times Paul came here to worship and to sing because he was always welcome here. Paul sang within these walls, 'Freedom, freedom, freedom over me, and before I'll be a slave, I'll be buried in my grave and go home to my Lord and be free.' "

As the clergyman's words resounded, it seemed that Robeson himself was saying the words. Robeson was far ahead of his time. His admirers and detractors would have agreed about that, at least. His statements about injustices in the 1930s and 1940s became commonplace by the time of his death. He was pretty much out in front by himself at a time when dissent was equated with Communism, and he was vilified.

At the World Peace Congress in 1949, Robeson said, "It is unthinkable that American Negroes will go to war on behalf of those who have oppressed us for generations against a country [the Soviet Union] which in one generation has raised our people to the full dignity of mankind." He said later that his statement had been taken "slightly out of context." Still, the comment was in keeping with his admiration for the Soviet Union.

Robeson's remarks so agitated a nation aflame with anti-Communism that no less a figure than Jackie Robinson was trotted out before a congressional committee to attest to the loyalty of black Americans. Robinson, while acknowledging respect for Robeson, affirmed the allegiance of black people to the United States. He later came to regret his appearance and echoed militant beliefs about racial injustice that were in the Robeson tradition.

One eulogist at the memorial ceremony, Samuel Rosen, said he always thought of Robeson as "Big Paul." Robeson, known as "Robeson of Rutgers," was an All-American football player, a four-sport man. In any historical roll call of American black athletic titans, the list would start with Jack Johnson and continue with Robeson, Jesse Owens, Joe Louis, Jackie Robinson, Bill Russell, Jim Brown, Muhammad Ali, Michael Jordan, and LeBron James.

For a long time, Robeson was not voted into the College Football Hall of Fame. During the cold war years, some sports publications even deleted his name from the early Walter Camp All-American teams. For a long time, the Hall of Fame hardheads kept Robeson out, claiming that "a man must have proved his worth as a citizen carrying the ideals forward into his relations with the community and his fellow man." And where was the College Football Hall of Fame housed? At Robeson's own Rutgers.

Some years after his death, Robeson was voted into the Hall. Jim Brown, also inducted at the time, said what an honor it was for him to be admitted the same year as Robeson.

At the end of the funeral service, as the coffin draped in red carnations was carried out into the pelting rain, the streets filled with the mournful strains of Robeson singing "Deep River" over a loudspeaker. Unforgettable. I walked over to Lenox Avenue and headed south toward my car. Two older white women who had been at the service walked slightly ahead of me. As they walked, young black men in their twenties heckled them from the shadows, using words like "white trash." They did not harm them, but they were menacing. The women ignored them and scurried along to a subway stop.

I went to my car. I agonized for the women because I knew they were the kind of stout hearts who had long fought for the rights of black people. For all I knew, they might have been at the Peekskill concert in 1949 that featured Robeson, at which local ruffians beat up left-wingers in attendance. (I was working at the *Compass* at the time, and some of the bloodied victims came down to our office to report what had happened.)

I have regretted that Robeson column because of how I handled it. I wrote about the service and the touching and inspiring moments. But I did not mention the galoots in the doorway menacing the women. I thought it would have taken away from the service, and at that point I was reluctant to insert any anti-black aspects. That was dishonest. My liberalism betrayed me. I should have written about the irony of the service and the indignities suffered by those women. I did not.

* * *

The 1968 Olympics in Mexico City are best known for the celebrated black power salute that was part of the protests by American runners. Tommie Smith and John Carlos ran one-three in the 200-meter race. In the victory ceremonies they raised black-gloved fists and kept their heads bowed during the playing of the "Star-Spangled Banner" as a protest against racism in the United States. There was a furor about this from American officials. They ordered the runners home and demanded their medals.

I respected Tommie Smith because I believed idealism motivated his actions. I had some doubts about Carlos. I felt he was a publicity seeker who liked the attention that came from being a loudmouth. When I first met him months earlier at San Jose State, I conveyed that I was sympathetic to the concerns of black athletes. Still, Carlos told me, "If you don't write what I like, I'll cut you, man." I knew this was just bluster, but his comments served to alienate people needlessly. Smith's comments were more thoughtful.

I had remembered my pieces from the time as somewhat critical of the young men. Not so. In the main, I was supportive. I wrote: "The sprinters also wore no shoes. When somebody complained about their lack of shoes, a British reporter said, 'Well,' Ibsen said, 'you don't wear your Sunday trousers when you go off to fight for truth and freedom.'"

I noted somewhat of a three-way split among American blacks. There were the militants; those who went along with the protestors for the excitement; and those who thought the Olympics were not the place for such a protest.

I quoted Harold Connolly, the thirty-seven-year-old high school teacher and veteran hammer thrower, a much-respected white Olympian. He said, "I think what they did was great. They are not downgrading America. They are speaking up for the dignity of the black man, and that's part of what the Olympics is about, the dignity of the human race, isn't it?"

His wife, a discus thrower, the former Olga Fikotova, a Czech he had met at the 1956 Olympics and later married, singled out a comment by the Russian track coach, Gabril Korobkov. He said, "The Americans have too much freedom; they're allowed to get away with too much." Ms. Connolly said, "Ah, but that is the beauty of America, that we have that freedom."

My feelings about Carlos came through in citing a British reporter who "was taken aback by the angry pose of the blacks. 'I can understand one man making his noble protest,' he said, 'but this has too much flavor of a putsch. I look at these fellows and I think of Camus' remark, 'Nothing worthwhile is ever achieved through hate.' "

I ended the piece about the protest with this: "In the eyes of Carlos and Smith black dignity is more important than the Olympic Games and running races. They came here partly to win gold medals, but mainly to carry the torch, to propagandize, if you will, for a passion that is at the heart of what shapes this nation today. They are not very couth; they have little grace; and they know not nearly as much as they think they do about what is involved in all of this. But the Englishman's Ibsen line keeps coming back. And didn't Teddy Roosevelt once call Thomas Paine 'a filthy little atheist'?"

I was glad to learn that in this case, what I wrote was *not* on the wrong side of history.

* * *

I *did* come up a bit short another time, when I interviewed Marv Albert, the peripatetic sports broadcaster. Albert lived in Sands Point on Long Island, not far from me. I was a guest at his house a few times, sometimes to interview him, once to play tennis on his court. On this occasion I wrote a column about him because illness forced him to take a day off from working a Knicks game. The hook that tickled me was that his wife Benita, a rabid Knicks fan, went to the game with their daughter, even though her husband was not there.

I watched the game on television with Marv and duly noted some of his comments. I kidded him about his wife choosing to go to the game rather than stay with him. He accepted the jibes good-naturedly enough, heaping some of his own sarcasm on Benita. I did not pick up that Albert's digs at his wife were more than light-hearted humor. He already was on the way out of his marriage. He left Benita a little while later. His life then exploded into a sex scandal and sensational court case.

It was obvious from my questioning of Marv, which included an emphasis on the closeness of the Albert family, about the direction of the column. In view of our long relationship, he should have taken me into his confidence to steer me off a column on the Close Family Alberts. He didn't. He later apologized. I lost respect for him for misleading me, but I also kicked myself for not picking up the signposts that all was not well with the Alberts.

* * *

I have never been a scoopmeister. Too often an exclusive consists of a story that tells what is about to happen anyway. As Russell Baker wrote in his memoir *The Good Times,* "I have never been much interested in getting 'inside information' and scoops. Such information was important to a newspaper, but it wasn't what I did well." I have always admired writers who can explain the whys and wherefores of a happening rather than a breathless revelation of what is in the works.

This is all a way of saying how I may have missed a minor scoop.

At the end of the 1959 season, the Los Angeles Dodgers were battling the Milwaukee Braves and San Francisco Giants for the pennant. I was in Chicago for the Giants' finale, a series with the Cubs. The Giants faded because their pitching staff fell apart. Manager Bill Rigney said he would choose his pitcher for the season's final game by rolling a ball down the middle of the clubhouse and "whoever picked it up would start the game."

After the game, I was planning to hustle up to Milwaukee on a short train ride to cover the nighttime finale between the Dodgers and Braves. It meant I was writing about two games in different cities—a neat, if not overly taxing, stunt. If anybody asked me about it, though, I acted as if I deserved a medal of honor.

On the way out of Wrigley Field after the game, I spotted the Cubs' manager, Bob Scheffing. He was an amiable guy. I had enjoyed being with him over the years and had spent some time with him in that final series. I thought about hailing him and chatting. Though I am a fairly gregarious guy, I often am reluctant to engage in small talk when I don't have a specific reason for talking to an athlete. I decided against calling out to him.

A few days later, I read that Scheffing was through as Cubs manager. I might have found that out by chatting with him and had my minor scoop. Nobody's perfect.

Another example of my fallibility came when I was a judge for the Eclipse Awards, sponsored by the Thoroughbred Racing Association. I was one of a panel of three judges to choose the best feature story on racing. We chose a piece by reporter Stephanie Diaz about Braulio Baeza, the one-time great jockey who was now down on his luck. The young woman described how Baeza had gone from glory as a jockey to an unsuccessful career as a trainer to the position of valet in the jockey quarters at the New York racetracks. A valet is, in effect, a manservant to jockeys, taking care of their gear.

Diaz described Baeza handing out clean towels and polishing the boots of jockeys. It was a poignant story. I liked it; so did the other judges.

When Diaz was awarded the prize, some keen reporters objected. A lovely story for sure, they acknowledged, but it was not true. People quoted in the story denied they had talked to the reporter. Baeza worked in the clerk of scales department, which meant that he made sure jockeys carried the proper weight for handicapping. But he did not service them, as the story suggested.

I was sorry to have been hoodwinked this way, but in retrospect, I didn't see how I, as a judge, would have been able to know the truth in this instance. The story passed the copy desk of the *Riverside Press-Enterprise* in California and there was no stink about it until the prizes were announced. The woman, it turned out, had some previous dalliances with journalistic fiction. I have not been selected as a judge of racing journalism since. I quite understand that.

Another embarrassing goof—of sorts—also involved horse racing, and this time an actual horse. The horse was Worlsigold, a terrible name. Nobody is more permitted to call it a terrible name than I am, because I am the bloke who named her.

I was a member of the LSI Gold horse syndicate of small bettors. I invested $2,000 and joined a partnership of thirteen people who had shares in a horse named Bullpen Carr that cost $70,000. He won his first race, paying $31. For me, on that day, he was the noblest beast of them all. He came rushing out of the pack with a glorious late run and passed the leaders just before the finish line. I had a few bucks bet on him, as did some friends I had invited to join us. It was a thrill to pose for a photo in the winners' circle with all the syndicate members. We looked like a cast of thousands.

The noble Bullpen Carr won only one more race; it was all downhill from there. He wound up at the Finger Lakes racetrack, home of the tired, the poor, the huddled, broken-down horses. Bad legs were his undoing. He eventually was claimed from LSI Gold. I hate to think about what happened to him in the end.

I had thought I could write a magazine piece, or maybe even a book, on the experience of owning a horse. The story went downhill owing to disaffection among the syndicate people and the trainer. This robbed the story of the feel-good human-interest angle that it needed. I dropped the project. Because I had written about the LSI Gold syndicate for *Newsday,* I was given a share in another horse. I think the syndicate head still had hopes I would write a book about my experiences.

It also may have been because I named Worlsigold. Fascinated as I am with horses' names, I accepted the offer to name LSI Gold's young horses. I didn't have any inspiration for this filly from the names of the sire and dam, so I decided, what the hell, I'll get LSI Gold into the name of the horse. Hence WorLSIGOLD. I was sure somebody would come up with something better, but nobody did. So it was Worlsigold.

Worlsigold turned out to be as uninspired as her name. She lost her first few races, running worse, it seemed, each time. I became completely disenchanted with her when I spent an afternoon accompanying trainer Mitch Friedman on race day. She ran dead last. After that I didn't bother to check with the LSI Gold office to know when she was running. She won her very next race and paid $131. None of the people at LSI Gold or the people at the barn or any of the owners bet on her that time.

She probably has joined Bullpen Carr at the great racetrack in the sky.

* * *

Enough of my foibles. I now slyly turn to what I call "My Three Greatest Picks."

Most predictions by sports experts are pretty poor. Or to be more precise, downright lousy. I'd love to be a bookmaker taking bets on the predictions in print of most of my colleagues. A bookie would have made a small fortune booking bets off me from my picks.

But I had my moments.

First, there was the first Floyd Patterson–Ingemar Johansson fight on June 26, 1959. Patterson was a huge favorite against the relatively unknown Johansson, though the Swede was undefeated in more than twenty fights. I went up to the Catskills to watch Johansson train. The most striking part of his training camp was the presence of his fiancée, the gorgeous Birgitte Nielsson. She was the stereotype of a blue-eyed, buxom Swedish blonde come to life. And she was charming. They obviously were breaking all the boxing taboos about fighters living monastic lives, refraining from sex before a bout.

Watching Johansson spar, I was impressed. I enjoyed the talk about his *toonder and lightening* punching power. I couldn't quite explain it, but I had a feeling there was something about him. I picked Johansson, the big underdog, to win the fight. I was one of the few. Johansson proceeded to knock Patterson out in the third round. I had not bet on Johansson. It is far easier to pick an underdog in the paper than actually risk money on him.

The story of my second triumph began in 1968, when I covered a track meet at Madison Square Garden. At the end of the three-mile run I made it a point of talking to one of the losers because of his distinctive name: Ambrose Burfoot. I was struck by his comment that he thought the distance of three miles was a bit too short for him. At that time, marathons were not the rage that they became later, so it seemed quaint that he thought three miles was "too short."

When I was up in Boston for its famed marathon that spring, I covered the race by riding the press bus that accompanied the runners. I joined the group of raucous Boston reporters who enlivened things with their colorful comments. They made merry at the expense of the runners, the scene, the characters involved in staging the race. But at heart they adored the amateurism of the event.

They ran a pool in which each bus rider put up five dollars to try to pick the winner of the race. Some Korean and Japanese runners were favored. In looking over the field I spotted the name of Ambrose Burfoot, a relative unknown. I recalled his comment about three miles being too short a race and figured that the 26-mile, 385-yards of the marathon should be long enough for him. For five bucks, it was easy to choose Burfoot.

I was the only one to pick him. Soon after the race started, he was among the leaders. And before the race was half done, he was in the lead. As he ran past the girls at the Wellesley College gate and the boys outside Boston College, I took some ribbing from the broad-A accented Boston scribes. "Isaacs, how the hell did you know anything about Ambrose Burfoot?" I laughed, in effect, all the way to the bank. Burfoot never faltered. He won the race handily. I won more than $100.

It turned out that Burfoot was a roommate at Wesleyan College of Bill Rogers, who would win the Boston Marathon three years in a row a decade later. Burfoot became a writer about track and field. I later met him and told him about my five-buck affection for him. He didn't ask me for a share of the swag.

My third feat occurred during the 1971 World Series between the Baltimore Orioles and the Pittsburgh Pirates. I went deep into my prediction reveries, thinking long and hard. I picked the Pirates to win in seven games. Though the Pirates were the underdogs, that was not a particularly daring prediction. But I also said that one of the games would be rained out. That is defying the fates a bit because for the World Series, neither rain, nor snow, nor gloom of night will get a baseball commissioner to postpone a game.

Baltimore won the first game. And then, *the second game was rained out.* Hah.

I was not quite in the catbird seat because the Pirates had to win in seven to confirm my genius. Baltimore then won the second game. Pittsburgh came back to take the next three. I needed Baltimore to win the sixth game and the Pirates to rebound in the seventh to win the series in the manner that I predicted. Baltimore fell behind, 2–0 in the third inning, but came back to tie and win 3–2, in 10 innings. I was enjoying the developments for sure.

Could Pittsburgh win the seventh game and the Series for me? The Pirates scored a run in the fourth and another in the eighth, enough to offset an Oriole run in the home half of the eighth. They won, 2–1. My Pirates-in-seven-games-with-a-rainout prediction had come through.

I had not bet actual money on it. No matter. The derring-do of pulling off such a precious piece of prognostication enriched me more than mere money could have. I think.

23

Righties and Lefties

At the time of the 1969 All-Star game in Washington D.C., President Richard Nixon hosted a White House reception for baseball people. One of the most striking aspects of the gathering was Nixon's feat of recalling the happenings in the 1929 World Series. The Philadelphia Athletics, behind the Chicago Cubs 8–0 in the seventh inning of the fourth game, roared back with a 10-run rally to win 10–8, and went on to beat the Cubs in five games.

Nixon said he was a student at the time listening to the game on the radio. He said the rally made such a great impression on him that he could remember it to this day. He then recited a batter-by-batter description of the ten-run rally. It was an astounding performance that dazzled the old ballplayers on hand.

I was somewhat suspicious about it at the time and glossed over it in the column I wrote about the affair. I could imagine a fan recalling the rally, but not every detail like that. My suspicions were confirmed later. I learned that his son-in-law, David Eisenhower, a rabid baseball fan, had contacted the San Diego columnist Jack Murphy before the gathering and gotten the exact details of the rally so that Nixon could recite them to the baseball people.

Nixon was a true baseball fan; he didn't have to impress anybody about that. But he had to be in character, the consummate flim-flammer.

In that East Room of the White House were, among others, Casey Stengel, Jackie Robinson, Joe DiMaggio, Carl Hubbell, John Galbraith, Bob Feller, Lefty Grove, Sandy Koufax, and Henry Aaron. (Standing next to Grove, I asked him what his highest salary was; he was insulted at the question.) For sports page devotees, this was a knockout of a gathering, though not quite enough to wake up the echoes of another time when President

John Kennedy hosted a large dinner party for intellectuals and said, "This is the greatest gathering of intellects to eat in the White House since one evening when Thomas Jefferson dined alone."

Baseball personalities, who usually are so cool in public they can freeze people in their tracks, turned goo-goo eyed in the face of the audience with the president. The four hundred or so guests waited patiently in line and gave their names to a White House aide, who passed them on to baseball commissioner, Bowie Kuhn; he introduced each guest by name to the president.

I was torn about joining the line because of my long dislike for Nixon and his red-baiting tactics, but I did it out of curiosity. The guests later received a photo of their interaction with the president. I think mine showed the ambivalence I had about being with him. My mother disapproved of my shaking his hand.

Nixon noted that some of the great political columnists started out as sports columnists. He said, "And I don't know if that's going up or down. I think if I had to live my life over again, I'd like to be a sportswriter." This inspired Maury Allen of the *New York Post* to say, "Mr. President, I'd like to exchange jobs with you, but I can't afford the pay cut." Nixon beamed and said, "That's funny."

* * *

The FBI once had me in their sights.

When the Freedom of Information Act allowed citizens to request their FBI files, I thought I should see if I was a target because I had once worked on the red-tainted *Compass*. But the procedure required some paperwork that I was too lazy to do, and for a long time I delayed making the request.

Then, in the summer of 1998, the CBS station in New York broke the story that the FBI had investigated Mickey Mantle. It also revealed that I was a target of an FBI investigation along with Mantle, Billy Martin, and Mrs. Branch Rickey. What a Murderer's Row! The report cited some correspondence between Richard Nixon's domestic adviser, John Ehrlichman, and the FBI.

When Nixon threw the party for baseball people and the press in connection with the 1969 All-Star Game in Washington, the White House had asked for an FBI check on the guests. The FBI report stated, "the central files of the FBI reveal no pertinent derogatory information regarding the following individuals." Some names included baseball commissioner Bowie Kuhn, Kansas City Royals owner Ewing Kauffman, NBC executive Carl Lindemann, and Pittsburgh Pirates broadcaster Bob Prince. It also included

Dodgers owner Walter O'Malley, who many of us regarded as a true enemy of the people.

There was another section that said, somewhat ominously, "attached are separate memoranda regarding the following individuals: Stan Isaacs, Mickey Mantle, Billy Martin and Mrs. Branch Rickey." I like to think I was listed first because I was the most suspicious character, but I concede that the names were listed in alphabetical order.

The FBI monitored Mantle because he had received threatening letters in the mail and because in 1956 he reportedly was blackmailed for $15,000 after being caught with another man's wife in a compromising position. Also, his name—and probably Martin's too—had come up in connection with gambling. A 1963 entry has a source telling the FBI that Mantle received telephone calls from a known gambler.

It is difficult to comprehend why Jane Rickey, the gentle wife of the general manager of the Pittsburgh Pirates, also was worthy of special treatment by the FBI. I'd hate to think it was because she approved of her husband's celebrated role in breaking the color line in baseball by signing Jackie Robinson.

After the CBS report and a column by Richard Sandomir in the *New York Times* mentioned my sudden notoriety, I sent for my FBI file. After several months, I received it. The letter, signed by James J. Roth, Chief Division Counsel for the FBI, informed that "pursuant to your request, 15 pages were reviewed and are being released. Notations have been made in the margins of the enclosed pages indicating specific examples applied to excised portions of the material. The enclosed material is from the main investigative file in which the subject of your request was the subject of the investigation."

I was sure the report would include some juicy stuff from my days at the ill-fated left-wing *Daily Compass,* when anti-Communism rode high. I wrote such subversive stuff as arguing with a passion that the great black pitcher, Satchel Paige, should be put in the baseball Hall of Fame.

It turned out my file included not a word about the *Compass*. The file started when I was at *Newsday*. It gave my address in Elmont and where we had previously lived in Manhattan, even noting my telephone number there.

I have to admit, I was a disgustingly upstanding citizen because it was recorded there were no "negative reports" on me from the Credit Bureau of New York, the New York Bureau of Motor Vehicles, and the Bureau of Criminal Identification.

There were many blacked-out lines, most of them to protect the scurvy informer who gave the FBI the information about me. I can't figure out what would have been subversive about me at *Newsday* other than the fact that I once wrote a glowing piece about the football team the Red Devils of Freeport High School. My wife thinks it's because the title of my column was "Out of Left Field."

It is outrageous, of course, that ordinary citizens could be investigated by the FBI on the word of anonymous informers. It is of some comfort now that the Freedom of Information Act has opened up the FBI files to some degree. But too much of the information is blacked out. There is no reason why my anonymous informer should have his or her identity protected.

* * *

My stint on the *Compass,* when some superpatriots saw Communists under every bed, left some psychic scars. When I started writing a city-side column at *Newsday,* I needed to obtain a press pass to move through police lines while covering a story. When I learned I would have to be fingerprinted to get the pass, I desisted. It was not that I had anything to be afraid of; it was just that I had never been fingerprinted and I regarded it as an intrusion on my rights. I came to terms with the situation by doing without the press pass. It never mattered.

Several years later, the younger reporters at *Newsday,* who were more militant in opposition to restrictive government policies, challenged the need for fingerprinting. They won. The Nassau County officials had to award press passes without requiring fingerprinting. I looked with admiration upon those who won the day. I wondered if I would have done the same had I been born twenty years later and not had the experience of working for a left-wing paper during a hostile time in the United States.

In 1978 I was invited to a party for I. F. Stone, marking the twenty-fifth anniversary of the birth of his dynamic, important little weekly, *I.F. Stone's Newsletter*. Stone, the bulwark of the *Compass,* started the weekly shortly after the *Compass* folded. An early opponent of the Vietnam War and a longtime spear carrier of the Left, Stone emerged as a hero among old-time liberals and students. The party in a restaurant in Manhattan's Chinatown celebrated a man who came to be regarded as one of the great independent journalists of the twentieth century.

I had been a copy boy and editorial assistant before getting promoted to sports reporting at the *Compass*. I occasionally brought a piece of wire service copy to Stone or included him in a coffee run.

Later, at *Newsday,* I wrote a long feature piece on him and his newsletter. I interviewed him in his cluttered offices in Washington. His thick glasses and short, chunky body gave him an owlish-like mien. His dress, an open vest and shirttails sticking out of rumpled pants, matched the disarray of papers and oddments in his office. I reminded him that I had been a copy boy at the *Compass*. We had a cordial session, and I wrote a glowing piece about him.

I intended to go to the celebration but forgot to respond to the party invitation. Just after the deadline, I called his office. His wife answered. Somewhat to my surprise, she was elated to hear from me and assured me there would be a place for my wife and me at the restaurant.

At the party, we were seated at what appeared to be a VIP table. When Stone got up to speak, he introduced with some pride the left-wing eminences in attendance. He then said, "And we are pleased that the long-time independent Republican who has been such a force for good in New York City is here too." He pointed to our table and said how delighted he was that Stanley M. Isaacs, the former borough president of Manhattan and only Republican member of the city council for many years, was present.

It dawned on me then that he had confused me, Stan Isaacs, for the respected Stanley M. Isaacs. When I didn't get up, Stone seemed miffed and said, "I guess Mr. Isaacs's representatives do not wish to be associated with this assemblage." I understood then why I was able to get a late invitation and why Mrs. Stone was so effusive when I called. Anyway, it was a grand party.

* * *

One of my heroes was the legendary liberal columnist of the 1920s and 1930s, Heywood Broun. We gave our oldest daughter, Nancy, the middle name of Broun to honor him.

Broun would have one-upped today's chorus quick to cry "socialism" at government policies marked by compassion. He said that as a student at Harvard he took a course that studied socialism and capitalism. He said, "During the fall term I heard the esteemed professor lay out all the good points of socialism. He was going to knock down those arguments for socialism and extol capitalism in the spring term. But came spring, I was not in the stuffy classroom learning about the glories of capitalism; I was out in the sunshine at Fenway Park watching the Red Sox." Hence, he became a socialist.

Broun was a driving force in starting the Newspaper Guild labor union. In an arbitration session about cutting working hours, management scoffed, "What would the workers do with the extra time?"

Broun said, "Can I suggest polo?"

24

Triple Threats

I have been interested in politics since at least age seven. Franklin Delano Roosevelt was a god in my family. I thought it was an outrage that Alfred Landon would even run against FDR in 1936. So one day on the way to school, I chalked on the wall, "Fuck Landon."

I probably didn't know what the word actually meant, but I knew it didn't compliment Landon. The graffiti remained there for the next few months. Whenever I walked past the wall, I nodded in sly recognition of my work. I never told anybody.

My politics have been fairly obvious: pro-FDR, devotedly pro–Eleanor Roosevelt, anti–Richard Nixon and all of his henchmen, anti–Vietnam War from the beginning, increasingly suspicious and angry about President Bush's lying that got us into the Iraq quagmire, disillusioned by President Obama's Afghanistan escalation—and dead-set always against the designated hitter.

In the summer of 1968, while the Democratic convention was taking place in Chicago, I went out to Arlington Park and wrote about a horse, Dr. Fager, winning the Arlington Mile in record time. I stayed on to cover the Yankees playing the White Sox. While I was there, managing editor Bill McIlwain, a wonderful guy with a soothing southern drawl, suggested I seek out some pieces at the Democratic convention. "We'll unleash mah man Stan on those politicos," he said, "and he'll treat them lahk jocks."

I had written about Eugene McCarthy, the Minnesota senator who was challenging President Lyndon Johnson on the Vietnam War. He had charmed people with his many sports references during the campaign. He was a glib guy. He talked about not wanting to go into the corners when he played hockey. He said first base was so easy that when Mickey Mantle was on his last legs, it was the only place Casey Stengel could put him.

I learned McCarthy was staying at a motel in the suburbs, not far from the Arlington racetrack. I made an appointment to see him the following afternoon just before the convention started. As I was getting out of my car in the motel parking lot, a man approached. He asked if I knew if Senator McCarthy was staying at the motel. I recognized him as Russell Baker, the respected *New York Times* correspondent.

I identified myself and told him I had an appointment to see McCarthy. He asked, somewhat diffidently, if he could join me. I figured it would not hurt at all to have a *Times* man help elicit comments from McCarthy. When we arrived, McCarthy perked up upon seeing Baker, whom he obviously knew well. During the interview, McCarthy responded to my questions by addressing his answers only to the *Times* man. Baker, obviously a bit uncomfortable about this, tried to shift McCarthy's gaze to me, but the senator was seeing only the *Times,* not the sports reporter from suburban *Newsday*.

I departed after a while, leaving McCarthy with Baker. It was an entirely unproductive meeting from the standpoint of writing a column, because I didn't think the readers were interested in my discomfort. I became disenchanted with McCarthy as a person and was not surprised by the dog-in-the-manger attitude he took toward the Democratic Party once he faded from center stage. I came away admiring Baker for the way he tried to avoid upstaging my interview.

Many years later, Baker spoke at a meeting of the Silurians, a gathering of newspaper people in New York. I told the group how classy he had been in trying to keep McCarthy's focus on me. He seemed pained.

* * *

McIlwain obtained a floor press pass for me at that convention. I moseyed about looking for sports-related angles. I interviewed, among others, the biggest man on the convention floor: six-foot five-inch Roosevelt Grier, the former defensive tackle of the New York Giants.

Giants such as Grier, Y. A. Tittle, Frank Gifford, Roosevelt Brown, Sam Huff, and Andy Robustelli were the darlings of New York sports in their time. It became an in-thing to go over to bar/restaurant P.J. Clarke's on Third Avenue to be a part of the Giants scene. (I was more comfortable at home with Bobbie and the kids in Roslyn Heights.)

Grier attended the convention because of his association with Bobby Kennedy. He had been enlisted in Kennedy's cause by his friend, Olympic decathlon star Rafer Johnson. Both men were at the scene when Kennedy was assassinated as he made his way from a primary victory party at a hotel in Los Angeles. They helped disarm the assassin, Sirhan Sirhan. The two later accompanied Kennedy's body on the plane back east for the funeral.

Grier and Johnson were put on the California delegation after Kennedy's victory in the state. Grier spoke of Kennedy with reverence, calling him, "The Senator." He said, "I'm in this only to see some of the plans of The Senator fulfilled so that the little man gets an even break. He was the only guy in the world who turned me on."

Grier said he now was for Ted Kennedy—or George McGovern if Ted didn't get into the race. He came away disillusioned after one of the crucial proceedings, when the convention voted against equal representation by blacks in Georgia. Grier was dismayed that many of the northern state delegations didn't support seating the black Georgia delegation led by Julian Bond.

"They say you can't settle things in the street," he said. "Well, I'm not for violence in the streets, but how can you tell people they can do things legally when a convention like this doesn't give them a chance to vote? They say you have to be tricky in football . . . but in politics . . ."

* * *

During the roll call, when each state announced its delegates' votes for the party's nominee, I settled in the Alabama delegation. Alabama passed its turn on the first call. While the other states were reporting their votes, a big, bluff man sat in a wheelchair, shaking his head. A plastic straw-like hat with a red, white, and blue band perched on his balding, gray head.

When one of the states cast some votes for Rev. Channing Phillips, a black minister from Washington, D.C., the big man in the wheelchair turned to a bystander and asked, hesitantly, "Is that a colored man?"

"Yes."

"My, my, what the Democratic Party has come to."

The vote rolled on through the states and came back to Alabama. "Listen to this," the man in the wheelchair said. The head of his delegation announced, "Humphrey 23½ votes, Ted Kennedy 3½, [North Carolina Gov.] Dan Malone half-a-vote, Paul Bryant 1½—and 3½ not recorded."

The man in the wheelchair roared, "Bear, Bear, Bear." He poked a friend. "Roll, Tide, roll," he shouted. "Bear would show them." Paul "Bear" Bryant was the favorite son of Alabama, the coach of the University of Alabama football team, the man who hardly lost, a god of southern football.

The secretary of the convention didn't quite hear the vote and it was repeated. This time the Alabamian responded, "Coach Paul (Bear) Bryant," and there was another shout in the delegation.

"I got another half-vote with me," the old man cried. "Bear would be the man all right. He'd wreck the line. We need somebody to crash the New York–California line."

I asked the man in the wheelchair his name.

"Connor," he answered.

"Mr. Bull Connor?"

"No 'Mr.' about it. Just Bull Connor. Roll, Tide, roll."

Bull Connor gained worldwide notoriety for setting dogs upon black adults and children in Birmingham in 1963. Delegates complaining about Richard Daley's police riot tactics in the city during the convention actually compared the Chicago mayor to Connor. The man in the wheelchair, a token figure here, regretted that he was unable to get around in the chair "to see old friends like Mayor Daley."

The half-vote for Bryant came from Jim Kahaley, a hotel owner in Mobile. "I voted for him as a tribute to a great man," he said. Few doubted that Bryant would sweep the state for any political office. "In Alabama," a man said, "an atheist is a man who doesn't believe in Bear Bryant."

Bryant was so celebrated in his bailiwick that he was seen on advertising billboards endorsing three products at once. He was smoking a cigar, holding a soft drink in one hand, and a hot dog in the other. Talk about triple threats.

I don't know if Bear Bryant was the first major sports figure to get votes for a major party's presidential nomination. And Bryant wasn't on hand to say whether he would run if nominated or serve if elected. Roll, Tide, roll.

* * *

The convention was notorious for the violence inflicted on demonstrators by the Chicago police. At one point, I was in Lincoln Park watching some of the action and was menaced by some cops who didn't like anybody seeing what they were doing.

While all this was happening, Humphrey, the eventual Democratic nominee, remained in his hotel room, a prisoner of President Lyndon Johnson's calamitous policies in Vietnam. Humphrey secured the nomination, but he had such little support even with his own party. He looked sure to lose to Republican nominee Richard Nixon.

I will always remember the scene after the convention voted down a minority plank in the party's platform, which would have laid a path toward peace in Vietnam. The playwright Arthur Miller headed a march of antiwar supporters along Michigan Avenue. I joined the march myself, and we walked about a mile, solemnly and silently holding lit candles. Above us were the hotels where most of the delegates were staying.

I didn't vote for Humphrey that November in the general election. In retrospect, that was a mistake, but when I went into the voting booth, I couldn't shake the image of an impotent Humphrey looking down upon the demonstrators from his hotel room.

* * *

I had my innings with Edmund Muskie one night when I was writing the column "Stan Isaacs' Long Island" (as opposed to anybody else's Long Island, I suppose). Muskie spoke at the annual Nassau County Democratic Party dinner in Garden City in June 1971, when the Maine senator was the front-runner for the 1972 Democratic presidential nomination.

He seemed quite glib about criticizing others, particularly the Republicans, but he had nothing to say about the Vietnam War, including his support of President Johnson and the war. It seemed to me that he should have said something about his own role in not speaking out against the war, as other Democrats had done. I asked him about his war stance.

He resented the question. He lost his temper with me. I had upset athletes, managers, and coaches before, but never a would-be president. I backed off. I wrote a column that in retrospect was deficient because I didn't zero in on my confrontation with Muskie. There is always a disinclination to make yourself a part of the story, but sometimes you should. Muskie later blew the race when he was ridiculed for showing tears during a campaign appearance in New England.

The Muskie incident came not long after a wrenching column I wrote about Robert Muller. He was a young ex-Marine who had been paralyzed in battle in Vietnam from the chest down. He was hit by a round of fire while attempting to lead a reluctant company of South Vietnamese men against a suicide squad of about a dozen enemy soldiers who couldn't be dislodged by artillery or aerial bombardment. Muller's lungs were pierced and his spinal cord severed.

He was slightly built, with a shock of brown hair and clear blue eyes. His body almost shook as he worked himself up about his experiences. He was bitter about the war, about what happened to him, about the government that lied to him. Wheeling about expertly in his wheelchair in his apartment in Great Neck, he offered me a cup of coffee. "Instant, I'm afraid," he said, puttering about almost as if he were not in a wheelchair.

"Before I went to Vietnam I didn't have any political feelings," he said. "I didn't question anything. I had only revulsion for peace people. I felt they were subverting our effort in Vietnam by raising dissent that only inspired the Viet Cong to fight harder." He lifted himself out of his seat to get into a more comfortable position and said, "Now, I look upon myself as a putz to a dimension you could hardly imagine."

Muller came back from Vietnam an antiwar activist. Almost every afternoon, he wheeled himself out of his apartment, drove off in his manually operated car, and spoke in ringing tones at peace meetings against the war and the policies of the government. When he finished there was, invariably, a moment of dead silence. Then the audience would burst into an ovation.

He related his experiences. "When I got hit, I must have been conscious for about ten seconds. I said to myself, 'I can't believe it, I am going to die in Vietnam.'" He was evacuated to a hospital ship, and the doctor later told him he had come within a minute of dying. He said, "When I woke up there were seven tubes in me and I was paralyzed, but the fact I was alive was so overwhelming that it made it relatively easy to accept what had happened to me. The joy of life is so great, the sorrow of being a paraplegic is nothing."

I saw Muller speak one night at a gathering in East Meadow. He leaned forward in his wheelchair with his elbow on a table and said, "This country fed me a line of malarkey." Fury rose within him. There was a faint resemblance at that moment between this slight, dark fellow and the angry Montgomery Clift in *From Here to Eternity*. He apologized for his anger, saying, "I'm a very emotional person about Vietnam. I can't help it. It has touched me too personally not to be affected by it."

At a rally in Roslyn, I heard him say, "Vietnam is all over for me. I have no sex life. I can't have babies, even by artificial insemination. I have no control of my bodily functions. I try to eliminate on schedule, but I still have accidents." He was quite free with me about his relations with his girlfriend. He smiled and said, "You know there are other ways to please a woman beside the conventional way."

A Marine major had told him, "What you are doing is wrong. It's irrelevant to ask why we are there; we should just go all out."

Muller disagreed. "It's never out of place to question why. It burns me up now to hear guys capitalizing on the dead and disabled as a rallying cry to justify winning this insane war. I can't talk for the dead, but I can talk for the living. I've been in the VA hospitals and I tell you the majority of the severely disabled are against the war despite their own strong need to justify their losses."

Muller said he joined the Marines because "the only way for me to go was the best way possible. I don't settle for mediocrity. I said, 'Why should this great country lie to me about being in the war?' It was the only thing my girl and I disagreed about. I accepted that it was my duty as a citizen to fight, and I demanded the Marines and the infantry."

"People say I'm bitter because I was shot. I was well aware of the casualty rate. I am bitter that I was lied to and exploited like a pawn in a chess game. We don't belong there. The South Vietnamese people don't want us there. I saw the poverty and corruption. When I returned I had time to reflect and understand that too many Americans are comforted by their blind faith in the government. They don't question as I didn't question, and look where it has gotten us."

Muller was twenty-five. He had just missed cum laude honors at Hofstra. He expected to enter Hofstra law school that fall. He said, "My girl and I are closer than ever in another way, but marriage is not a part of the picture now. My family wanted me, but I took my own apartment because I wanted to be completely independent. I am."

He was tireless in his efforts. We've heard that Vietnam veterans were spit at when they returned from duty. That is not substantiated, but I know that at one peace march, somebody came out of the crowd to spit at Muller. That is an image I have never been able to get out of my head: a paraplegic veteran being spit at because he was speaking out against a terrible war.

We went to the racetrack one afternoon. I saw him there with some of his friends another time. He kept speaking out and became an effective and honored activist. Robert Muller became president of the Vietnam Veterans of America Foundation. He was a cofounder of the International Campaign to Ban Land Mines, which won a Nobel Peace Prize in 1997.

Decades later, in the midst of the war in Iraq, I saw Muller at a program on Vietnam at the Museum of Natural History. We hugged. He said, "The same thing is happening all over again. Don't we ever learn?"

25

Newspaper Lore

The best comment I ever heard about reporting came from McCandlish Phillips, a fine *New York Times* reporter. Phillips said that if he were a journalism professor, he would send his students to a brownstone address in upper Manhattan. "I'd have them sit on the stoop for several hours. Then I would have a woman in an upstairs floor pour water down on them, after which they would return to the office."

His point was, of course, that reporters spend most of their time waiting around and suffering at the hands of people who take a fiendish delight in inflicting indignities upon them. So much for the glory of Woodward and Bernstein.

I did my share of waiting around. I figured out fairly early, though, that I probably would not amount to much as a city-side reporter. During the interlude between when the *Daily Compass* folded and I hooked on with *Newsday,* I was desperate enough at one point to seek work at the *National Enquirer,* a sensationalist rag.

I was assigned to go out to the Park Slope section of Brooklyn and interview the mother of a boy who had been slain. I dutifully took the subway to the neighborhood. That is as far as I got. I didn't see what good purpose was served in hectoring a woman at the time of her tragedy. I reported back to the editor that the woman wasn't available. Nor was I anymore at the *Enquirer*.

Reporters often have to pursue such dirty work. I respect them for being able to do it. It toughens them and they go on to better things. I could never do it, and I still wince when I see TV reporters harassing citizens who have just suffered tragedy. I believe that an ordinary citizen has the right to ask for money when approached by a print or TV reporter in situations like these. Celebrities frequently get paid big sums for their exclusive "as told to" stories to publications. Ordinary people are more deserving of money—the more the better, if it is from some media conglomerate.

* * *

When I started out with the *Compass,* I was impressed by I. F. Stone's bird-dog ability to spot a small item in a press release or budget proposal and develop a story behind the story. I wasn't in that league, but I did enjoy spotting small items in the paper and developing them into interesting columns.

In 1983 I saw an obscure one-paragraph obituary in the Sunday *New York Times* noting the death of Connie Desmond. I did a double take because I knew Connie Desmond as the one-time popular Brooklyn Dodgers radio broadcaster. The item said that Desmond had died ten days earlier in Toledo, Ohio, his hometown, at seventy-five.

I knew that alcoholism had done him in a long time before that. Stoking my memory, I made phone calls to people who worked with him. I developed what could stand as a more complete obituary of Connie Desmond.

Desmond came out of Toledo, where he had broadcast minor league Mud Hens baseball and college sports. He worked a year for the Giants and Yankees, then hooked on with the Dodgers as Red Barber's sidekick in 1943. There was a nice-guy quality to him. He was easy on the ear, sort of like Bing Crosby. He worked for the Dodgers until 1955, when his drinking was so bad that the Dodgers couldn't carry him anymore.

He drifted about New York for a time, cadging money from friends until there were no friends left. At one point, he started a Connie Desmond radio sports report aimed at people riding in taxis, but it was short-lived. Somebody said he had heard that Desmond may have been working as a tour guide on the Circle Line tourist boats around New York. People might say, "Connie Desmond, didn't he die?"

Barber, who had retired to Tallahassee, had heard the news of Desmond's death. He told me, "I am deeply troubled, but I have to say for him that I am glad it is over." Vin Scully, by then the longtime Los Angeles Dodgers broadcaster, had not heard the news. "Ooh," he said over the phone. He paused a moment. "Sad. I guess it wouldn't be in the papers out here because nobody would have known of him."

Barber said, "I never worked with a better person. We seemed to understand each other. He had a warm personality, a warm pleasant voice. He knew his business impeccably. We fit together like a hand and glove. I last saw him at Yankee Stadium. What happened to him after that I don't know. In the last seven years we worked together I had to be extra careful with him, but I never discussed his drinking."

Scully joined the Dodgers crew as the third man in 1950 fresh out of Fordham, replacing Ernie Harwell, who had moved to the Giants. Scully said, "Red was very much the father figure. I might have been the son he never had. Connie was like the older brother. Where Red might chew me out—rightfully—Connie, the older brother, would stroke me and pep me up."

Desmond and his wife and two children lived in Flower Hill in Roslyn, where he had several friends among the airline pilots who lived there. "The thing he did better than almost anyone," Scully said, "he could chuckle on the air and it came over so warm that you could relate to it. He was as good as anybody in all-around ability. He could do all sports well, if none exceptionally well. He had a remarkable flair."

Scully added: "He was a guy who lived in the fast lane, with the glamor, the recognition, the money, and the exposure to anything if you want it. The drinking danger lurks over everybody in this business because you have all that time. Then finally, you wind up dead like everybody else."

Dodgers' owner Walter O'Malley had hired a member of Alcoholics Anonymous to accompany Desmond to the ballpark. The Dodgers let him work as much or as little as he chose. He couldn't break the habit. It was heartbreaking. "The last vestige of pride may have been that he would never ask me for a nickel," said Scully. "I would have liked to help, but I was sort of the younger brother and he wouldn't ask. It is kind of remarkable, though, that he lived to seventy-five, considering the bumps and bruises."

Desmond went back to Toledo in 1960. He worked the Mud Hens games again. A friend reported he was still drinking. "He wanted to be paid in the morning so he could start drinking early. I told him I wouldn't loan him money anymore."

Divorced, he lived with his sister, Bette Sullivan, until she and her husband retired to Scottsboro, Arizona. "Connie preferred to stay in Toledo," she said after the funeral. At the end, "He was in good health. We talked on the phone all the time. On Wednesday we laughed and acted foolish together. We always did. I remember that people once said that if Connie ever ran for mayor of Brooklyn he would be elected."

He was living in apartments subsidized by Catholic charities. When *Toledo Blade* columnist Jim Taylor interviewed him in late 1982, he looked good. "He still had that good voice," Taylor said. Desmond fondly recalled the old Dodgers such as Gil Hodges, Duke Snider, and Roy Campanella. Asked if he had a favorite sport, he told Taylor, "I'd do football on a crisp fall day, free. Say the Bears against the Giants. Bulldog Turner against Mel Hein. What could be better?"

Frank Gilhooly, a sportscaster in Toledo, delivered the eulogy. "He was a super guy who goofed," Gilhooly said. "I was afraid that nobody might show up at the funeral, but about a hundred people were there, friends and people from the church."

And the obituary made just one short paragraph in the *New York Times.*

* * *

In an episode of high foolishness, *Newsday* once was sued for libel because of me. It involved a column about a moveable feast orchestrated by a friend.

Len Bernstein, one of the stalwarts of the New York Wine and Food Society, conceived the idea of staging a food tasting of the fast-food establishments on Old Country Road in Westbury, Long Island. He enlisted five couples with a sense of adventure, particularly when it involved eating, to participate in what he called, "The Old Country Road Food and Wine Society Take-Out Restaurant Clambake." He invited me along to be a taster.

The group visited twelve take-out/eat-in restaurants along a mile-and-a-half stretch of Old Country Road. We munched at America's most ubiquitous eateries: McDonald's, Arby's, Carvel, Friendly's, KFC, Pizza Hut, Dunkin' Donuts, and Jack-in-the-Box as well as local stalwarts Berger's Deli, Alie's, Tony's Hero Shop, and the Lollypop Drive-In. Afterward, the group, stuffed to the gills, straggled like General Lee's ragamuffins at Appomattox back to the Bernstein home in Westbury to make evaluations. Bernstein decreed that the establishments be rated for "food quality" and "food quality adjusted for other factors," such as ambience and service.

Reactions were mixed. "Most of the food was good when you consider availability and price," said one feeder. A key comment came from one of the female gourmands: "On the whole," she said, "I thought it was a pretty unappetizing group of eating places. It was mostly all fake food, ground-up *schmutz."*

I wrote about the adventure in a column that included a box score called "The Gluttons Report." Carvel won, followed by Arby's and Berger's Deli. Lollypop Drive-In came in last.

Not long after, the Lollypop Drive-In sued *Newsday*. It was a ridiculous suit. You might as well sue a food or movie critic for a nasty review. But a shyster lawyer, seeing *Newsday* as a fat, rich, vulnerable target, persuaded the Lollypop owner that he might be able to make some money suing the newspaper.

Newsday's lawyer assured me there was no chance of losing the suit. He mentioned other cases where *Newsday,* by my lights, had so hurt people with irresponsible stories that it *should* have lost in the courts, but it hadn't. It is close to impossible to win a libel suit against a newspaper. At a hearing, I was grilled by the opposing lawyer. Some of his questions were so ridiculous I would have laughed, except that the poor schnook owner of the eatery sat next to him and I thought it would hurt his feelings.

A key aspect of the libel charge was the Yiddish phrase "ground-up *schmutz,*" which had been uttered in the evaluations. Their side argued that she was calling the food "shit," while we interpreted it as meaning "dirt." The case went to a judge who ruled there was no libel in the case. He had a good time with the *"schmutz"* issue, citing Leo Rosten's dictionary of Yiddish terms, which came down on the side of "dirt."

The rogue-in-robes obviously thought of himself as a wit, because he had fun at my expense. "Isaacs meant all this to be funny," he said, "though I am not sure he succeeded."

* * *

I am often amused when citizens complain about the weak performances of reporters trying to grill politicians at formal press conferences. They don't realize that experienced politicians hold almost all the cards. They can take a question in any direction they please. They can avoid some reporters, reward others, seek softball questions when they need one. They can cut off questions whenever they want.

Once in a while, a person will goof, like President Gerald Ford saying at a debate that there was no Soviet domination of Eastern Europe. But that is rarely the case. The odds are stacked so much against the reporters that even sports figures do quite well at controlling press conferences. Casey Stengel was a master of any session with the press; he would resort to Stengelese to obfuscate a delicate situation.

Stengel also had a way of using the press to drive a point home to his players. He would shout advice or suggestions to puzzled reporters that were not meant for us, but for players who happened to be in the vicinity. It would become a "why wouldn't you?" lecture. After I got used to it, it amused me when Stengel barked at me, replaying a situation for the benefit of his players. If the opposing pitcher was dominating the Yankees, he'd yell, "Why wouldn't you bunt?" I was tempted sometimes to answer as if I were one of his uniformed minions.

If Stengel used the press one way, his successor on the Yankees, Ralph Houk, went in another direction. He tried to ingratiate himself with his players by setting himself up as a buffer between the press and the players. Where Stengel treated his players as adults able to withstand fair criticism, Houk turned a false face to the world. He was a dull dude and the players liked it that way.

He was most comfortable with reporters considered "house men." They were so happy to be a part of the Yankee caravan that they frequently were obsequious to gain Houk's favor. In one typical instance, a young reporter new to the beat didn't quite grasp the protocol of when to ask a pointed question in a postgame situation. You usually waited until Houk had gotten some banalities out of the way. The young guy directed a query to Houk about some faulty Yankee play. Houk ignored him and addressed an answer to one of his sycophants.

I may have not agreed that the question was a good one at the time, but I felt that in such a situation the young reporter had to be supported. So I repeated his question, not winning any points with Houk. Leonard Shecter of the *Post,* the toughest guy on the beat, would also back up an irreverent questioner in such a situation. I often thought I lost Houk for good after one leisurely press gathering during spring training. I kiddingly asked him if he wore Yankee pin-striped pajamas. He thought I was serious.

* * *

I got some interesting advice one day from Kyle Rote, the outstanding end for the New York Giants. The Giants were staging a day for quarterback Charlie Conerly. In those days when a player was given such an honor, it was not enough that he was bestowed with gifts from the team, teammates, and friends; the team actually asked the general public to contribute money for a gift of appreciation to the athlete.

Now, it is fairly obvious that it is ridiculous for the team to be asking ordinary blokes to contribute money for an athlete who was making ten times more money. As salaries increased, and cranks like me pointed out such inequities, team managements wised up and stopped asking citizens to contribute.

Rote was the highly regarded leader of that Giants team. A few teammates even named their sons after him. I believed that Rote, ostensibly a class guy, would understand the incongruity of asking ordinary folk to contribute to a fund to heap goodies on a well-paid professional athlete. I asked him about the requests to contribute to a Conerly fund. It took him a few moments to grasp the thrust of my question. Finally, he said, "If you feel that way you shouldn't be in this business."

26

Forgive Us Our Press Passes

Probably the most famous sign on a baseball fence was the "Hit Sign Win Suit" sign of Brooklyn clothier Abe Stark on the scoreboard in right-center field in Ebbets Field. Stark later became borough president of Brooklyn and most agreed that the sign provided an eminence that helped get him elected. Stark would bemoan all the suits he had to give away. He said the sign was hit "many times, at least five times a year." Actually the sign was hit rarely.

Situated along the bottom strip of the scoreboard, it was not an easy sign to hit. A hitter needed to place a line drive into the right-center field gap to hit the sign, and few achieved that. Visiting players also had to deal with Carl Furillo, the Dodgers' strong-armed right fielder. Furillo snagged any ball hit in that direction. It occurred to him one day that he wasn't deriving any benefit for protecting Stark's inventory. "I ask the man for a pair of pants or something for guarding the sign," he said. "He never gives me anything."

Bill Roeder of the *World Telegram* was assigned the task of notifying Stark if a ball hit the sign. When Harry Walker hit the sign on a bounce, he asked if that wasn't at least good for a pair of pants. Roeder took up his cause in the paper, and Walker got the pants.

Roeder was a likable guy who wrote sparely, but with a neat turn of phrase. We lived in the same town of Roslyn Heights, Long Island, and often drove to Ebbets Field together. On the way, he stopped at the Barricini candy shop on Eastern Parkway, not far from the ballpark, and introduced me to one of life's wonderful delicacies: dark chocolate almond bark. Though Barricini is long gone, I will snap up dark chocolate almond bark whenever I see it.

When I first broke into the field, I liked Roeder for another reason. He was the slowest writer on the beat. When a sports reporter first starts out, they frequently are concerned about being fast enough to meet a deadline. At Ebbets Field, I didn't want to be the last one writing, holding up the impatient Western Union operators who transmitted stories to newspapers. I didn't have to worry about that because Roeder was sure to be the last one to finish his story. This took the pressure off me until I developed enough speed to finish my stories without trying the patience of the Western Union guys.

Roeder and Dave Anderson, then of the *Journal-American*, were the last writers still working after the final game ever at Ebbets Field. Anderson wanted to have the distinction of being the last reporter to leave the press box. So he delayed long enough for Roeder to finish and allowed Bill to precede him out the door.

Roeder was an odd duck. He and his wife had at least a half-dozen children. But at a point in his midfifties, he had a midlife crisis, suddenly walking out on his family and taking up with a younger woman. It was a shock. A few years later, when he had left the *World Telegram* and was working for *Newsweek,* he died of a heart attack.

It was the worst funeral I ever attended. The priest did not know Roeder, so he mouthed a set spiel that had nothing to do with him. Worse, with Roeder's wife and his children sitting in the front row, the priest went on at length about what a fine family man Bill Roeder was. I felt for his wife.

* * *

The line that politics make strange bedfellows applies, in a way, to the sports beat. We spend considerable time on the road and in the press box with people with whom we otherwise might not be involved—or want to be involved. Among reporters, a camaraderie develops, for better or worse. I think one of the things a retired sportswriter misses, just like an athlete, is the give-and-take of the press box, the locker room, the newspaper office. And we do tend to embellish memories of those times.

Jimmy Cannon was a big-time columnist of my era. He was a peerless, much-imitated stylist. I admired his writing but didn't accept many of his takes on sports figures. Like many people in the business, he tended to glorify people who hardly needed glorifying—what Stanley Woodward derided as "godding them up." I found that some of the people Cannon lauded—Joe DiMaggio, Toots Shor, Ralph Houk—were less than the exalted guys Cannon made them out to be.

I became so suspicious of Cannon's heroes that it was a bit of a jolt to me the first time I met Billy Conn, the old fighter. When I met Conn at a boxing training camp, I was prepared to dislike him because Cannon had made so much of him. Conn turned out to be a charmer with an infectious what-the-hell attitude about life.

Cannon was a kid from the New York streets, a reformed alcoholic. He had an ego to match his talent. He was highly entertaining to be around—at least for a short time. After a while, his self-involvement became wearying. One thing galled him most: the Pulitzer Prize awarded to the pedestrian columnist at the *New York Times,* Arthur Daley. Cannon would bray that it should have gone to Red Smith or him—though you knew he really thought he deserved it most.

One of Cannon's most popular columns was the "Nobody Asked Me, But . . ." spray of opinions about matters of the world. He was a terrific one-liner guy, particularly apt at put-downs. I certainly qualified for one. He had a penchant for needling me about my attire. I wasn't quite of the Heywood Broun unmade-bed school of dress, but I leaned toward an overly casual style. Cannon, a dapper dresser of a conservative bent, hit on this frequently.

One year I had an urge to wear a corduroy sports jacket. It was out of style, for sure, because none of the stores I frequented carried corduroy sports jackets. I searched far and wide, even going to upscale stores. One afternoon I was in the Brooks Brothers store on Madison Avenue looking at the racks of jackets. As I turned a corner, I bumped into none other than Cannon. He looked at me in mock disgust and said, "What are you doing here? A rag picker wouldn't put his hook in you." It was a bulls-eye line that my wife, the other critic of my *deshabille,* loved.

Many years later I was watching an old Frank Capra movie, *A Pocketful of Dreams,* a remake of a Damon Runyon short story. It was a so-so movie, Capra's last. It involved a bunch of Broadway characters sprucing up an old beggar-like lady to make her look like a grand dame to fool her daughter. One of the characters says, "a rag picker would not put his hook in her."

Flash! I checked the background notes of a biography of Capra and discovered that Cannon was one of the uncredited script writers for the film. Did Cannon get the line from the Runyon story or was it his own? I looked up the Runyon story, "Madame La Gimp." The line was not in it. Cannon probably inserted that line into the movie—and he definitely draped it on me.

We were in Cincinnati covering the end of the 1964 pennant race, in which the Phillies would blow a big lead. I was sitting with Stan Hochman of the *Philadelphia Daily News* and Cannon, then with the *Journal-American.* We were joined by Joe King of the *World Telegram,* who was fresh from touring the pro football training camps. He bubbled over about various prospects and teams he saw.

Cannon started chomping at all this. Finally he could stand it no longer. He pounded the shelf and announced, "Baseball, gentlemen, baseball!" The phrase has been repeated often as a rallying cry when conversations stray from the main thread.

Dick Young was probably the best baseball writer in New York. He was colorful, imaginative, courageous. I often repeated his press box line that "Isn't it wonderful that you can work at a job where you can be laughing all the time?" He was an early idol, but that wore off as he became an embittered right-winger, disillusioned about athletes, about younger newspaper people, about life.

Young wrote for the *Daily News,* a morning paper, so he finished his stories not long after a game ended. *Newsday* had an afternoon paper deadline in my day, so I could work the postgame clubhouse and then come up to the press room to write. Young, who had already finished, would come into the press room and schmooze in his garrulous way with people who were still writing, no matter that some would have preferred a bit of quiet.

For big games like the World Series, Young would write details while the game was still on. In one such situation, a few afternoon paper guys—who didn't have to write while the game was on—were bantering, wisecracking. Young, of all people, had enough of this. He turned and said, "Guys, is the sound of my typing getting in the way of your conversation?"

* * *

Sports reporters have an admonition: "No rooting in the press box." This is generally adhered to, at least in New York. Most of the time.

Once, Al Kaline of the Detroit Tigers was having a great game in right field at the old Yankee Stadium. He played in front of the low right field fence almost like a goalie, hauling down a few line drives and fly balls by Yankees that would have been home runs. This nettled Jim Ogle of the *Newark Star Ledger,* a man who could well have worn Yankee pinstripes, so much was his heart with the Yankees. (He eventually wound up in charge of the Yankee player alumni, a fitting job for a man whose loyalty to the team invariably outweighed his responsibility to readers of his newspaper.)

At a point late in the game, I ambled down to the end of the press box to sip from the water cooler near where Ogle sat. Just as I did, a Yankee, Roger

Maris, hit a drive well back into the right field stands to win the game. As the ball flew well beyond Kaline into the seats, I heard Ogle mutter, "Let's see the prick catch that one."

Foul balls occasionally flew back into the open press box at Yankee Stadium. When I came up with a ball, I would throw or hand it back to a kid seated in the mezzanine behind the press box. Years later, Len Berman, who became a sports reporter on the NBC evening newscasts, told me he had gotten a ball from a reporter at the stadium and had asked around to find out who it was. He told me, "It was Stan Isaacs."

* * *

Bill Corum, the *Journal American* columnist, said, "I don't want to be a millionaire; I just want to live like one." Sports reporters of my day could be a spoiled lot. Our traveling arrangements and luggage were taken care of by traveling secretaries who eased our registration at hotels. We were minor celebrities just by our association with major league teams. We had free food and liquor in press rooms, and we were wined and dined at press conferences. We often had goodies heaped on us at Christmastime.

At *Newsday* we held to some kind of standard by not accepting Christmas presents. One year the Giants handed out field glasses to reporters who covered the team regularly. My often-skeptical coverage of the Giants displeased somebody in management to the extent that I was the only one not to be bequeathed the glasses. This bothered me no end because it deprived me of the pleasure of returning the field glasses in keeping with *Newsday* policy.

Some people were so accustomed to the red-carpet treatment that they became arrogant and demanding. It became a joke in relation to one particular scribe—Mike Gaven of the *Journal American*. He was the hardest to please in all matters relating to creature comfort. When a new minor league ballpark opened in Miami after World War II, it was regarded as the most up-to-date arena in many aspects, including press box facilities. The Miami people burst with pride about their stadium and awaited the acid test—when Mike Gaven arrived with the Brooklyn press contingent for a Dodgers exhibition game. After receiving a guided tour of the stadium, Gaven and the other Dodger reporters settled into a press box that consisted of private booths for each scribe.

At the end of the game, after the writers had filed their stories, the Miami people approached Gaven somewhat breathlessly for his verdict. Gaven looked at them unsmilingly and said, "No pencil sharpeners."

Gaven was a man who could be accused of seeing only the bright side of things involving the Dodgers. After Bobby Thomson hit the home run that won the 1951 pennant for the Giants over the Dodgers, Gaven's story ignored any aspect of the game; it previewed promising prospects the Dodgers had coming up from the minor leagues the next season.

Early in my career, I was impressed by what I thought were the eloquently simple lead paragraphs of Rud Rennie of the *Herald Tribune.* Rennie might write, "The Giants beat the Dodgers, 4–3, yesterday. It was a good game."

I thought this was an economical, spare way to treat a baseball report from time to time. After a while, I learned Rennie's modus operandi. He was a man who liked to get out of the ballpark as quickly as possible. So he would prepare his lead in the ninth inning as the game was drawing to a close. He might write, "The Giants beat the Dodgers, 4–3 yesterday. It was a—game." He would leave the adjective blank until the last out. Then he would insert "good" or "exciting" or "suspenseful" or whatever before scooting out of the press box almost as the final out was made. If a team came from behind in the ninth inning to change the score, Rennie would curse, tear up his lead and prepare another one.

Lester Rodney was the sports editor of the *Daily Worker,* a Communist newspaper. When Leo Durocher was managing in Brooklyn, he once got into a protracted conversation with Rodney. After a while, Durocher said, "You know, for a fucking Communist, you sure know your baseball."

Rodney became disillusioned with the Communist Party around the time that the Soviet Union invaded Hungary in 1956. He quit the *Daily Worker* and relocated to the West Coast, just after the Dodgers left Brooklyn for Los Angeles. One day Gil Hodges on the field looked up and spotted Rodney in the press box. Hodges threw up his hands in mock horror and shouted, "The Communists followed us."

* * *

Joe King, who inspired Cannon's "baseball, gentlemen, baseball" tirade, was short with a clipped, reddish mustache. He was a likable guy, but something of a loner. Sometimes after covering a Yankee–White Sox night game on Chicago's south side, I would head over to the near north side to listen to Dixieland jazz at the Jazz Ltd. nightclub. Frequently, King was there. I would nod to him, respecting the feeling that he didn't want company, and take a table by myself.

King was at the celebrated National Football League 1967 championship game when Green Bay beat Dallas, 21–17, on the last play of the game in what has come to be referred to as the Ice Bowl. King, in Green Bay most of the week, liked to take a drink. He imbibed all week. On this climactic Sunday he started drinking early—and often. By the time the game started he was, in the expression of the day, four sheets to the wind. By the end of the game, he was in no position to write.

He somehow got himself back on the press bus to hotel headquarters. The *World Telegram* was an afternoon paper, so he had a late deadline; he didn't have to file a story immediately after the game. In the press room it became evident to his colleagues on other papers that he was not up to his appointed task. Somebody sat down and started writing a story for Joe.

It developed into a group project. Dick Clemente of *Newsday* would write one paragraph; Dick Joyce, a wire service guy, would write another. Several took turns at this inspired task. King, who had the habit of rocking on his feet when he was soused, stood looking over the shoulders of the collaborators, rocking and saying, "Yeah, that's good, that's good."

I didn't drink. I recall my shock the first time I made a western trip with a ball club when Leonard Shecter invited me to stop at his room and pick him up on the way to dinner. When I arrived, he pulled a bottle of scotch out of his suitcase and offered me a drink. I knew that some of the other veteran reporters drank—some too much—but was surprised that Shecter did. He was the first Jewish assimilationist of my acquaintanceship, as far as drinking was concerned.

An example of what a nondrinker I was: In my early twenties, on my first vacation from the *Daily Compass,* I hitchhiked across the country. I was inspired by reading about people riding the rails during the Depression. I wanted to get a sense of the United States, to meet and talk to people. I went to diners, to YMCAs, to college campuses, to the 1950 Republican political convention hotels. I talked a lot with the drivers who gave me lifts. I went from New York to California and not once in that time did it occur to me that a good way to meet and talk to people was to go to bars.

* * *

Harold Rosenthal, a pudgy man with an infectious laugh and a graceful writing style, once said, "The road will make a bum of the best of us." He was referring especially to romantic shenanigans. That was a world I never made.

I was disgusted by the actions of one of the guys on the beat. He was single, but not much of a Beau Brummel. He spent much of his time on the road with Shecter and me, two married guys content to eat well and see movies. I wondered why he didn't go out with some of the hounds looking for women. Eventually he married. It was then, given the confidence his wife provided him, that he became Mr. Macho Man, on the make. So long, Shecter and Isaacs.

Another reporter, Paul Horowitz of the *Newark News,* had been cuckolded by his wife. In turn, he became a lothario with older women. He told about the time he and a lady friend were dallying in a motel room while the Super Bowl game was on television. The lady said, "Imagine this, making love while watching the Super Bowl." Horowitz said, "Watching the Super Bowl? I'm *in* the Super Bowl."

* * *

One year, before the running of the Preakness Stakes at the Pimlico Race Course in Baltimore, a few of us writers were gabbing. Somebody mentioned the rumor that the *Baltimore Evening Sun* might fold. Joe Hirsch of the *Racing Form* said, "I'd hate to see the Evening Sun go down."

27

Inside Stuff

I was much more gung-ho about sports than any of my teenage friends. It wasn't unusual for me to go to games alone. So on December 26, 1947, the night tennis player Jack Kramer turned pro against Bobby Riggs, I bucked the snowstorm that brought New York City to a standstill. I took the subway up to Madison Square Garden. So did many New Yorkers because a sellout crowd of 15,114 customers tromped through the blizzard to see if the crafty Riggs could handle the Californian who had been dominating the so-called amateur tennis ranks.

I rooted for Riggs because he was smart, colorful—and small. He won the ballyhooed opener, 6–2, 10–8, 4–6, 6–4. As the tour continued, Kramer began to catch on to Riggs's style. His big game dominated, and he finished with a 69–20 advantage.

Riggs made his next big splash with the celebrated "Battle of the Sexes" showdown against Billie Jean King in 1973. Riggs, fifty-five, played the male chauvinist to help create interest in what became an extravaganza. King, twenty-nine, beat him easily enough, 6–4, 6–3, 6–3. It gave the irrepressible Riggs another moment in the spotlight and a considerable payday.

I had been going to the U.S. Nationals at Forest Hills since before the Riggs-Kramer match. In those days, it seemed to me when I rode the "E" subway line out to the Continental Avenue stop that I was going to the end of the world, or at least to the end of Long Island. Actually, Forest Hills was in the middle of Queens, some sixty miles from the eastern end of Long Island. I enjoyed stopping at the Addie Vallins ice cream shop on my short walk from the subway to the entrance of the grand old club.

The West Side Tennis Club at Forest Hills was an elitist enclave featuring row upon row of grass tennis courts. It had leisurely charm, and, for commoners like me, it was a joy to amble about and watch the action close-up at the many side courts between the stadium and the ivy-covered clubhouse. Some neighborhood people resented the annual invasion of their precincts. They were sorry, though, when the tournament grew into an extravagant commercial enterprise and moved to Flushing Meadow Park.

The U.S. Open became such a big deal at Flushing Meadow, it wouldn't have had room for the unheralded player that I once stumbled upon. Shail Kumar was a young man from Nepal studying in a United Nations internship program in New York in 1960. He told me he saw a subway poster announcing the U.S. Nationals poster, and not knowing any better, submitted an entry. He was, after all, one of the best tennis players in Nepal. When he filled out the entry form, he noted that he would be the first Nepalese player to compete in this American championship. That must have impressed the officials because they accepted his entry.

Kumar had never played on a grass court because there were no grass courts in Nepal. And he was one of the best players in Nepal because there were only about three dozen tennis players in the mountainous country. He was the nephew of the prime minister of Nepal. He said he didn't put that bit of information on his entry form because "I didn't see that it had anything to do with my tennis."

Kumar played Don Rubell of Brooklyn in the first round. He was beaten, 6–0, 6–2, 6–1. Afterward he said, "I think I would have done better if it had not been on grass."

* * *

When reporting on the Boston Marathon in the 1960s, I grew fond of a man named Kurt Steiner, who was a Nazi concentration camp survivor. Steiner would muscle his squat body into a spot at the front of the start of the Boston Marathon and sprint into the lead for the first one hundred yards of the 26-mile, 385-yard jaunt. This enabled him to make the early edition photo of the *Boston Globe*.

In 1966 Roberta Gibb slipped into the race as an unofficial runner and became the first woman ever to complete the Boston Marathon. A few of us interviewed her in the basement of the headquarters building. She was shy, bewildered by the attention. The *Boston Record American* put her story on page one the next day.

The next year Kathy Switzer entered as K. Switzer and ran with a male friend. When steward Jock Semple became aware of her, he jumped off the press bus to remove her from the field but was tackled by her boyfriend, to the cheers of the rascally Boston press guys on the bus.

Soon after, women were permitted as official entries. None other than Semple became the man who shepherded and encouraged women preparing for the race.

* * *

Jack Nicklaus was one of the titans of the national sports landscape. I found him an intelligent man with a good sense of proportion about golf and life. He had a tough time early in his career. He was a phenom, but his success was at the expense of Arnold Palmer, the golfer so beloved by many. "Arnie's Army" whooped it up for him on golf courses, and they resented this fat kid from Ohio State. They openly rooted against him with catcalls during the action.

Nicklaus easily could have become embittered by this treatment. But he was a smart man; he understood the dynamic of seeing a hero dethroned. He played his game, became friendly with Palmer, and emerged as a beloved man in his own right. He is the greatest golfer of his generation, perhaps of all time.

I generally covered a big golf tournament by walking with a golfer during his entire round the first day. I would position myself at a hole or two for the second round. I would walk about the course the third round and cover the last round by watching the action on television in the locker room. I enjoyed and often used the entertaining comments of the golfers who finished early and watched the closing action on TV.

In 1967, during the British Open at the Royal Liverpool Golf Club, Hoylake, I followed Nicklaus the first day. After he hit his drive, I ambled down the fairway toward the first green, daydreaming. I had already covered the Wimbledon tennis tournament, and I felt fortunate to be in England covering these big events. I even got to see the nightclub in Liverpool where the Beatles got their start.

My reverie was broken by a tap on the shoulder. It was Nicklaus walking toward the green.

He said, "Hi Stan, what are you doing here?" I was pleased that he remembered me. Earlier that year, I had covered the U.S. Open Tournament at Baltusrol in New Jersey, which Nicklaus had won.

He said, "Have you seen the sweaters?" I didn't know what he was talking about.

He said, "They have these great Pringles sweaters at one of the merchandising tents at the course. You can get terrific bargains on Pringles sweaters."

It struck me that this millionaire was excited about getting bargains on sweaters. I thanked him. And I later made my way to the Pringles tent. I bought four sweaters, one for my wife and one each for preteenage daughters. Guess who was long the favorite golfer in the Isaacs family?

* * *

On Opening Day in 1969 at Yankee Stadium, the songwriter/singer Paul Simon threw out the first ball. He told the press that he grew up as a rabid Yankee fan. The talk led to a grudge stickball game at a schoolyard in Manhattan. Larry Merchant rounded up the legendary filmmaker Woody Allen, who brought along his friend, Mickey Rose, who wrote for *The Tonight Show* with Johnny Carson. A show business vs. sports columnist match-up might have seemed appropriate, but when it turned out that Allen had been a Giants fan and Rose a Boston Braves fan, I joined them on a National League team against the two Yankee rooters, Merchant and Simon.

Simon wore his Yankee cap, which he recently had stolen from a locker at Yankee Stadium. Simon said he once went the whole season without striking out in stickball, so it was a source of satisfaction when Rose fanned Simon his first time up. Simon mumbled something about not having his eye, yet—which is what I would have expected from a Yankee fan, poet or no poet.

The game might have settled into an epic battle except that some of the handball players in the schoolyard intervened. They offered a challenge. We would play for twenty-five cents a man, the Handball Players vs. the Interlopers.

It was something of a new experience. For one thing, some of our opponents were young mod types who sported beards. I had never before played stickball against guys with beards.

I had always admired Allen's professional work. Now I came to truly respect him as a stickball player. He didn't try to hog the good positions. When others suggested a seven-inning game, Allen insisted on the regulation nine innings. He also showed a little disgust at the kidding attitude of our opponents. "They're just a bunch of clowns," he said.

We got off to a one-run lead in the second inning. Simon walked, I hit a weak pop fly that was dropped, Rose walked, and Merchant lined a single. In the second inning, Simon ran back from his third base position and made a sensational over-the-shoulder running catch of a pop fly.

Allen came to play. In the third inning he swung and missed and sent the stickball bat flying. It hit Simon in the groin and ricocheted off Merchant's cheek. Simon went to his knees. Gutty little guy that he was, he got up and said he would continue playing. "That never happened to me before," he said.

People moved well to the side when Allen batted again. He swung and missed and somehow the stickball bat split in his hand. He got a long splinter in his left hand. It bled. He said, "That never happened to me before." We agreed they just didn't make stickball bats the way they used to.

I gave Allen a bandage, which I always carry in my wallet. For some reason the guys found it funny that I had a bandage. They, of course, had dirty minds, thinking about the long-unused item they had carried in their wallets when they were coming of age.

Allen was so shaken up by the blood streaming from his hand, he played too far back in the infield, and the opponents' only two hits came because he was standing too deep to catch grounders. We ended up winning, 5–0. I was pleased that I played the entire game without striking out. We collected our quarters.

One of the opposing players said he owned a beauty parlor where they also cut men's hair. He offered to cut Simon's hair. This really disgusted Allen. "We beat a bunch of hairdressers," he said.

28

Flights of Fancy

Through the years, I have made excursions into American history. In what felt appropriate for a seeker of truth on the sports pages, I pursued the name of Paul Revere's horse. The more I thought about it, the more I persuaded myself that this was probably the most significant horse in American history for carrying Revere on his ride through New England on that wondrous night in 1775. Yet, as far as I knew, we didn't know the name of the horse.

I hopped on my own curiosity-driven steed and reviewed the Revere saga.

The basic story is that Revere, forty at the time, rode from Charlestown to Lexington on the night of April 18, 1775, to warn his countrymen the British were coming. The ride was immortalized by Henry Wadsworth Longfellow's poem—which was admirable though full of inaccuracies. Longfellow did not note, among other things, that William Dawes also rode to warn New Englanders about the British, or that Revere was captured by the British on his way out of Lexington en route to Concord. Longfellow was, in effect, an unpaid public relations guy for Revere.

The primary source in the matter, I learned, is Revere himself. He wrote three accounts of his ride. The first two probably were written in 1775, the same year as the ride. The third and most complete account was a letter to a friend, reputedly written in 1778.

Revere's mission started in Boston. He rowed across the Charles River to Charlestown for the beginning of his ride. He wrote in the 1778 letter, "When I got into town I met Colonel Conant, and several others; they said they had seen our signals. I told them what was Acting and went to git me a Horse; I got a Horse of Deacon Larkin . . . I set off upon a very good horse."

Revere rode to Lexington and warned John Hancock. Then he galloped on and was captured outside Lexington. A British major ordered him to give up his horse to a sergeant.

"I dismounted," Revere wrote, "the Saarjint mounted my horse . . . and they told me they should make use of my horse for the night and rode off down the road."

Revere had to walk back toward Lexington. There is no further mention of the horse. This seemed to me a terribly anonymous end for this great steed, so important in American history. She is more significant, I have written, than our most famous thoroughbreds—Man O'War, Citation, or Secretariat. She deserves more honor than even Silver, Rex, or Champion of cowboy movie fame.

I found out that the identity of Revere's horse is the question most asked of the Boston Public Library. How about that?

I have uncovered bogus names assigned to the horse. A secretary of the Boston Society grew so tired of answering questions about the horse that he was moved by a puckish spirit to invent the name "Sparky" because in the Longfellow poem there are the lines:

The fate of the nation was riding that night;
And the spark struck out by that steed in his flight,
Kindles the land into flame with its heat.

Others have felt free to bestow names on Revere's horse just because they felt like it. In his book *Paul Revere,* Emerson Gifford wrote, "That night's work was the last which good old Dobbin was ever called to undertake. Before daybreak he had been ridden almost to his death in his country's service." In the poem "Tribute to the Horse," which appeared in the February 1, 1909, issue of *Horse Journal,* W. A. Paxson wrote:

Take Tam O'Shanter and his famous mare, Meg
And Paul Revere and his famous Peg

In "Fugue for Tinhorns" from the Frank Loesser musical *Guys and Dolls,* it says, "I got the horse right here, his name is Paul Revere." That, of course, is a bit of poetic license in the tradition of H. W. Longfellow. The horse couldn't be named Paul Revere because, as I learned from Revere's letters, the horse belonged to Deacon Larkin, who only lent the horse to Revere for his famous ride.

I was pleased to discover others who cared as deeply as I did about this. James A. Rhodes, who later became governor of Ohio, wrote these words when he was mayor of Columbus:

Wake up historians! Have you no remorse?
Tell us what became of Paul Revere's horse.
Tell us what became of this gallant horse
After he finished his courageous course.
Can't you recall or remember his name,
Or tell us his color from tail to mane?
How did he die or where was he buried?
To your grave these secrets you have carried
If you historians cannot trace his source
We Americans will call him "Freedom's Horse."

In the course of my pursuit, I read books on Revere and visited the New York Public Library, Boston Public Library, Massachusetts Historical Society, and Massachusetts State Archives. At the state archives, where I stopped during a trip to cover the Boston Marathon, the staff met my request with a pained look. Leo Flaherty, the head archivist, said, "If people would only pay as much attention to important matters as they do to unimportant ones . . ." Politely, I begged to differ, questioning his sense of what was and was not important.

What about the English sergeant who took the horse from Revere? Was it possible that Revere told him the name of the horse as he surrendered him? In England I took a train out to the suburb of Kew to check out the national archives. It was a bit overwhelming to look at the stacks and stacks of material, but a solicitous clerk guided me to the section on the Revolutionary War. Sure enough, I came across a handwritten diary by the major who had ordered Revere down from his horse. Reading his handwriting was not unlike negotiating a maze, but I made things out enough to grasp that he did not mention the name of the horse when he took it from Revere.

My continuing correspondence on the matter led to a letter from Mr. George Vincent of Oceanside, Long Island. He wrote, "May I offer you some historical notes on Paul Revere's horse. Based on a book published by Knickerbocker Press, N.Y., 1930, entitled 'Some Descendants of Edward Larkin' (plus some other immigrants from England & Wales) the following occurs: 'Samuel Larkin, born Oct. 22, 1701, died Oct. 8, 1784; he was a chair maker, then a fisherman and had horses and stable. He was the owner of Brown Beauty, the mare of Paul Revere's ride. . . . The mare was loaned at the request of Samuel's son, Deacon John Larkin, and was never returned to her owner.'"

Mr. Vincent was a descendant of Samuel Larkin, hence his interest. The unknown author makes no attempt to document the name of the horse, yet it is the closest thing to a reliable source on this pressing matter. It persuaded historian David Hackett Fischer. He mentioned Brown Beauty three times in his 1994 book *Paul Revere's Ride*. He cites erroneous votes for Meg, Sparky, Scheherezade, and the lot; he comes out definitively for Brown Beauty.

So that is how it stands. Even though Brown Beauty sounds a little too pat, Brown Beauty it is. But should any scholars out there have any other leads . . .

* * *

I often had flights of fancy involving horse racing. One of my favorites was a holiday column on "The One and Only Christmas Stakes." I conceived a race among the eight reindeer in Clement Moore's revered poem, "Twas the Night Before Christmas."

I put top jockeys on the reindeer: Ted Atkinson on Comet, Isaac Murphy on Dancer, Angel Cordero on Prancer. I set up an odds line with Dasher/Eddie Arcaro the 8–5 favorite, Blitzen/Jerry Bailey 4–1. I made Cupid/Willie Shoemaker a 50–1 longshot because he might have his mind on other things beside racing.

With Santa Claus as the starter, they raced a mile around the north pole. At one point the air resounded with the cries, "On Comet, on Cupid, on Donner and Blitzen." It all ended suspensefully in an eight-reindeer dead heat. And Santa Claus rode off saying, "Happy Christmas to all and to all a good night."

* * *

I have had fun over the years by clocking renditions of the "Star-Spangled Banner." This was inspired by Marvin Gaye's performance at the NBA All Star Game in Los Angeles in 1983, which long has been regarded as a classic. An instant hit, it made the All Star game's play-by-play press notes for the first quarter, which began, "Marvin Gaye rock 'n rolled today's anthem in 2:33.4." Gaye didn't just rock it. He gave it a slow, soulful caress that left some folks agape. It had the Forum crowd—and both teams—clapping in rhythm, roaring in tribute.

Gaye's delivery was arguably the longest anybody had ever taken to sing the song without any repeated lines. It led me to time other renditions.

Aretha Franklin outdid Gaye by clocking in at 2:44 before a Thomas Hearns–Dennis Andries fight in Detroit in 1987. But I rule her out because she threw in introductory phrases and riffs that were strictly self-serving.

If others have eclipsed Gaye, I am not aware of them, because I retired from anthem clocking. Sometimes performers with little of Gaye's talent set out to top him, often by repeating lines. Gaye, who was shot and killed by his father the year after his All Star game performance, stands supreme for me among anthem singers.

My penchant for anthem clocking fostered my curiosity in "Star-Spangled Banner" lore. It was penned by Francis Scott Key the night of September 13–14, 1814, while watching the bombardment of Baltimore's Fort McHenry during the War of 1812. His poem, called, "Defence of Fort McHenry," was put to the music of "To Anacreon in Heav'n," which was written as a bawdy drinking song by John Stafford Smith for a London social club, the Anacreontic Society. It was sung by rakes and roues at the Crown and Anchor tavern in London.

It was favored during the Spanish-American War of 1899, and it was declared the national anthem by President Woodrow Wilson in 1916. In 1931, 117 years after it was written, an act of Congress officially designated it as the national anthem. There have been some attempts to replace it with other songs, such as "God Bless America" and "America the Beautiful," but it has stood as our anthem.

According to the Baseball Hall of Fame, the first pregame "Star-Spangled Banner" was sung in 1913 by a New York opera star, Anna Fitziu. It became a fixture at sports events during World War II.

This bothered Kenny Smith, a dandy little man who covered baseball for a few decades at the *New York Daily Mirror* and later became a curator for the Baseball Hall of Fame. Smith was no curmudgeon, but he didn't like the idea of baseball—a commercial enterprise—wrapping itself in the American flag by playing the anthem. Smith grumped, "When Macy's and Gimbels open their stores in the morning, they don't play the national anthem, do they?"

The anthem has had its critics. Richard Rodgers: "It's impossible to sing." Godfrey Cambridge: "It has no meaning for the black man." Meredith Wilson: "It violates every single principle of songwriting." Joan Baez: "It is just so much trash." Westbrook Pegler: "It's just terrible." One critic wrote that the song, which ranges from a low B-flat to a high B-flat, can't be navigated without the risk of a hernia.

I think it would be unfair, though, to lay the difficulty of singing the song on what happened to a Long Island mail carrier in August 2000. Percy McRae, sixty-five, who was in Chicago to attend a mail carrier's convention, sang the anthem at a Cubs game and suffered a fatal heart attack in the first inning. It was revealed afterward that he had hypertensive cardiovascular disease.

Robert Goulet, a Canadian, botched his version of the anthem at the heavyweight championship fight in Lewiston, Maine, on May 25, 1965, when Muhammad Ali knocked out Sonny Liston in the first round and referee Joe Walcott mishandled the count. Somebody wrote, "Three people didn't belong in that ring: Liston, Walcott and Goulet."

Frank Sinatra, Eddie Fisher, Willie Nelson, and Johnny Paycheck have blown the words. So did Nat King Cole and, later, his daughter Natalie Cole, which prompted writer Jack Wilkinson to call it a first- and second-generation "Star Mangled Banner." Cab Calloway forgot the words at Madison Square Garden, but the hi-de-ho man bailed himself out with a scat rendition the rest of the way. And Roseanne Barr made a fool of herself with vulgar actions while squeaking away at a San Diego Padres game in 1990. Perhaps the fans at Chicago Blackhawks games at the United Center know best how to handle the tough anthem: they cheer nonstop through the heartfelt renditions of Jim Cornelison.

José Feliciano, the twenty-three-year-old blind guitarist and rock singer, broke the mold with a hip, soulful rendition before the fifth game of the 1968 World Series in Detroit. Though many overwrought people at the time protested his version as a desecration, Feliciano opened the song to different interpretations, some of them magnificent, many of them an assault upon the ears.

Ella Fitzgerald sang it well at one Sugar Bowl. "So well," said college football maven Beano Cook, "that everybody in the press box was silent, nobody was eating. That's how good she was."

I once heard a terrific rendition at an All-Star Game at Yankee Stadium. I loved it. A few years later, I was covering the World Series in San Francisco with my pal and *Newsday* colleague, Steve Jacobson. He was a jazz buff, and he told me, "Carmen McRae, whose 'Star-Spangled Banner' you loved so much at the All-Star Game, is performing at a club in North Beach. Want to see her?" We went. She didn't sing the anthem, and I didn't enjoy her at all. I was perplexed. I realized only later that it had been Della Reese and *not* Carmen McRae who had sung the anthem at that All-Star Game. I periodically remind Jacobson of that.

The athletes generally want the song to be over quickly so they can get on with their pregame preparations. The champion advocate of the quickie rendition was Paul Zimmerman, a lovable zany at the *World Telegram* and *Post*. He carried a stopwatch with him as basic equipment. "I carry it for hang-time punts," he once said at a football game, "but I get the anthem that way, too."

Zimmerman inspired one of the quickest renditions ever by Fenway Park organist John Kiley. He once described to me how it came about:

> Yankees–Red Sox series, 1977. Friday night, I heard two bars and said to everyone "He's on a record pace," my record being the Princeton band's 53 seconds. Kiley came in at 0:55 without raising a sweat. I immediately visited his booth. A nice, old, bald-headed guy. I told him, "Mr. Kiley, you can break the record if you pick it up at the end." He said he'd already been criticized for playing it too fast. I told him, "I'm not telling you what to do, but just think about it." Next day the entire press box was primed. (Okay, about three guys were). He came out of the blocks flying. I screamed, "He's going for it!" Sure enough, he breezed by Princeton and would have hit 50 seconds except that he held the last note, as a gesture of, what? Defiance. Time: 0:51. I ran over to his booth. He was beaming. I told him, "Mr. Kiley, this is a great moment for me and I want to sincerely thank you." He said he'd done it for me, but that was the last time.

Inspired by Zimmerman, I tried to get some locals to go for the record. Joe Duerr, the anthem singer at New York Islander hockey games, told me that he shaved it down to fifty seconds in practice. He tipped me to a major try at an upcoming game and I alerted readers. He choked, however, and went over a minute. An Islander official told him not to try it anymore—something about it desecrating the song. I almost got John Amirante, the anthem man for the New York Rangers, to try to set a record one night, but he begged off at the last minute, cautioned by a Madison Square Garden bluenose.

Gladys Goodding, who probably played the anthem on the organ as much as anybody, became the answer to the trivia question: "Who played for the Dodgers, Knicks and Rangers?" She played for the Dodgers at Ebbets Field and the Knicks and Rangers at the Garden. She said it couldn't be done in less than 1:10, but the television people, anxious to get to commercials, persisted. She got it down to fifty-nine seconds.

I interviewed Goodding. She was a nice, matronly woman. She had one request. "Please spell my name with two 'd's," she asked. When she died, I wrote an obituary that ended with the words, "Please Mr. Typesetter, that's Gladys Goodding with two 'd's." It came up in the paper as Gladdys Gooding.

29

Stuntsmanship

I have seasoned my columns with various off-beat pursuits over the years. One of them was a caper vaguely inspired by Paul Gallico, a columnist for the *New York Daily News* who later became a successful fiction writer. Gallico once got into the ring with heavyweight champion Jack Dempsey and lived to tell the tale.

My pal Larry Merchant and I did not want to fight a champion; we just wanted to see what it was like to be in the ring trading punches with boxing gloves and ring gear.

In the early 1960s, when middleweight champion Emile Griffith was training at one of the Catskill Mountain hotels for a defense of his title, we persuaded Griffith's manager, Gil Clancy, to let us go at each other in the ring. Clancy, a terrific guy, was amused. He also agreed that it was a good idea for those who wrote about boxing to get even a slight taste of what it was like to be a pug.

Clancy agreed to referee the match, and he provided us with gloves, headgear, and mouthpieces. My first hurdle was the mouthpiece; it cut into my gums. I immediately had new respect for boxers, since they could keep the damn thing in their mouths.

Larry and I were fairly evenly matched physically, both in our thirties, in the 155 pound range, around 5'7". We started out cautiously. When we moved in to throw punches, I believe Merchant got the better of it. It was so tiring after only a few moments of flailing at each other, I felt as if I were throwing punches underwater.

Midway in the round, I threw a right-hand punch that hit Merchant squarely on the chin. He went down. I am not sure who was more surprised:

Merchant, Clancy, or me. Larry then got up and dominated the rest of the round.

Merchant probably would have won had we fought, say, a four-round fight. But on the basis of the knockdown, Clancy awarded the round to me. He said, "When you hear that somebody hit somebody on the button, that's what you did to Larry. It wasn't that you hit him so hard but that you hit him just on that spot on the chin."

I later learned that Clancy, recognizing how tired we were, cut the round from the regulation three minutes to two.

* * *

In 1964, I was covering the U.S. Open golf tournament in the Washington, D.C. area. *Newsday* did not publish on Sunday at the time, so I decided to play hooky from the golf tournament on Saturday to check out the legend of George Washington throwing a silver dollar across a river.

I wrote a column about the sport that I called, "Throwing a Dollar Across the Rappahannock." I pointed out with some fervor that it was the Rappahannock and not, as often erroneously written, the Potomac or the Delaware River that was the scene of Washington's legendary toss. If it happened, it occurred near his boyhood home, Ferry Farm, outside Fredericksburg, Virginia.

I tooled down to Fredericksburg to the alleged spot of his toss. At that spot, some vendors were selling a special Spanish piece of eight, which they claimed would have been the kind of coin Washington threw. There was, of course, no American coin in those pre-Revolutionary days, even if people insist on saying he threw a silver dollar.

Numerous books say Washington threw a stone. They had a supporter in Ellie Milliken, who ran the tourist shop at Ferry Farm that called itself "the site of the legendary cherry tree and dollar-thrown incidents." Milliken said it was probably a stone "because George was too level-headed a boy to be throwing dollars away."

She pointed to a clearing near the spot where Washington is supposed to have made the throw. I picked up ten stones just right for throwing and made my way down to the bank of the Rappahannock. And to be as authentic as possible, I also came armed with one of those Spanish pieces of eight, which cost me a dollar.

The river was serene. Two boys fished lazily on the other bank. As I started warming up to throw, I judged the width of the river at that point to be about equal to the distance from home plate to right field in the Polo Grounds, some 250 feet or so. It was about 11:30 in the morning. The temperature was already in the nineties. I figured that was just the kind of heat to loosen up my thirty-five-year-old soupbone.

My first toss plunked into the water, only halfway across the Rappahannock. My second toss went a little farther. So did my third and fourth. My fifth went three-quarters the width of the river. That was my best throw. My only hope of emulating the father of our country lay with the piece of eight. I rested up for the big throw, got a good toehold and let fly a beautiful skimmer. It was my best throw by far. I watched with the excitement that comes with a sense of history.

It plopped into the drink, at least fifteen feet from the opposite bank.

I could be a sourpuss and say my experience illustrated that Washington could never have hurled anything across the Rappahannock. But I won't, because there is evidence it *can* be done. Milliken told me that an annual "Throw Across the Rappahannock" was held on Washington's birthday for Fredericksburg's Boy Scouts. "They use large washers instead of dollars," she said. "This year thirty boys took part and seven cleared the other bank."

The sign outside Ferry Farm reads, "George Washington developed here the intensity and moral strength that later forged a nation."

"The good arm, too," I wrote in my column.

* * *

Among the wacky columns I most enjoyed was the one recording the actions of motorists at the Throgs Neck Bridge tollbooth in the Bronx. I stationed myself next to the basket into which motorists threw coins (I think it was fifty cents in those days). I saw coins fly with abandon with different thrusts worthy of any big-time basketball arena. Among others, I noted these actions:

The Leaner: He leans all the way out of his car window and reaches across his body with his right hand to drop the coin into the basket. He rarely misses—but he sacrifices a quick getaway from the tool booth.

The Loose Wrist: He is timid, without authority, as he lets the coin go. He is most likely to miss the basket.

The Rainbower: She shoots with a sense of style. She throws the coin up, so it arcs into the basket. She watches the coin plunk into the basket with a smile of satisfaction.

The Slob: He usually parks too far from the basket. He has trouble getting the coin out of his pocket. He holds up the line of cars. He frequently misses.

The Ernie Calverly Shot (honoring a last-second long-distance basket made by Rhode Island State's Ernie Calverly at Madison Square Garden many years ago): The passenger in the right front seat throws the coin over the top of the car trying to sink it into the basket on the left side. The guards at Throgs Neck told me nobody was on record making this shot. It was frowned upon by the authorities.

A guard told me about the time a husband came out of the passenger's seat to pick up the coin after his wife missed the basket. "Just as the husband got out," the guard said, "I told the woman to drive on, that I would pick up the money. She was flustered, she didn't see her husband, and drove off. Her husband started chasing after her, yelling, 'Stop, Sarah, stop, wait for me!' She never heard him. She just kept on going. The guy was fuming. We had to put him on a bus to get him home."

* * *

In 1981 I realized a horse player's fantasy by persuading *Newsday* to stake me to a week's betting at Belmont Park. I could do this because one of the editors had become a degenerate horse player.

As I explained to readers, the accepted wisdom is that you can beat a race, but you can't beat the races. My own financial balance sheet over a few decades punting at racecourses certainly substantiates that. But the point of the stunt was to test my theory that I could do better if I had a larger bankroll with which to assault the mutual machines.

I noted that I was always the cautious $2 bettor, afraid to wheel and deal, to operate, to plunge, to throw that old devil "Caution" to the winds. What would happen, I pondered, if for at least one week I could go to a track with a bankroll worthy of a tycoon and patiently, scientifically attack the mutual machines, to wait when the waiting was good, to swashbuckle when the opportunity presented itself?

Many horse players feel this way. My editor did, too. The paper agreed to bankroll me with $1,000. The stipulation was that whatever I won that week would be mine, while returning the $1,000 to the company. *Newsday* would absorb the losses. Paradise found.

My big week started on Sunday, June 1, and ended on Saturday, June 6, the day of the 102nd Belmont Stakes. I prepared by reading racing books by respected writers: Dick Sasuly, a friend; Tom Ainslie, an alias for Dick Carter, an outstanding reporter and former colleague at the *Daily Compass;* and the redoubtable Andy Beyer, probably the most renowned of all handicappers, who brought an infectious joie de vivre to his writing.

Going into detail might make people's eyes glaze over, so here is a box score of how I did leading up to the day of the Belmont Stakes.

Sunday: I won $468.40
Monday: I won $69 (bankroll: plus $537.40)
Tuesday: no racing
Wednesday: I lost $236 (bankroll: plus $301.40)
Thursday: I lost $103 (bankroll: plus 198.40)
Friday: I lost 124.50 (bankroll: plus 73.90)

I rode an emotional roller coaster. I enjoyed winning bets, fretted over losing bets. I had the satisfaction of laying off losing horses that tempted me; I despaired about bets that I should have made but did not. On Saturday, after betting on four races, I was down $6.10 for the week, leaving me with a bankroll of $993.90. What to do?

I decided that to give some weight to the story, I should make a huge bet on the Belmont Stakes, the highlight event of the week. I had seen every Belmont since Bounding Home won in 1944. It was my favorite race and one of my favorite sporting events. It seemed appropriate to end the caper with a bang—or a simper.

All week long I had felt that Codex, the winner of the Preakness, would win the Belmont. My sentimental heart, though, was with Genuine Risk, the valiant filly that won the Kentucky Derby. I would have preferred to bet on her, but it seemed to me that if ever I was to be a racetrack pro, this was no time for sentiment.

A night of rain had produced an off-track, which meant that it was slow. My colleague, Vic Ziegel, then of the *New York Post,* noted that Codex had never done well on an off-track. Others talked about Rumbo loving an off-track. I noted, though, that these observations were based on just one race in California. I was reassured by Joe Tanenbaum, the Gulfstream Park publicity man. "An off-track in California is nothing like an off-track in New York," he said. "I love Codex."

I faced the ambivalence that attacks every horse player almost every time they try to make a decision. I figured I should have faith in my own opinion rather than be swayed by the comments of others. I tried to stifle the sentimental voice within that said, "How would you feel if Genuine Risk won and you *did not* bet on her?"

No other horse in the field tempted me. I screwed up my courage. I would go out with a splash, even though this broke all the rules of good money-management betting. I proceeded to make a $400 win bet on Codex, the

8–5 favorite, the biggest bet of my life (on company money, of course). And I uttered a silent prayer that if I lost with Codex, he would not be beaten by Genuine Risk.

The race started. Codex was a dud. He ran poorly, making only a slight move from the back of the pack on the backstretch, never getting into contention. He finished seventh in the field of ten.

As the horses pounded down the stretch, it looked like Genuine Risk was going to be the winner. In that split second my heart filled with a thousand "I-told-you-sos." This would have provided a smashing ironic note to my story, but Temperence Hill, a 53–1 shot, came out of the gloom and beat Genuine Risk by two lengths.

Codex's defeat meant my losses for the week totaled $406.10. Of the fifty-three races that had been run, I had bet on thirty-six and won ten of them. My handicapping had been fair; my money management, topped by the folly of plunging on the Belmont Stakes, poor. I turned in my $593.90 to the *Newsday* financial department and wrote the story of my caper for *LI Magazine* in advance of the next year's Belmont Stakes.

I went back to making $2-based bets at the races. I still feel stupid about that Codex bet.

* * *

For decades, I attended the Brown-Columbia football game in New York. I had dual loyalties there. Press lunches for Columbia football were one of my first assignments as a cub sports reporter at the *Daily Compass*. I later attended a one-week sports editors' conference at Columbia during my checkered regime as sports editor at *Newsday*. My Brown University loyalties stemmed from the allegiance that came from underwriting the costs of sending our youngest daughter, Ellen, to Brown.

I would trek up to Baker Field every other year and bask in what is one of the gorgeous spots in all of New York City. From the press box situated above Leonard Wien Stadium, I looked out at a leafy green park and the confluence of the Harlem and Hudson Rivers at the cut in the land that is called Spuyten Duyvil. A magnificent vista.

One year, my interest in Columbia football inspired two bright lads in the Columbia band. They extended me an invitation to be a guest musician with the band. I performed on a glorious instrument known as the lengthopipe, which consisted of a toilet plunger at one end, attached to a long piece of garden hose, connected to a trumpet mouthpiece. I blew a noise that sounded like "oomph" to punctuate designated points in a particular rendition. As a youth who was barred from singing in grammar school assemblies, this was the one and only musical highlight of my existence. I assure one and all that no one blew with more gusto to produce those "oomphs."

I would tell everyone that I looked forward to being at Baker Field on the great day when Brown and Columbia, who wind up their seasons against each other every year, play for the Ivy League championship. People laughed and told me I would not live that long. They probably were right.

I have been tireless in coming up with ideas to elevate Columbia football. I have argued that far too much space and attention is given to insignificant postseason games strictly because the label "bowl" is attached to those games. For example, a Waste Management Bowl, say, between Mississippi State and Tulsa might receive some notice in many newspapers for no other reason than it is listed as a bowl game. To that end, I have urged that the annual meeting between the two New York State Ivy schools, Columbia and Cornell, be labeled the Empire State Bowl. (New York is the Empire State.)

A group of raucous Cornell alumni had the same idea. They even issued sweatshirts proclaiming the need for an Empire Bowl. I encouraged them by offering a trophy for the game: a two-foot plastic statue of King Kong that I had received as part of a promotion for a movie. What better symbol of the Empire Bowl than that magnificent Empire State building climber, King Kong? I am hopeful the Empire State Bowl will come to pass. I await the day the King Kong trophy will be presented at midfield to the winning team after an Empire State Bowl showdown. But I am not holding my breath.

30

Leaving *Newsday*

Since my start at *Newsday* in October 1954, our sports section had emerged from a small-time operation into one of the best in the country. Though *Newsday* had come a long way, it was regarded as a suburban paper. Out-of-town sports editors and columnists were more aware of us than the sports editors in New York, who tended to be insular in their view of sports journalism.

It was a drawback not to be as dominating a presence on the sports scene as the New York papers. The stories in the city papers were seen each day by management and athletes. A *Newsday* story might not be seen at all, or it might be talked about a few days later. This frustration about recognition led to a stream of writers leaving the paper. We lost, among others, George Vecsey and Pete Alfano to the *Times* and later Bill Nack and Tom Verducci to *Sports Illustrated*.

I carved out a respected niche for myself and, in truth, could be regarded as a big fish in a small pond. I won a "National Headliners Award" for sports column writing in 1962. I had a story selected for the annual "Best Sports Stories of the Year" book collection eight years running from 1960 through 1967. During that stretch Joe Falls, a Detroit sports guy, said to me, "I asked someone I respect who is writing the best stuff in New York and he said, 'Stan Isaacs is." Falls would never tell me who said that.

On a few occasions, I was approached by the *Times* about joining the sports staff. Sports editor Jim Roach, who lived in Douglaston, Queens, often praised my work. His successor, Jim Tuite, sounded me out a few times about a job. I was invited to have lunch with managing editor Arthur Gelb in the *Times* executive dining room. Gelb seemed more eager to talk about how great the *Times* was—I couldn't help but agree with him—than talk about me and what I could bring to the paper.

The offer from Tuite was to join the sports staff as a reporter. I decided to stay at *Newsday,* where I had the freedom of a columnist to choose my own subjects. At the *Times,* I would have had the name recognition that likely would have enabled me to land big-time book contracts. But I chose a better quality of life over the status the *Times* would have provided.

* * *

In retrospect, there has never been much doubt that I made the right choice, because I had a varied career at *Newsday*. I wrote the columns "Out of Left Field," "Stan Isaacs' Long Island," and later "TV Sports," as well as longer pieces for *LI Magazine,* plus fumbling around as sports editor for a year-and-a-half.

Newsday and the newspaper business went through some dramatic changes during my career. In late 1966 Harry Guggenheim brought in Bill Moyers, the former press secretary to President Johnson, to be publisher of *Newsday*. We didn't know what to expect with Moyers because of his association with Johnson, who had imploded with his deceit about the Vietnam War. We would learn much later that Moyers had a falling-out with Johnson in the latter days of the administration because he disagreed with Johnson about the war.

Early on, Moyers called me into his office and asked, "How can the sports department be improved?" I didn't know him well enough to be entirely candid with him, so I shilly-shallied, making some relatively mild suggestions. I realized in a short time what a special hombre he was.

Moyers moved slowly at first, but within a few years he had shaped the paper into one of the most liberal newspapers in the country. It astounded some *Newsday* veterans and Long Islanders to see the paper take such radical positions as expressing sympathy for the Black Panthers and coming out against Suffolk police wearing American flags on their uniform sleeves.

Inevitably, there was a falling-out between the conservative Guggenheim and his new prodigy. While Guggenheim lay near death with prostate cancer, his Republican friends urged him to take the paper away from "that Communist." Guggenheim proceeded to freeze Moyers out of the paper and his will. He sold it to what he thought were the safe, conservative hands of the Times Mirror Company. That was the old *Los Angeles Times* of Norman Chandler.

His son, Otis, was of a more modern and liberal stripe. He allowed *Newsday* to go its own way editorially, while updating its technology and business procedures. A liberal pension plan would later prove a boon to veteran staffers. The paper slid downhill when the Times Mirror sold it to the Chicago Tribune Company, and it deteriorated into ignominy when it became the property of Cablevision.

* * *

While I was writing the feature column, I pursued something that I would never have been able to try for at the *Times*. I won a one-year National Endowment for the Humanities fellowship at Stanford University for the school year 1976–1977. My wife and I called it our "Year in Paradise." It was the greatest year of our lives.

The fellowship chose fifteen news people from the United States and three foreign journalists. It provided us with a year on campus away from the hurly-burly of daily journalism to recharge our batteries. We could audit whatever courses we chose—as could our spouses—and were responsible only for writing one essay for a philosophy course. With our eldest daughter Nancy off to college, my wife and I and two younger daughters, Ann and Ellen, drove across the country in late August 1976 and settled into graduate student housing, a garden-apartment duplex on campus.

Participants in the fellowship were asked to select an area of study that would enrich them for future journalistic application. My application specified interest in women's studies for preparation to write about the burgeoning women's movement. There was no rigidity to any of this. I took women's studies courses along with history, art, introductory law, philosophy, literature, and Jewish studies.

A standout course was "American History since World War II" with historian Barton Bernstein. He laid the responsibility for the cold war on the United States as much as the Soviet Union. The professor was particularly hard on President Truman for detouring from a course of dealing with the Soviets that President Roosevelt had set. He has frequently written pieces questioning the rationale for the United States dropping not one but two atomic bombs on Japan.

Bernstein lectured to a large audience. The course included a seminar with a small group of students presided over by a graduate student, Michael Kazin, the son of author Alfred Kazin. He went on to a professor position at Georgetown University, a chronicler of leftist movements. In one session, we were talking about the red scares of the 1950s and how Senator Joe McCarthy rode roughshod over people. One student, acknowledging my seniority, said, "Mr. Isaacs, you were there at the time. How could you people allow McCarthy to get away with what he did?" I was flabbergasted.

I tried mightily, if not well, to explain the frustration of not being able to discredit McCarthy.

We loved Stanford—the beautiful campus, the courses, the many guest speakers on campus, and those who specifically addressed the journalism fellows. Our group included Soveig Torvik of the *Seattle Post-Intelligencer,* Dick Foster of the *Des Moines Register,* Paul Jablow of the *Philadelphia Inquirer,* Frank Ashley of the *Louisville Courier Journal,* David Corcoran of the *Record* in New Jersey, and energy fellow Paul Andrews of the *Seattle Times.* The foreign journalists were Maciej Wierzynski from Poland, Josef Szasi from Hungary, and Russell Skelton from Australia. We became good friends with many and later visited Szasi in Budapest, learning that he, a reluctant member of the Hungarian Communist Party, was rabidly anti-Soviet.

I had expected that the professors at Stanford would be superb, better than any from my long-ago days at Brooklyn College. I was surprised that except for Bernstein and maybe one other, the teachers did not impress me. They were likable, but hardly as brilliant or inspiring as two Hofstra professor-friends, historian Michael D'Innocenzo and literature scholar Ruth Prigozy.

My one required paper stemmed from a course in which the professor and the graduate students extolled William Faulkner's *Absalom, Absalom.* I found the novel turgid, unreadable, with some of the longest sentences ever forced on poor, suffering readers. Faulkner was a hot item on the Stanford campus at that time—maybe he still is—and I wrote a paper entitled "Effluvium, Effluvium," in which I lampooned the novel and his convoluted style. This inspired a roasting from a few of my colleagues. Kay Mills of the Newhouse papers later sent me a T-shirt labeled, "Faulkner Fan Club."

* * *

While at Stanford, we took off one day for the old gold-mining country of northern California. We drove to the Calaveras County Fair to watch the annual frog jumping contest. The contest stems, of course, from the Mark Twain story, "The Celebrated Jumping Frog of Calaveras County," which details some skullduggery over a frog-jumping bet. The fair promoters were smart enough to resurrect the frog jump as an attraction to lure Twain fans.

Years before my Stanford sojourn, I had become aware that it was possible to enter a frog in absentia. I sent in a $5 entry fee with the understanding that an area youth would jockey my frog. I gave my frog the name of Rumpelstiltskin. A few days later, I received a postcard informing me the distance my frog had jumped, which, regrettably, was not long enough to win the contest. It was more than enough, though, for me to write columns about it. Whitey Ford, the only Yankee living on Long Island, asked me in the clubhouse one afternoon, "How did your frog do?"

On this day, I opted for the fair over my wife's objections. She had a feeling that the fair wouldn't be much and noted that we would be missing a good speaker scheduled to address the assemblage of journalists in the fellowship program at Stanford.

We drove into gold country toward the fair. I tingled with the idea of jockeying my own frog this time, Rumpelstiltskin II. As we approached the fairgrounds, platoons of motorcyclists whizzed by us on the road. The closer we got to the fairgrounds, the more motorcycles, the louder the cacophony. It was as if we were joining a convention of Hells Angels.

The grounds appeared to be as scraggly as the garb and facial hair of the motorcyclists. We pressed on toward the frog jump, concerned that it did not have a featured place in any of the literature and billboards. When we finally found it in a far-off, tree-less corner of the grounds, we came to a half-assed, half-hearted activity in which the officials, if that is the correct term, conducted the competition in a bored, lackadaisical manner before a gaggle of spectators.

There was no sense of Mark Twain's fun and frolic. It didn't matter that I was present; I could not participate with my frog. I gave my entry fee and waited until a boy picked out a frog and readied him for his turn. Rumpelstiltskin II seemed no more interested than the officials. He had to be roused for his first hop, took a small jump, then had to be roused for his third hop. I don't recall what his distance was. I probably could have jumped farther myself.

* * *

I paid a price for my Stanford sabbatical. When I returned to *Newsday,* my feature column was gone. As sports editor, I had proposed a column on television and sports. Now I settled into the challenge of going back to sports and writing the TV Sports column. I followed the path pioneered by Jack Craig of the *Boston Globe,* a classy guy who was nothing but encouraging when I called to ask for advice.

I fashioned a dual role: I wrote as critic and reporter. I critiqued telecasts and the style and language of announcers.

* * *

I was an early fan of John Madden, not only because he was the best football analyst on television, but also because he had a quirky way of looking at things. He was, like me, a numbers freak.

I interviewed him early in his career as an announcer. In a casual conversation, I was delighted to hear him talk about numbers. He said that everyone was born to wear a number. In his mind's eye he gave numbers to people based mostly on their body build, but also on other factors like what they did, how they did it, their spirit of joie de vivre or gloom-and-doom, the cut of their jib.

He had a high regard for number 12. In his mind it was the ultimate number for a quarterback. Kenny Stabler, his star quarterback when he coached the Oakland Raiders, wore 12. So did quarterbacks Roger Staubach, Terry Bradshaw, Joe Namath, and Bob Griese.

Madden didn't stop with football or just sports. He had ready answers in most cases when I fed him the names of other figures.

President Jimmy Carter got a 5; Jack Kennedy an 18, Bobby Kennedy a 19; Muhammad Ali an 87; Ronald Reagan a 16; Robert Redford a 19; Katherine Hepburn an 88; Mae West a 64; Winston Churchill a 61; Franklin Roosevelt a 16.

He said Dolly Parton was "a true 64."

Why not a 66?

"A 66 would be for a taller person."

He couldn't envision a number for Joseph Stalin and chose to pass on the villain of the moment, the Ayatollah Khomeini. He gave Hitler a 22, the same number he assigned the assassin-minded defensive back Jack Tatum, who played for him in Oakland.

He gave Santa Claus a 78 because "he's big and blocky and 78 is an offensive player's number, which would be more passive and happy than a defensive number like 74." Madden was a 74 in his career. "I was slow but deliberate," he said.

He would make Secretariat a 12. "I don't know much about horse racing, but here's a horse who had charisma and projected leadership. and that makes him a perfect 12."

He drew a blank on Adam and Eve. Others might see them as 1 and 1A. Madden said, "I can't envision their bodies so I can't give them numbers."

I asked him what number he would give me. He said, "I see you as a 9."

That was the number of Ted Williams, Roger Maris, Gordie Howe, Maurice Richard, and Bobby Hull. I would give it to Thomas Jefferson, Humphrey Bogart, Citation, Cyrus Warmheart, Eleanor Roosevelt, and Wolfgang Amadeus Mozart. I liked it.

* * *

I visited trucks and control rooms to report the whys and wherefores of TV production. Ted Nathanson of NBC, one of the best producer-directors, once told people he respected me because I had come to the production truck to learn how TV sports worked.

Most networks allowed me access to their trucks for behind-the-scenes looks at telecasts. Some did not. ABC's Howard Cosell, in particular, did not want me to see the workings of his telecasts. Cosell excoriated newspaper people for not understanding TV, yet wouldn't permit us the access that would provide a better understanding of his work and the industry.

Thanks to the redoubtable director Chet Forte, his longtime colleague, I occasionally snuck into a production truck without Cosell's knowledge. Getting an inside view of Cosell and the ABC people only enhanced my appreciation of the technical skill of Cosell and all involved, though I had a different overall view of Cosell.

Cosell was brilliant. He was a bully. He had almost total recall, but he would not admit a mistake. He was paranoid about any criticism. If an obscure paper in Podunk, USA, had a line critical of him, he would find out about it and react as if it were read by everybody in the country. Cosell was a consummate salesman who sold 1) himself, 2) ABC and the sponsors, and 3) the sport he was covering.

He was a hypocrite, as well, because he praised pro football and blasted baseball when he worked pro football, then lauded baseball when he was off pro football. He reveled in boxing, basking in the limelight provided by Muhammad Ali, then deplored it later, though boxing was no more corrupt than it had been when he was making a name for himself. He deserved credit for supporting Ali during his draft troubles, but he acted as if he were the only journalist who championed Ali when the great one had his championship taken away for refusing to serve in the army during the Vietnam War.

Cosell made an Olympic sport out of blasting newspapermen. On one occasion he called me to praise an article I had written, which criticized another member of his craft for a conflict of interest. Within a few seconds, he was into a rant about newspapermen. My wife, who heard my side of the conversation, said, "I thought he called to praise you."

I once wrote a column praising his daughter Hillary for her work as a producer on an NBC report. Later, when she produced a flowery piece about Al Davis, whom her father liked, and then followed it up with a hard-hitting piece on football commissioner Pete Rozelle, whom her father disliked, I wrote a piece critical of her one-sidedness. Cosell never forgave me for this. He called me "Sleaze One." Ira Berkow of the *Times,* who had also criticized him, was "Sleaze Two." Berkow said, "I want to be Sleaze One."

By visiting production facilities, I developed a better understanding of the techniques and the problems of the technical people. I probably was more understanding of their difficulties; I reminded readers that live television people didn't have the support of a copy desk to correct errors. I came to have great respect for Nathanson, Forte, Rick Gentile, and Don Ohlmeyer, among others.

Mike Weisman of NBC was easily the most creative of all the producers I met. He generated a classic pregame feature piece the day after a gimpy-legged Kirk Gibson hit a dramatic, game-winning home run in the 1988 World Series. Weisman matched shots of Gibson swinging and running the bases with clips of Robert Redford in the movie *The Natural.* I still tingle with the memory of that brilliant piece.

I was in the truck for an ABC telecast of a Brown-Yale football game before a sparse crowd at the cavernous Yale Bowl. I was impressed by a director's shrewd trick that disguised the paucity of people in the stands. When a punter kicked the ball, the director held the camera shot on the punter. He then shifted to the returner catching the football. He did *not* show the ball in the air because the relatively empty stands would have provided the backdrop.

Bud Collins, the garrulous *Boston Globe* columnist, was an informative and entertaining tennis expert on TV. Collins started on PBS in Boston and then worked Wimbledon for many years on NBC. His highlight moment may have been when the camera picked up a member of the party in the royal box at Wimbledon picking her nose. Collins said, "Nice backhand."

On one occasion, I tailed Marv Albert on one of his many appearances on the David Letterman show. We sat with Letterman afterward. This was at the time of Wimbledon, and Letterman mentioned to Albert how much he disliked Collins's work. Albert gave an unintelligible grunt. I decided to have fun with it; I wrote a light-hearted column trying to drum up a mock feud between Letterman and Collins. A little while later, Collins showed me a letter to him from Letterman in which the funnyman denied he had ever said what I had quoted.

Early on, I recognized the brilliance of Bob Costas. I was pleased to see him rise to become the most outstanding broadcaster in sports television. I was an early booster, as well, of Mary Carillo and Al Trautwig. I touted Keith Olbermann early, too, and looked on with amusement as Olbermann emerged as a cocky and controversial figure wherever he went.

* * *

In the late 1970s and 1980s, when I was the sports TV critic for *Newsday,* I had a short and lucrative spell moonlighting as a columnist for *Sports Illustrated.* I wrote pieces on the state of golf and pro basketball on TV; bowling; the ABC telecast of a Division III college football game; and a mirthful critique of Howard Cosell dominating the 1979 World Series telecasts.

SI had gobs of money to throw around. In 1980 it sent me out to Los Angeles to cover Super Bowl XIV between the Pittsburgh Steelers and Los Angeles Rams at the Rose Bowl. But I wasn't to attend the game itself. No, my assignment was to watch the game *on television* in Los Angeles. I dutifully flew out, hung around with the television people early in the week, and then settled down in a handsome room at the Beverly Wilshire Hotel and wrote my piece afterward.

When ESPN went to twenty-four-hour programming for the first time, publicity man Joe Goldstein suggested I watch the first twenty-four hours and write a piece about it. I holed up in a motel room not far from ESPN headquarters in Bristol, Connecticut, and lay on a bed for twenty-four hours, gaping at basketball players leaping, hockey players high-sticking, go-karts buzzing, and karate figures flailing.

The lowlight was a canned program on China's Fourth National Games, a sort of Sino Spartakiad. For two hours I looked on with increasing giddiness at a gaggle of gymnastic events, motorcycle races with sidecars, a parachuting competition, and model-boat and model-plane races. I drank enough coffee to keep me awake throughout. The mind reeled. In retrospect I'm not so sure all of today's non-stop presentations of college football and basketball on ESPN are any more worthy.

* * *

Back at *Newsday,* I had worked under several sports editors. Bob Zellner, who hired me, was followed by Jack Mann, Ed Comerford, Dick Clemente, and a few others. It is the pattern of newspapers that old stars don't always mesh with new editors. In a sense I was an old star, accustomed to doing things my way, and I was never as comfortable in the latter days at the paper as I had been in the dynamic days with Mann, Comerford, and Clemente.

I wrote the TV Sports column from 1978 on, and by the early 1990s felt I had done all I could do with the column. I also recognized that the column should be handling the business side of sports as well as TV. I did not have that background and admired how well Richard Sandomir was combining sports television and business writing at the *Times.* When *Newsday* came up with a handsome buyout offer for its older employees in 1992, I took the money and ran. I was sixty-three.

31

Life in Isaacstan

If I was concerned about how I would spend my time in retirement—and I was—I need not have worried. After leaving *Newsday,* I kept busy with various pursuits, such as speaking at libraries and men's clubs. Once, on a cold, dreary, rainy day in November when I was scheduled to speak at the Elmont Public Library in Long Island, only one man showed up. I apologized and said the talk would be canceled. "No way," he said. "I came to hear you and let's get on with it." So I gave my spiel, but he had so many sports remembrances spinning in his head that it was more of a dialogue than a talk by me. I loved it almost as much as he did.

My first writing project in retirement was a collaboration with sportscaster Marty Glickman on his autobiography, *The Fastest Kid on the Block.* Glickman was a prince of fellows who had long been a respected and beloved figure in New York broadcasting.

We had met for the first time when I was at Brooklyn College. At that time Glickman hosted a sports quiz show on WHN that pitted groups of contestants against each other. On this night, I competed with my Brooklyn College *Vanguard* mates against staff members of the NYU newspaper. We won.

I recall my contribution was answering correctly the final question about the Triple Crown of horse racing. It was, "The Kentucky Derby is held at Churchill Downs. Where is the Preakness held?" This was ridiculously easy for a sports fanatic like me. I trumpeted the answer, "Pimlico," and nailed down the prize for our team, a $15 gift certificate at the Buddy Lee men's clothing store in Brooklyn. The NYU losers had to settle for a paltry $10 gift certificate from the sponsor's store. Buddy Lee's slogan was, "The Store Where Style Begins." Glickman would add (off air) "And Ends."

I had long resisted teaming with sports figures to write their autobiographies because I rarely felt close to the people with whom I might have collaborated. Close quarters for extended periods with some of the bozos of the sporting life is not something I relished. And I suppose the feeling would be mutual for some people who found my company less than thrilling.

But Marty Glickman was somebody I had known and respected for a long time. He had been a star athlete at Madison High in Brooklyn. He had been a world-class sprinter who had made the 4 x 100 relay squad on the 1936 Olympics team. He and Sam Stoller, the only Jews on the track squad, were dropped from the relay at the last moment. This action reeked with anti-Semitism by assistant track coach Dean Cromwell and U.S. Olympic head Avery Brundage.

Marty went on to a long, distinguished career in broadcasting. He made his mark in radio on college basketball; the pre- and postgame Brooklyn Dodgers baseball shows; the nightly recap of baseball games called "Today's Baseball;" and Giants, Knicks, and Jets broadcasts. Glickman worked everything from marbles tournaments to wrestling. He was a grand guy.

Many people wondered why Glickman had never written his life story. When I talked to him, he said, "I have tried but I don't have the patience to sit down and do it." I said I would be happy to work with him. He agreed, and we formed a partnership.

It was easy and pleasurable working with him. I mostly taped his recollections at his apartment on East 74th Street in Manhattan. Glickman occasionally drove out to my house in Roslyn Heights for working sessions. He impressed me by swimming forty laps at our less-than-Olympic-sized pool.

I was as respectful as I could be about his wishes; he bowed to my professional writing judgments. There was only one case where he overruled my judgment. That was inspired by his wife, Marge. She was concerned about an episode involving Marty's father.

His father was a problem gambler. Marty told me about his father breaking into his boy's piggy bank to help pay off a gambling debt. His father also did poorly in business, and once, when he couldn't pay his creditors, he was sent to debtor's prison for a short time. Marty described the anguish of that time to Peter Levine, who wrote about it in an excellent book, *Ellis Island to Ebbets Field: Sport and the American Jewish Experience.*

Marge objected to my including the prison incident because she didn't want her children and grandchildren to read about the family disgrace. When I pointed out that this story already had appeared in Levine's book, she said it was unlikely that the young people would read that book. She didn't want it in Marty's life story. She was a gracious woman whom I liked very much. I complied with her request without rancor.

Our book did not attract any of the large publishers. Glickman, who made his mark in radio, didn't have the name recognition of TV sportscasters, even though his story was more significant. We eventually found a more-than-willing publisher in Syracuse University Press, which did an excellent production job on the book, fashioning an attractive cover. *The Fastest Kid on the Block* was not a huge seller, but the important thing to me was that the book was done honestly, and we got Marty Glickman's story told.

* * *

A regular paycheck is a wonderful thing, but the ability to fly fancy free when you don't have to worry about earning the daily bread is as close to workaday heaven as I could ever have imagined. The handsome buyout moolah from *Newsday,* invested in the market during the boom days of the 1990s, put me on the sunny side of the street. I wrote when I wanted for whom I wanted. I could shrug off the inevitable turndowns from fickle editors, which was the typical bane of freelancers.

I sent off pieces to a grab bag of publications. The list of outlets in which I appeared did not reach Olympian status, but one never loses the buzz that comes from seeing one's byline on a page, no matter the eminence of the address. This is the list of publications that my less-than-precious prose graced: *The Complete Handbook of Pro Football; The Complete Handbook of Baseball;* the *Silurian News;* the *New York Times* Op-Ed page; the *New York Times* Sunday Long Island section; the *New York Times* Metropolitan Diary; the yearbooks and programs for the New York Mets and Knicks; *Delta Airlines Magazine;* the *Thoroughbred Daily News;* the *Northern Sentinel;* the *Roslyn News; Business; Long Island Voice; Giants Jottings;* the *Bregman Times;* the dinner journal for the Baseball Writers Association of America; *Eve's Magazine;* the *Philadelphia Inquirer;* and the sports and op-ed pages of *Newsday.*

I wrote a regular column for the ESPN Zone website for two years, along with Roger Kahn and Frank Deford. After that, I moved on to a regular column for a site called www.thecolumnists.com.

This enterprise was started by a few former *San Jose Mercury* staffers and edited by the irrepressible Ron Miller, a former movie critic who put to use his near-encyclopedic knowledge with provocative essays on movies and movie stars. He was the best editor I ever had, because he allowed his stable of writers to do what they wanted. Miller was funny, irreverent, nurturing of writers, ever encouraging. To turn around an old saw, he separated the wheat from the chaff and kept the wheat. It was a privilege to write for the site. When asked about my remuneration, I answered, "I am paid in the high zeros."

I was inspired by words of wisdom from Leonard Koppett, my old press box colleague. He said, "It's important to write; it doesn't matter where, as long as you keep writing." I got back into my old "Out of Left Field" swing, tripping the light fantastic in sundry directions. Art Buchwald's advice was a big influence: "Be funny about serious things and serious about funny things."

In various columns, I promoted the mythical country of Isaacstan, which I placed in a narrow corridor somewhere between Uzbekistan and Tajikistan on the Afghanistan border with a dogleg to Kazakhstan on the right. I think I began to believe the People's Republic of Isaacstan actually existed. I extolled the nation that "lived up to the ideals of Benjamin Franklin, Tom Paine, and Groucho Marx."

I fleshed out significant facts about Isaacstan. The country covered 95,000 square miles, about the size of Oregon, with a population of some 480,000, about the same as Wyoming. Its chief industries were yogurt processing, the production of goatskin clothing, and farming. It was rich in livestock, with thirteen million goats, ten million chickens, and 209,000 pigs, but not many sheep. The second-largest city was named Islamgood. The capital was Stantinople. And the country was unique for being 33 percent Muslim, 33 percent Catholic, and 33 percent atheist. It had some former Protestant missionaries who converted to Judaism after watching Mel Brooks movies.

Isaacstan was an ally of the United States, but it wasn't always that way. During the height of the cold war, when Isaacstan was having economic difficulties, it cuddled up to the Soviets, shipping goatskin overcoats to the Kremlin. This prompted the U.S.A. to put Isaacstan on its foreign aid list, and the economic crisis was averted. The American dollars allowed for the upgrading of its education system, now up to 99.99 percent literacy; there was one old woman who refused to learn how to read and write because she would not take any time away from sewing goatskin overcoats.

The monetary unit of Isaacstan was the brick. There were a thousand bricks to one U.S. dollar. Ron Miller, the masterful editor, ran a graphic of two somewhat bedraggled, turbaned characters standing in front of a wall of bricks: "the national treasury, which contains more than a million bricks."

The first Isaacstan column proved such a hit there were demands for more. I obliged, with alacrity. At a time when Osama Bin Laden was reportedly hiding in the hills of Tora Bora on the Pakistan border, I entitled the second piece, "They Don't Do the Hora in Tora Bora."

I made political points not too subtly: When the United States was on the verge of war with Iraq, Isaacstan stepped in with an offer to provide asylum for *both* Saddam Hussein and President George Bush. "Certainly a good portion of the world would be happy to see both Bush and Hussein put away in a safe place," said Ali Ali, the Premier of Isaacstan.

There was consternation among Isaacstanis when they read that the United States was offering $25 million for the capture of Osama Bin Laden. "In this poor region," a scholar said, "wouldn't $5 million be enough of an incentive? Or a thousand dollars? Why even $37.50 would be enough for my cousin Ahmed."

"Hell," said a wizened shepherd at a town meeting. "My nephew Looie would go after that bandito for 30 goats and a new tent."

* * *

One of the columns I am proud of was the piece entitled "The Goat That Inspired a President." It was a scoop of sorts, because it uncovered for many the story that President George W. Bush was reading to elementary school students in Florida on September 11, 2001, when he was informed that planes had hit the World Trade Center buildings in Manhattan.

Scholars and news people were unable to track the story because it was mislabeled "My Pet Goat." I discovered that it was "The Pet Goat." And it was not a standalone story. It was one of many stories in the workbook *Reading Mastery II: Storybook I*. Some of the other stories in the book: "The Fox Wants Ice Cream," "Meet Spot," and "The Elephant Gets Glasses."

"The Pet Goat" was written by Siegfried "Zig" Engelmann. He was seventy-three, a professor of education at the University of Oregon. He told reporters he didn't remember the story because it was one of more than a thousand he had written in the past thirty years.

"The Pet Goat" is about a little girl and a mischievous goat who did bad things. He ate pans and cans. Her father wanted to get rid of the goat, but the girl made the goat stop being mischievous.

A video of Bush's reading shows him sitting to the side of the teacher, listening raptly to the recitation. At one point his aide, Andrew Card, comes to whisper something in his ear. Bush nods, but continues to sit and listen even though he had been told about what Card called "an attack on America."

To some he seemed to look off in space, dazed perhaps. He sat listening for seven minutes while the nation was hearing about the attack. When the reading was finished, Bush did not rush from the room immediately. He told the children they were "great readers."

The story measures 372 words. The shame of it is that Bush had to leave before he finished the entire story. He heard the first 184 words; he wasn't around for the final 188 words.

I would suspect that Bush never learned how the story turned out. He left just when a "car robber" came to the girl's house. He probably would like to know that the goat foiled the robber's attempt to steal the family's car by attacking him.

The story continued: "Just when the goat stopped playing, he saw the robber. He bent his head down and started to run for the robber. The robber was bending over the seat of the car. The goat hit him with his sharp horns. The car robber went flying. . . . The girl hugged the goat. Her dad said, 'That goat can stay with us. And he can eat all the cans and canes and caps and capes he wants.'"

After Bush left the White House, he was busy developing a memorial library at Southern Methodist University that celebrated his administration. When he puts books into the library shelves, I hope he will have a place of honor for *Reading Mastery II: Storybook I,* featuring the immortal "The Pet Goat."

* * *

A tip from an old Stanford friend, Harry Press, led to a column that I loved doing. As the NCAA basketball tournament approached in March 2001, Press let me know that a statue of Hank Luisetti outside the Stanford gym had been vandalized and only recently been repaired. Luisetti was a Stanford immortal, one of the most important figures in college basketball for popularizing the one-hand shot.

What the Baltimore Colts–New York Giants "greatest game ever played" was to pro football, Stanford's 45–31 victory over Long Island University in 1936 was to college basketball. Stanford came into Madison Square Garden and snapped LIU's forty-three-game winning streak before a full house. Historians recognize that this game launched college basketball as a big-time national sport.

Luisetti unveiled to the East his running one-hand shot and dazzled with all-around play. He scored fifteen of his team's forty-five points in the face of skepticism about anybody shooting with one hand. Though others out

West shot one-handed, it was Luisetti who revolutionized the sport. Kids all over the country started to shoot one-handed, just as many years later they all took to the jump shot that changed the sport anew.

Like most people, I thought Luisetti had died. Harry tipped me off that he was still alive and put me in touch with him and some of his old teammates.

He was eighty-four and living quietly in Foster City, a few miles up the road from Stanford's Palo Alto campus. I was told he was never comfortable with reporters, shy about talking about himself. I was delighted to find he was quite cordial, happy to talk with me about the old days.

He explained that he had started shooting one-handed as a six-year-old on the playground in San Francisco named after the tennis great Helen Wills. "In those days the basketball had ridges on it," he said, "It didn't bounce cleanly as it does now, so we had to learn all the basics to control the ball. I was a little scrawny and when I tried to shoot two-handed, it was easy for others to block the shot. So I shot one-handed and I kept shooting that way."

Born Angelo Enrico Luisetti, he became Hank "because kids would call me 'Angel' and I didn't like that. So I came up with 'Hank' out of the blue and that became it."

Luisetti was a 6'2" forward, far ahead of his time. He made All-America his three varsity years and was named national Player of the Year his last two seasons. When the Associated Press conducted a poll on the game's great players of the first half of the twentieth century, Luisetti came in second to George Mikan, though the majority of voters had never seen him play.

He was born too early to cash in on the big bucks of a pro career. After graduation Luisetti played with the AAU champion Phillips Oilers and served three years in the navy. Spinal meningitis ended his playing days. He went on to coach a Chevrolet dealership team to an AAU championship. He was in the automobile and travel businesses before retiring.

In the 1970s Stanford commissioned a statue of Luisetti. The artist Phil Zonne, his old Stanford teammate, fashioned it, working without a fee. In 1999 the left arm was broken off the bronze statue. Because it occurred on the eve of the traditional Big Game between Stanford and California, the vandalism was thought to be the work of some overenthusiastic Cal freshmen. None of the culprits were found.

Bob Oakford, another Stanford teammate, spearheaded the statue's repair. The arm was fashioned and reattached to the bronze. It has Luisetti shooting one-handed with the ball twelve feet in the air. "Naturally, I'm pleased about that," he said.

Luisetti died December 17, 2002, at eighty-six, a little more than a year after I spoke with him.

* * *

I started going to the theater when I was fourteen. On December 29, 1943, six of us in Mrs. Weiss's art appreciation class at Junior High School 50 attended the theater as part of an art assignment. We were there to witness in the flesh the architectural aspect of theaters that Mrs. Weiss had laid out. I most recall her talking about the proscenium, the area at the front of the stage. I don't think I've heard the word since.

We saw *Arsenic and Old Lace,* then in the early stages of a long run at the Hudson Theater on West 47th Street. We bought the cheapest tickets and sat in the nosebleed reaches of the second balcony.

I was captivated. There was an electricity in the interaction between the actors and the live audience, and the language was bawdier than was permitted in movies. Somebody actually used the word "bastard." I reveled in the laughter that rocked the house. The play is, of course, a broad farce about two old ladies in Brooklyn who poisoned old gentlemen as acts of charity. They then had their loony brother Teddy (who thought he was Teddy Roosevelt) bury them in the cellar (the locks of the Panama Canal).

I was so taken by it all that I made a point of saving the Playbill and making notes on it. I wrote down the date I attended, the names of my classmates, and a brief critique. I wrote, "Very good. Very funny."

Within a few months I saw *Angel Street* ("Just fair. Mysterious"), *Three Is a Family* ("Very funny. I liked it"), and *One Touch of Venus* ("Very elaborate. Good show.").

I moved into high-blown criticism with *Death of a Salesman,* in which Gene Lockhart portrayed Willie Loman. I still wince as I read my verdict: "This play must take its place in the history of the drama as one which reflects an important aspect of American thought, of American life. Miller puts it all there for us to see. . . . Such a play makes theater drama the highest and most important art form in the United States. . . . Mildred Dunnock gives a fine performance. Arthur Kennedy is one of the most natural actors I have seen." I had come quite a way, not necessarily for the better, from "Very funny."

My one hundredth play was *The Matchmaker,* on March 31, 1956. Number two hundred was *Beyond the Fringe* on October 24, 1962. Number three hundred: *Julius Caesar* on July 17, 1972, in Stratford, England. Number four hundred: *Albums* on November 29, 1980.

From the beginning, I noted my companions at the plays. The first play I ever attended with Natalie Bobrove, my wife-to-be, was *Male Animal* (number forty-two) on October 11, 1952. During our honeymoon week, we had our only daily double. On December 23, 1953, we saw the forgettable *Prescott Proposals* (number fifty-eight) at a matinee and the short-lived *Dead Pigeon* (number fifty-nine) on opening night. I usually am Mr. 87th-or-so-Nighter at a play; this was the only time I ever made an opening night.

I was surprised that *Clandestine on the Morning Line* (number 158), a shrewd comedy about horse racing by my Brooklyn College classmate, Josh Greenfield, which we saw in Washington's Arena Theater, never made it to Broadway. Former *Newsday* colleague Joe Treen's *The Best Reporter There Ever Was* (number 446) was at a converted garage in Soho. The most unusual evening was an amateur production of Genet's *The Maids* (number 168), staged and acted by our friends Fran Dincin and Tybee Oesterreicher in the basement rec room of Dincin's home in Teaneck, New Jersey. We saw the play again in San Francisco (number 176) and came away impressed by what professionals could do with staging.

My Playbills range from A to Z: *Absence of a Cello* (number 216) to *Zulu and the Zayda* (number 233). The best one-man show was, undoubtedly, Hal Holbrook's *Mark Twain Tonight* (number 149). I have liked playwright Herb Gardner early and often: *A Thousand Clowns* (number 199), *Thieves* (number 327) and *I'm Not Rappaport* (number 443). And there really was *An Evening with Jake LaMotta* (number 208). The former pug grunted, groaned, huffed, and puffed excerpts from *Born Yesterday, On the Waterfront, Of Mice and Men,* and *Marty,* among others. He was no Shakespeare.

As play number five hundred approached, we talked about making it a special occasion, doing it up in a big way. An initial suggestion of mine was to invite all the people who had ever attended a play with me, buy up the theater for a performance of an off-Broadway production, and make a theater party out of it. The logistics of locating many of the people I no longer knew was daunting enough. And when my wife suggested it would be too expensive to pay for all those people, and I argued that we would not have to pay for them because people would be delighted to be invited to such a gala affair, she said that was cheap, and she would have no part of it.

We instead decided to make number five hundred special by going to London, where we had seen several plays over the years. Fortuitously, friends of ours, Marilyn and Bernie Bookbinder, were spending the summer in England. They agreed to join us for the historic occasion. They were in London during July and Bernie kept me apprised of the plays there. No choice shouted out to us, because most of the good dramas had closed for the summer. A showy musical did not appeal to us. I would have opted for the long-running *The Mousetrap* by Agatha Christie as a worthy number five hundred, but Bernie had seen it and didn't care to see it again.

In late July, when they were settled in a cottage in the south of England, Bernie noted there was a good regional theater in Chichester and that a play by Noel Coward was scheduled. The play was *Point Valaine,* which I had never heard of. But it was by Noel Coward. Why not make that number five hundred?

We arrived in England on a Friday. Bookbinder had purchased tickets for *Point Valaine* at the Minerva Studio Theater in Chichester on the following Tuesday night. Terrific. On Sunday morning Bookbinder and I went to Chichester to play tennis on the town courts. After I absorbed my usual shellacking from Bernie's well-placed winners, we walked over to take a look at the nearby theater. It turned out to be a complex holding two theaters-in-the-round.

I noted *Point Valaine* and then checked the play schedule at the other house, the Chichester Festival Theater. There in bold letters was the listing for the play that would be on the boards the coming week: *Arsenic and Old Lace.*

It seemed like something of a million-to-one shot to have my number one play also come up as a candidate for number five hundred. Exultantly, I bought tickets for *Arsenic and Old Lace* for the next night, July 24, 1991. *Arsenic and Old Lace* was, glory be, number one and number five hundred.

From the Chichester theater program, I learned this was the first run for the play in England since its first appearance in the 1940s. Also, the producers of the original production, Howard Lindsay and Russell Crouse, had substantially rewritten large sections of the Joseph Kesselring original. The Chichester production featured one familiar face, Rosemary Harris, as one of the two old biddies. The others were top pros; some were familiar from PBS television productions from England. It was first-rate. The Chichester *Arsenic* was a worthy number five hundred.

I kept piling up theater visits—and playbills. By the time I approached six hundred, we were living in a retirement community in Haverford, Pennsylvania, called the Quadrangle, where some good folks staged script-in-hand readings. I prevailed upon them to do *Arsenic and Old Lace.* Guess who wangled his way into playing Teddy ("Charge") Roosevelt?

* * *

We made many trips after I left *Newsday*. We traveled with the Overseas Adventure Travel group to Costa Rica and Turkey and made a few trips to

England when we needed a British fix. We attended Hemingway conferences in Paris and Cuba. We walked in northern Italy with British Coastal Travels, cruised the inland waterway of Alaska, and visited with Stanford friend Solveig Torvik's relatives in Norway.

We went to Vietnam in 2002. One of the highlights was a day at the races in Ho Chi Minh City. During the war in Vietnam, I had read in the *Wall Street Journal* about the Phu Tho racecourse. I would say there may never have been a greater tribute to the passion for horse racing by a segment of the public than in Saigon during the war. While battles raged outside the city, racing continued in Phu Tho.

While preparing for the trip, I found out the Phu Tho track was still in operation. When the Communists liberated South Vietnam in 1975, gambling was outlawed as an example of bourgeois decadence. Then, as the country's political climate became more open and liberal, the course was reopened in 1989.

From our downtown digs at the Hotel Continental in Saigon, my wife and I took a half-hour taxi ride to Phu Tho on a Sunday afternoon. It showed the effects of wear and tear in a country that had been bogged down in conflict for decades. (Vietnam has been invaded something like sixteen times in its history, mostly by China. And shortly after the United States pulled out of Vietnam in 1975, it was back at war again with China, the country with which the United States supposedly went to war to protect the Vietnamese. So much for the Domino Theory.)

The peeling pastel grandstand held about three thousand people. The place was less imposing than even a bush-league racetrack in the United States. We gained admission inside a wire fence by paying one thousand dong, less than seven cents in U.S. money. We were told it would be wise to go to the equivalent of the turf and field club, so we paid an extra sixty-six cents to sit in the terrace area above the grandstand. To beat the heat, we sat at a table under an umbrella cooled by a small electric fan.

The track was about a mile in circumference. All seven races, from distances of five furlongs to a feature race of almost a mile and a sixteenth, went off from a creaky starting gate across the parched grass infield. I had read that in the days before there was a starting gate, it was not uncommon for a crooked starter, in on a fix, to wait until the favorite was turned in the wrong direction, then drop his flag for the start.

I had been told as well that a syndicate fixed the races, that horses were drugged, that jockeys got bribed, and that people outside the track would try to influence the outcome of a race by throwing stones at the horses. I saw no thrown stones, but I had no way of knowing how honest the races were. I do know that the universal language of losing horse players is the cry of "Fix."

Horses came out of the stable area with the jockeys up. They paraded in front of the grandstand to a paddock area at the far left end of the straightaway. The horses were small, perhaps a little larger than ponies, much smaller than thoroughbreds. The jockeys were as young as fourteen.

My first task was to find somebody who spoke English so that I could grasp the betting procedure. I came across a Vietnamese man from the United States who was in Ho Chi Minh City visiting relatives. He was an engineer from Kansas City in his thirties whose name was Guing. He clued me to the proper procedure. Phu Tho offered only exacta betting in five thousand dong ($0.33) or twenty-thousand dong ($1.33) denominations. I made my way to the betting area in the rear of the terrace. For sure this was not a parimutuel operation. The betting board consisted of a rack of paper slips attached to combinations of numbers, almost like a coat check rack at a restaurant.

My wager on the first race was on number four, My Ngoc (Beautiful Jade), and number six, Tan Long Huong (New Dragon). For the first race, the horses were sent off on a five-furlong jaunt some fifteen minutes past post time. Spectators could look at a large TV screen in the infield or TV sets around the stands. New Dragon led early. He faded to second in the last few strides. It turned out Beautiful Jade was the winner. So I had won the exacta—"always a 5–1 payoff," as my pal Guing explained.

Phu Tho ran every Saturday and Sunday afternoon. I estimated a crowd of two thousand. Men in jeans mixed with bare-footed street urchins, pajama-clad old men and women spitting out red betel juice. Women vendors in conical hats sold street food such as the universal noodle soup, "pho," as well as tea, sugar cane, eels, and sticky rice. Spectators milled about between races and then took up good viewing spots. In full voice, they urged on their favorites. Some things are indeed universal.

I bet exactas on a few more races. I did not win again. Some things never change.

32

A Craft and a Life

When I look back at a career in journalism that spans more than fifty years, I see one particular game serving as a metaphor for the world of fun and games that is not always just fun and games.

On November 9, 1969, I went up to Wesleyan University in Middletown, Connecticut, to write a column about the Wesleyan-Williams football game. I wanted to experience a green and leafy football scene involving two outstanding small schools that were traditional rivals. I got a bit more than I bargained for.

Wesleyan and Williams, along with Amherst, make up the Little Three, a rivalry that goes back to the 1880s. The richness of its traditions matches the Big Three of Harvard, Yale, and Princeton. It represents what I regard as the highest ideals of American college sports: excellent students playing hard, living up to the sound mind and sound body principles of amateur sports.

Wesleyan has long been the most liberal of the Little Three. On the Wesleyan team of that tumultuous time, football coach Don Russell told me, there were the extremes of beatnik-pseudo hippies and the full-blooded jocks. The previous year, star end Stu Blackburn took part in a protest against the Vietnam War and a sit-down in the president's office. At the same time, his pal, Steve Pfeiffer, the quarterback, was collecting signatures for a petition urging that the protesters be removed from the president's office.

The coach said, "Despite this they remained friends and they left here as friends. Blackman became a coach at a private school in Maine, Pfeiffer a Rhodes Scholar at Oxford. I think there is willingness on all sides here to respect the other fellow's views. We have differences, but some of our personality clashes on the team are as likely to be between two jocks as between two hippies."

I loved this. And I loved the game and the scene. The football field and temporary stands, seating about forty-five hundred, were laid out on a greensward in the middle of the campus, in a bower of huge oaks and elms ringed by century-old red brick buildings. Looming behind them were modern buildings. Behind one end zone, nonpaying tweedy and jeans-wearing spectators spread out on blankets on a grassy terrace amid some frolicking dogs.

At halftime, the Williams band straggled onto the field, all wearing outlandish hats, to serenade the crowd. Wesleyan's musical aggregation featured a swing band with an old upright piano in the front row of the stands. The Wesleyan cheerleaders, all long- and wooly-haired males, shouted the usual cheers, plus the chant, "Chastise them! Chastise them! Make them relinquish the ball."

The game was terrific. Williams, powered by Jack Maitland, a shifty runner who would have a brief stint in the National Football League, took a 14–0 lead in the second period. Wesleyan had a quarterback named Pete Panciera. He was a skinny, round-shouldered man who had the slouchy movements of Joe Namath. He couldn't run, he set up badly and he often threw badly, but he threw line drives and the Wesleyan ends made some remarkable catches. Wesleyan cut the lead to 14–6 at the half.

At one point in a topsy-turvy second half, Williams intercepted a pass; Wesleyan intercepted a pass a few moments later; on the very next play, Williams intercepted right back. Wesleyan went 80 yards and trailed 14–12 early in the fourth period. Williams surged back for a field goal and led, 17–12. Panciera then moved Wesleyan 80 yards to a touchdown and Wesleyan led by a point. It came down to a tingling, final play. Williams tried a thirty-yard field goal. It was blocked. Wesleyan won, 18–17.

Wesleyan walked off the field as champion of the Little Three. The players paraded the coach off the field. The swing band played. The students—long-haired and short—ran from the stands and the terrace to hug the players. The dogs scampered.

I couldn't ask for anything more. But there was a subtext to it all that provided a bit more than green and leafy football. Prior to the game, there had been a campus dispute typical of the late 1960s. There had been an incident on campus in which some black students beat up a white student because he had written what they regarded as an anti-black tirade letter to the school newspaper. The black students immediately were expelled by a dean. Militants then protested, objecting that the students had not been tried properly by a student disciplinary board. The protestors hinted they might disrupt every campus event, including the football game, unless the black students were reinstated.

Sides were taken. The captain of the football team was among those heading a drive supporting the dean. There was a bomb threat late in the game that emptied the press box.

At halftime, a representative of the black students addressed the crowd. Most of the students listened to his appeal, while many of the tweedy alumni tried to shout him down. The official in charge of the public address microphone said, "When Nixon and Humphrey were here last year, the kids were branded punks and rabble because they hissed and didn't give those men a hearing. Well, now this man has something to say and you should pay him the courtesy of listening."

The afternoon provided me with the joy of watching inspiring football action against a backdrop of controversy. I see that as reflective of the world of sports in a larger context. One can thrill to the splendid actions of the athletes and yet be disheartened by larger issues that go beyond the playing field. Sports is big business. It is rampant commercialism. It is a breeding ground for drug usage. It is a world where billionaire owners vie against millionaire players without much concern for the interests of the paying public. It is frequently discouraging to see how the ideals of sportsmanship are perverted in the willy-nilly pursuit of victory.

* * *

At my retirement party in 1992, one of the speakers was Dick Schaap, an impressive five-media man. He was an excellent newspaper columnist, magazine writer and editor, book author, and commentator on radio and television. I envied Schaap's ability to make friends with big stars in sports and entertainment and yet, to a considerable degree, maintain his journalistic integrity. While a reporter at *Newsweek* in the early 1960s, Schaap first brought *Newsday* to people's attention as a significant player in sports journalism.

At my party, Schaap noted there were no people of color in the crowd. That bothered me, of course. I thought long and hard about it. I think it reflected not a bias on my part but the fact that I never got close to athletes, whether they were black or white. I remember Milt Richman, a United Press International reporter who became buddy-buddy with many baseball players, asking me who were my best friends among athletes. I was somewhat startled by the question, realizing that I didn't have any "friends" among ballplayers. I didn't have "friends" because I believed in the separation that should exist between reporters and the people we covered.

I think I was the first reporter covering baseball who turned down the opportunity to be an official scorer. I believed that the press had to keep a distance from its subjects. That was more important than showing you had the guts to make tough calls and face aggrieved athletes afterward. *Newsday* then was the first paper to turn down the official scorer opportunity—I believe it paid $50 a game. A few years later, however, new *Newsday* baseball writers resumed the so-called plum assignment of official scorer. So much for progress.

I also believe I didn't have "friends" among athletes because I was not comfortable in a relationship with people who were accustomed to being the center of attention. Schaap could do it; I couldn't. Later, when I covered television sports, I did make friends with some people I covered because we were both in the business of journalism—and I never felt I had to pull back on criticism of any of them.

For all the mixed feelings about the distortions of what Robert Lipsyte called "SportsWorld," it has been an exciting place to make a career. As a youth I aspired to cover a major league baseball team and make $75 a week. I carved out a career in journalism and made more than $75 a week. All in all, I was satisfied. More importantly, I married well, and my wife and I raised a wonderful family.

People look upon a sportswriter's life as a glamorous one. It has been that for me. It is also a craft, a constant search to report fairly and honestly—and to write well. The down times were insignificant in the larger scheme of things. When airline travel was a trial, when athletes turned hostile, when owners lied, there was much bitching and moaning. But there was effective, enlightened reporting on important subjects, leavened with whimsy and tomfoolery. It was a helluva lot better than working as an accountant.

Index

STAN ISAACS (1929–2013) was a sportswriter and pioneering sports media reporter. His longtime column, "Out of Left Field," appeared in *Newsday*. He is the author of *Ten Moments That Shook the Sports World*.

ARAM GOUDSOUZIAN is the Bizot Family Professor of History at the University of Memphis. He is the author of *The Men and the Moment: The Election of 1968 and the Rise of Partisan Politics in America*.

The University of Illinois Press
is a founding member of the
Association of University Presses.

Composed in 11.5/13 Arno Pro Regular
with Kelson Sans display
by Jim Proefrock
at the University of Illinois Press
Manufactured by Sheridan Books, Inc.

University of Illinois Press
1325 South Oak Street
Champaign, IL 61820-6903
www.press.uillinois.edu